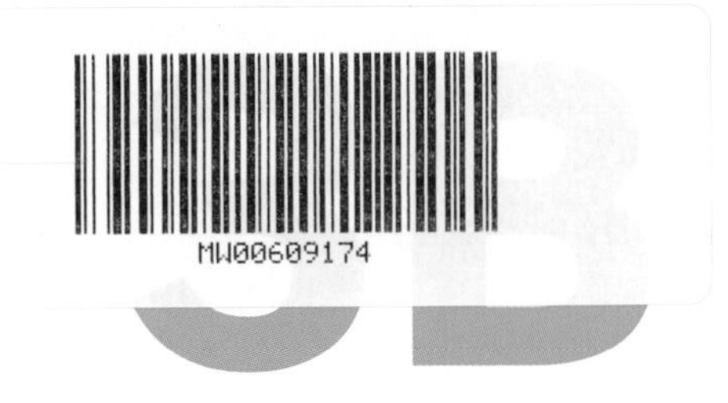

American ENGLISH FILE

Christina Latham-Koenig
Clive Oxenden

Paul Seligson and Clive Oxenden are the original co-authors of *English File 1* and *English File 2*

OXFORD
UNIVERSITY PRESS

198 Madison Avenue
New York, NY 10016 USA

Great Clarendon Street, Oxford, OX2 6DP,
United Kingdom

Oxford University Press is a department of the University of Oxford. It furthers the University's objective of excellence in research, scholarship, and education by publishing worldwide. Oxford is a registered trade mark of Oxford University Press in the UK and in certain other countries.

First published in 2014
2023 2022 2021 2020 2019
12 11 10 9 8

General Manager: Laura Pearson
Executive Publishing Manager: Erik Gundersen
Senior Managing Editor: Louisa van Houten
Associate Editor: Yasuko Morisaki
Associate Editor: James Power
Design Director: Susan Sanguily
Executive Design Manager: Maj-Britt Hagsted
Associate Design Manager: Michael Steinhofer
Senior Designer: Yin Ling Wong
Electronic Production Manager: Julie Armstrong
Production Artists: Elissa Santos, Julie Sussman-Perez
Image Manager: Trisha Masterson
Image Editors: Liaht Pashayan
Production Coordinator: Brad Tucker

ISBN: 978 0 19 479634 7 MULTI-PACK B
ISBN: 978 0 19 477591 5 STUDENT BOOK/WORKBOOK B (PACK COMPONENT)
ISBN: 978 0 19 436059 3 ONLINE PRACTICE (PACK COMPONENT)

Printed in China

This book is printed on paper from certified and well-managed sources.

STUDENT BOOK ACKNOWLEDGEMENTS

The authors and publisher are grateful to those who have given permission to reproduce the following extracts and adaptations of copyright material:

p.8 Extract from "He claims we used to play Cowboys and Indians. I recall him trying to suffocate me" by Tim Lott, The Times, November 20, 2010. Reproduced by permission of NI Syndication. p.8 Extract from "The seven ages of an only child" by Joanna Moorhead, The Guardian, March 4, 2006. Copyright Guardian News & Media Ltd 2006. Reproduced by permission. p.3–4 Extract from "The millionaire who couldn't write his name" by Karen Bartlett, The Times, February 4, 2011. Reproduced by permission of NI Syndication. p.7 Extract from "Blue Peter presenter Helen Skelton begins epic Amazon kayaking adventure" by Cassandra Jardine, Telegraph Online, January 23, 2010. © Telegraph Media Group Limited 2010. Reproduced by permission. p.7 Extract from "Blue Peter presenter Helen Skelton's Amazon diaries: week one", Telegraph Online, January 31, 2010. © Telegraph Media Group Limited 2010. Reproduced by permission. p.7 Extract from "Blue Peter presenter Helen Skelton's Amazon diaries: week two", Telegraph Online, February 8, 2010. © Telegraph Media Group Limited 2010. Reproduced by permission. p.5 Extract from "Gossip with the girls but men only have four subjects" by Peter Markham, The Daily Mail, October 18, 2001. Reproduced by permission of Solo Syndication. p.8 Extract from "New baby? No problem for Commando Dad" by Neil Sinclair, The Times, May 7, 2012. Reproduced by permission of NI Syndication. p.3–4 Extract from "Alex Rawlings most multi-lingual student in UK" by Hannah White-Steele, Cherwell.org, February 24, 2012. Reproduced by permission. p.6–7 Extract from "Debrett's guide to mobile phone etiquette", Telegraph Online, August 5, 2011. © Telegraph Media Group Limited 2011. Reproduced by permission. p.8 Extract from "Mother-in-law from hell sends harsh lesson in manners to 'uncouth' bride-to-be in email that becomes worldwide sensation", The Daily Mail, June 29, 2011. Reproduced by permission of Solo Syndication. p.2 Extract from "Very superstitious: Andy Murray, Wimbledon and sport stars everywhere" by Matthew Syed, The Times, July 1, 2009. Reproduced by permission of NI Syndication. p.5 Extract from "Sealed with a kiss and 35¢: how a singer and a toll booth operator set out on the road to love" by Will Pavia, The Times, February 14, 2012. Reproduced by permission of NI Syndication. p.5–6 Extract from "What does your profile picture say about you?" by Una Mullally, The Irish Times, October 29, 2011. Article Courtesy of the Irish Times. p.7–8 Extract from "Yes, Looks do Matter" by Pam Belluck, The New York Times, April 26, 2009 © 2009 The New York Times. All rights reserved. Used by permission and protected by the Copyright Laws of the United States. The printing, copying, redistribution, or retransmission of this Content without express written permission is prohibited. p.3–4 Extract from "The Chinese way of bringing up children" by Alexandra Frean, The Times, January, 10 2011. Reproduced by permission of NI Syndication. p.3–4 Extract from "Don't shout. Don't swear. And use pink envelopes drenched in aftershave: How to complain successfully by the King of the complainers" by Julia Lawrence, The Daily Mail, October 15, 2011. Reproduced by permission of Solo Syndication. p.9 Extract from "A real Good Samaritan" from BBC News at bbc.co.uk/news, December 24, 2010. Reproduced by permission. p.9 Extract from "Your Good Samaritan stories" from BBC News at bbc.co.uk/ news, January 7, 2011. Reproduced by permission. p.3 Extract from "Not exactly life-changing, is it…" by Matt Rudd, The Sunday Times, October 9, 2011. Reproduced by permission of NI Syndication. p.7 Extract from "A Maestro Sets the Tone" by David Masello, The New York Times, January 18, 2012 © 2012 The New York Times. All rights reserved. Used by permission and protected by the Copyright Laws of the United States. The printing, copying, redistribution, or retransmission of this Content without express written permission is prohibited. p.15 Extract from "The Importance of Doing What You Love" by Stephanie Lewis, www.workawesome.com, March 31, 2012. Reproduced by permission. p.19 Extract from "How Bob Dylan changed my life" by Bob Dylan, The Times, June 24, 2011. Reproduced by permission of NI Syndication. p.14 "Girls & Boys" Words and Music by Benji Madden and Joel Madden © 2002, Reproduced by permission of EMI Music Publishing Ltd, London W8 5. Source: p.3–4 The Times

We would also like to thank the following for permission to reproduce the following photographs: Cover: Gemenacom/shutterstock.com, Andrey_Popov/shutterstock.com, Wavebreakmedia/shutterstock.com, Image Source/Getty Images, Lane Oatey/Blue Jean Images/Getty Images, BJI/Blue Jean Images/Getty Images, Image Source/Corbis, Yuri Arcurs/Tetra Images/Corbis, Wavebreak Media Ltd./Corbis; pg.6 (market) Alessandro Della Valle/Keystone/Corbis, (Steve) Steve Anderson; pg.7 (escargot) Miscellaneoustock/Alamy, (shrimp) Yiap Creative/Alamy, (dessert) Davide Piras/Alamy, (chicken) Iain Bagwell/Getty Images, (mussels) Steve Anderson; pg.8 Gerard Fritz/Getty Images; pg.9 (bike) PhotoAlto/Superstock, (grandma) Rena Latham-Koenig; pg.10 Tim Lott; pg.11 (Sarah Lee) Loop Images Ltd/Alamy, (girl) ableimages/Alamy, (siblings) Inti St. Clair, Inc./SuperStock/Corbis; pg.14 (man) Judith Haeusler/cultura/Corbis, (car) Car Culture/Corbis, (woman) Alexey Tkachenko/Getty Images, (bkgd) Lostandtaken.com; pg.15 Steve Stock/Alamy; pg.17 Ringo Chiu/ZUMAPRESS/Newscom; pg.18 Jane Cadwallader; pg.20 (lizard) Martin Harvey/Alamy, (woman) BBC, (bird) John Cancalosi/Getty Images, (butterfly) Stockbyte/Getty Images; pg.21 (mosquito) Redmond Durrell/Alamy, (kayak) BBC, (dolphin) Kevin Schafer/Corbis, (fish) boryak/istockphoto; pg.23 (Goodwill) Goodwill Industries International; pg.24 (Miami) Murat Taner/Getty Images, (bkgd) Maciej Noskowski/Getty Images; pg.25 (Lotus) Nick Greening/Alamy, (Foust) Bo Bridges/Corbis, (seaplane) Jad Davenport/National Geographic Society/Corbis, (Wood) Frederick M. Brown/Getty Images, (Ferrera) Andres Otero/WENN/Newscom, (boat) OUP/Amana Images Inc.; pg.26 Don Mason/Blend Images/Corbis; pg.27 Belinda Images/SuperStock; pg.29 (men) Tim Klein/Getty Images, (women) Westend61/Superstock; pg.30 (camo) CollinsChin/istockphoto.com; pg.36 Michael Cogliantry/Getty Images; pg.37 (1) Carlo A/Getty Images, (2) Lilly Roadstones/Getty Images, (3) miya227/shutterstock, (4) Brüderchen & Schwesterchen GmbH/Corbis, (5) Tara Moore/Getty Images, (6) Radius Images/Getty Images, (Alex) OUP; pg.38 (old phone) Ninette Maumus/Alamy; pg.39 John Lund/Paula Zacharias/Blend Images/Corbis; pg.40 (left) Murray Sanders/SWNS.com, (right) James Dadzitis/SWNS.com; pg.43 (conductor) Charles Eshelman/FilmMagic/Getty Images, (bikes) Steven Greaves/Corbis; pg.44 (1) Richard Drury/Getty Images, (2) Carlos Caetano/shutterstock, (3) David Madison/Getty Images, (4) Kathy Quirk-Syvertsen/Getty Images, (5) Moe Kafer Cutouts/Alamy, (6) Urban Zone/Alamy, (7) Ray Moller /Getty Images, (8) Corbis Flint/Alamy, (9) Sami Sarkis/Getty Images, (10) Richard Watkins/Alamy; pg.45 (Crosby) Peter Diana/ZUMA Press/Corbis, (Terry) Albert Pena/Icon SMI/Corbis, (Toure) Adrian Dennis/AFP/Getty Images, (Wurz) Rick Dole/getty Images, (player) Simon Bruty/Sports Illustrated/Getty Images, (lines) Marc Debnam/Getty Images, (ball) OUP/Photodisc; pg.46 (referee) Graham Chadwick/Allsport/Getty Images, (marathon) David Madison/Getty Images, (soccer) Bob Thomas/Getty Images; pg.48 (toll) Shannon DeCelle, (couple) Stephen Lance Dennee; pg.54 (castle) Dov Makabaw/Alamy, (alley) Oleg Korshakov/Getty Images; pg.55 (Highclere Castle) Jeff Gilbert /Alamy, (Casa Lomo) Angelo Cavalli/SuperStock; pg.56 (War Horse) Dreamworks SKG/The Kobal Collection, (Indian Jones) Lucasfilm Ltd/Paramount/The Kobal Collection, (ET) Universal/The Kobal Collection, (Minority Report) 20th Century Fox/Dreamworks/The Kobal Collection, (Catch Me If You Can) Dreamworks/The Kobal Collection/Cooper, Andrew; pg.57 Courtesy of Dagmara Walkowicz; pg.58 (Martin) PhotoAlto/Alamy, (Phone) Cyberstock/Alamy, (Annabel) Mark Roberts/Getty Images, (Sean) Paper Boat Creative/Getty Images, (Sarah) Guido Mieth/Getty Images; pg.60 (Brand) V Labissiere/Splash News/Corbis, (1) Rex Features, (2) Suzanne Kreiter/The Boston Globe via Getty Images, (3) Allen J. Schaben/AFP/Getty Images; pg.61 (before) Charlie Gray/Contour by Getty Images, (after) Ken McKay/Rex; pg.63 (theater) Bob O'Connor/Getty Images, (Kong) AF archive/Alamy; pg.65 Shed-Media; pg.66 (envelope) Mark Bassett/Alamy, (music) Erin Patrice O'Brien; pg.68 (kitchen) Carolyn Barber/Getty Images; pg.69 (Vivienne) Tetra Images/Corbis, (Mauro) Tim Kitchen/Getty Images, (Andrea) Echo/Getty Images, (Carlos) Burke/Triolo Productions/Getty Images, (living room) David Papazian/Getty Images, (kitchen) Kim Sayer/Getty Images, (bedroom) Ryan McVay/Getty Images; pg.70 RIA Novosti/Alamy; pg.71 Radius Images/Corbis; pg.74 Devon Anne/Shutterstock; pg.75 (dress) Ivor Toms/Alamy; pg.79 (blood pressure) Ragnar Schmuck/Corbis, (bugs) Michael Freeman/Corbis, (meeting) OUP/zefa RF, (microscope) OUP/Deco; pg.80 (Corcoran) AP Photo/Jeff Christensen, (burger) CBS Foods, (John) Frederick M. Brown/Getty Images, (Cuban) Richard DuCree/USA Network/NBCU Photo Bank via Getty Images, (sharks) abrakadabra/shutterstock, (Perry) Perry's Music, LLC 2012; pg.81 Jorg Greuel/Getty Images; pg.84 Ekaterina Nosenko/Getty Images; pg.85 (street) Sven Hagolani/fstop/Corbis, (bike) Smith Collection/Getty Images, (bike bkgd) Stephen Smith/Getty Images; pg.86 (Beatles) Popperfoto/Getty Images, (Gates) Joe McNally/Getty Images; pg.87 Stefan Sollfors/Alamy; pg.94 (Jobs) Diana Walker/SJ/Contour by Getty Images, (1) oliver leedham/Alamy, (2) Tony Avelar/Bloomberg via Getty Images, (3) Jay L. Clendenin/Los Angeles Times/Contour by Getty Images, (4) Visions of America/UIG via Getty Images, (5) Laurent Fievet/AFP/Getty Images; pg.96 (Barbie) Teenage doll/Alamy, (Love) Charlotte Marie Marshall/Alamy, (sneakers) Peter Kramer/Bravo/NBCU Photo Bank via Getty Images, (Chrysler Building) Jorg Hackemann/Shutterstock.com; pg.97 (soccer) ALLSTAR Picture Library/Alamy, (Ikea) david pearson/Alamy, (toaster) Niall McDiarmid/Alamy, (rolex) John Henshall/Alamy, (building) Chris Ryan/Getty Images, (stopwatch) artpartner-images/Getty Images, (Vertigo) Paramount/The Kobal Collection/Bass, Saul, (Breakfast at Tiffanys) Courtesy Everett Collection/Rex; pg.98 (Wood) Steve Schapiro/Corbis, (Splendour) Silver Screen Collection/Getty Images; pg.99 (Walken) Trinity Mirror/Mirrorpix/Alamy, (Wagner) Phil Roach/Globe Photos/ZUMAPRESS/Newscom, (Davern) Paul Harris, PacificCoastNews/Newscom; pg.100 (Green) Popperfoto/Getty Images, (reader) David Paul Morris/Bloomberg via Getty Images; pg.103 (Dylan) Popperfoto/Getty Images; pg.104 Steve Stock/Alamy; pg.105 Craig Hibert/SWNS.com; pg.106 (Crosby) Peter Diana/ZUMA Press/Corbis, (Sorvino) Suzanne Kreiter/The Boston Globe via Getty Images, (Rutterschmidt) Allen J. Schaben/AFP/Getty Images, (Toure) Adrian Dennis/AFP/Getty Images, (McVey) Rex Features; pg.110 (Terry) Albert Pena/Icon SMI/Corbis, (feet) Mark Thompson/Allsport/Getty Images; pg.113 (Sofia) Westend61/Corbis, (Angela) OUP/Blend Images; pg.114 KidStock/Getty Images; pg.115 (subway) Juan Antonio/AGE fotostock, (metrocard) Bora/Alamy, (bike) Stan Honda/AFP/Getty Images, (bus) wdstock/istockphoto, (taxi bottom) hanusst/istockphoto, (taxi top) Songquan Deng/Shutterstock.com; pg.117 Paramount/The Kobal Collection; pg.118 (Thailand) Viacheslav Khmelnytskyi/Alamy, (Mexico) John Edward Linden/Arcaid/Corbis; pg.119 Creative Crop/Getty Images; pg.121 (car) CandyBox Photography/Alamy, (facebook) Erkan Mehmet/Alamy, (bus) Anna Peisl/Corbis; pg.152 (1) Dave King/Getty Images, (2) Gastromedia/Alamy, (3) jon whitaker/Getty Images, (4) studiomode/Alamy, (5) Food and Drink Photos/Alamy, (6) Annabelle Breakey/Getty Images; pg.155 (1 top) David Cole/Alamy, (2 top) Peter Titmuss/Alamy, (3 top) MkStock/Alamy, (4 top) Greg Balfour Evans/Alamy, (5 top) Dick Reed/Corbis, (6 top) Robert Harding Picture Library Ltd/Alamy, (7 top) Justin Kase ztwoz/Alamy, (8 top) imagebroker/Alamy, (9 top) Bill Cobb/SuperStock, (1 bottom) Tom And Steve/Getty Images, (2 bottom) Chris Ryan/Getty Images, (3 bottom) Stellar Stock/Masterfile, (4 bottom) Ian Dagnall/Alamy, (5 bottom) kickstand/Getty Images, (6 bottom) Michael Runkel/Alamy, (7 bottom) John Nordell/Getty Images, (8 bottom) Peter Ptschelinzew/Getty Images, (9 bottom) Tetra Images/Alamy, (10 bottom) AKP Photos/Alamy, (11 bottom) StacieStauffSmith Photos/shutterstock, (12 bottom) Bo Zaunders/Corbis, (13 bottom) Alan Schein/Corbis, (14 bottom) JTB Media Creation, Inc./Alamy; pg.157 (1) Caro/Alamy, (2 left) imagebroker/Alamy, (2 right) VisitBritain/Andrew Orchard/Getty Images, (3) Matthew Ashton/AMA/Corbis, (4) Corbis Super RF/Alamy, (5) Jonathan Larsen/Diadem Images/Alamy, (6) Mark Davidson/Alamy, (7) Dmitry Korotayev/Epsilon/Getty Images, (8) Stadium Bank/Alamy, (9) Scott W. Grau/Icon SMI/Corbis; pg.159 (1) New Line/The Kobal Collection/Bridges, James, (2) 20th Century Fox/The Kobal Collection, (3, The Help) Dreamworks LLC/The Kobal Collection, (4) Zoetrope/United Artists/The Kobal Collection, (5) Warner Bros./The Kobal Collection/Buitendijk, Jaap, (6) Hammer/The Kobal Collection, (7, 10) Touchstone Pictures/The Kobal Collection, (8) Warner Bros/The Kobal Collection, (9) Lucasfilm/20th Century Fox/The Kobal Collection, (11) Universal/Studio Canal/Working Title/The Kobal Collection/Sparham, Laurie, (12) Morgan Creek International/The Kobal Collection/Farmer, J; pg.160 (1) PBWPIX/Alamy, (2) Fancy Collection/SuperStock , (3) Jenna Woodward Photography/Getty Images, (4) Ocean/Corbis, (5) D. Hurst/Alamy, (6) Somos/Superstock, (7) altrendo images/Getty Images, (8) Philipp Nemenz/Getty Images, (9) OUP/Masterfile, (10) Win Initiative/Getty Images, (11, 18) OUP/BananaStock, (12) Karen Spencer/Alamy, (13) Silas Manhood/Alamy, (14) Lusoimages-Abstract/Alamy, (15) William Radcliffe/Science Faction/Corbis, (16) PhotoAlto/Alamy, (17) Aflo Foto Agency/Alamy, (19) Kris Timken/Getty Images, (20) Juan Silva/Getty Images; pg.161 (UK) keith morris/Alamy, (US) Will & Deni McIntyre/Corbis; pg.162 (modern) Fotosearch/Getty Images, (rustic) Southern Stock/Getty Images; pg.163 (crowd) Tomas Abad/Alamy, (beach) John Short/Design Pics/Corbis.

Commissioned photography by: Gareth Boden pp.26, 27, 30 (two dads in park), 38 (mobile phone) 68, 75 (Macbook pro, Tiffany heart necklace). Ryder Haske: pp.12, 13, 32, 33, 52, 53, 72, 73, 92, 93. MM studios pp.96 (Beatles album, Penguin books), p.152 (meat, fish and vegetable groups).

Pronunciation chart artwork by: Ellis Nadler

Illustrations by: Peter Bull: pp.20–21, 25, 116; Mark Duffin: 81; Alex Green/Folio Art: p.100–101; Olivier Latyk/Good Illustration Ltd: pp.34, 35, 90, 138, 162; Lyndon Hayes/Dutch Uncle: pp.16, 19, 30, 59, 76–77, 80; Astushi Hara/Dutch Uncle: pp.49, 79, 120, 133, 134, 135, 137, 138, 142, 143,144, 145, 148, 149, 150, 151, 156, 158, 161, 164; Sophie Joyce: p.47; Jonathan Krause: p.64; Tim Marrs: pp.50–51, 88–89; Joe McLaren: pp.4–5, 41; Matt Smith: pp.30/31.

Contents

G passive (all tenses)
V movies
P sentence stress

6A Shot on location

Where was the movie shot?

I think it was shot in New York.

1 READING

a Look at the photos with the article. Do they remind you of any movies or TV series that you have seen?

b Now read the article and complete it with a past participle from the list.

based designed inhabited inspired ~~owned~~
photographed transformed used welcomed

You are standing in *the place where...*

A Highclere Castle *near Newbury in Berkshire, UK*

The castle has been [1] *owned* by the Carnarvon family since 1679, and the Earl and Countess Carnarvon currently live there. In 2010, movie director Julian Fellowes, a close friend of the family, was planning a new TV series about an aristocratic family and their servants during the early 20th century. While he was staying at Highclere Castle, he realized that it would be the perfect place to set his historical drama, and the castle was [2] __________ into *Downton Abbey*, the home of the fictional Crawley family. The series was a huge success, and it has been sold all over the world. Both the interior and exterior scenes were shot in and around the castle itself.

In the second season of the TV series, the castle is used as a hospital during the First World War. These scenes are [3] __________ on a real-life event. In 1914, Lady Almina Carnarvon allowed soldiers who had been wounded to be taken care of in the castle.

Go there

Highclere Castle and gardens are open to the public during the Easter holidays and during the summer—from July to September. It is also open on many Sundays and holidays from 10:30 a.m. to 6:00 p.m. Visit the Egyptian Gallery, which contains many objects brought back from his travels by Lady Almina's husband, the fifth Earl of Carnarvon, who famously discovered the tomb of the young Pharaoh Tutankhamun. www.highclerecastle.co.uk

B Cortlandt Alley

New York City, USA

In Hollywood's version of New York City, the giant metropolis is full of secret alleys where crimes take place, and criminals are chased by the police. In fact, there are hardly any alleys in New York today at all. One of the few remaining ones, Cortlandt Alley, has been [4] __________ for almost all the alley scenes in movies and TV series that are set in New York City. Movies with scenes that were shot there include *Crocodile Dundee* and *Men in Black 3*, and TV series like *Blue Bloods*, *Boardwalk Empire*, *NYPD Blue*, and *Law & Order*.

Go there

Thousands of tourists want to be [5] __________ in Cortlandt Alley. It is on the edge of Chinatown, in Manhattan, between Franklin Street and Canal Street. In fact, it is a perfectly safe place to visit. In real life, it is not [6] __________ by gangsters, but is the home for perfectly respectable businesses such as the New York Table Tennis Federation Training Center.

C Casa Loma

Toronto, Canada

This Gothic Revival style building, with a spectacular tower, was [7]__________ by Canadian architect E.J. Lennox. The original owner, Sir Henry Mill Pellatt spent $3.5 million and hired 300 workers to construct the building. After three years, the castle was finally completed in 1914. Unfortunately, in 1933, the city of Toronto seized Casa Loma from Pellatt for nonpayment of taxes. After several years of neglect, the castle was scheduled for demolition, but it was saved by the Kiwanis Club—a service club that helps the homeless, the hungry, and other disadvantaged people. The club still holds meetings there today! During World War II, equipment designed to find underwater enemy boats was made in the castle. Because of its unusual look, the castle has been used as a location in several well-known movies such as *X-Men*, *Chicago*, and *Scott Pilgrim vs. the World*. In addition, author Eric Wilson was [8]__________ by this building to write the novel *The Lost Treasure of Casa Loma*.

Go there

Visitors are [9]__________ throughout the year. However, some areas of the castle may be closed to the public due to prebooked functions. The castle is open daily from 9:30 a.m. to 5:00 p.m. It's closed on December 25th, Christmas Day. Guided garden tours are available from May through October.
www.casaloma.org

c Read the article again. Answer the questions with **A** (Highclere Castle), **B** (Cortlandt Alley), or **C** (Casa Loma).

Which place...?

1 is not really as it seems in movies
2 has a permanent exhibition there
3 was used for the same thing both in real life and on TV
4 a place that inspired an author to write a novel about it
5 is one of the few places of its kind that still exists
6 is only open during holiday periods
7 was taken from its owner
8 was used to make equipment for a war

d Have you seen any of the movies or TV series mentioned? Which of the three places would you most like to visit? Why?

2 GRAMMAR passive (all tenses)

a Read the *Highclere Castle* text again. Underline an example of the present passive, the past passive, the present perfect passive, the past perfect passive, and a passive infinitive. How do you form the passive? What part of the passive changes when you want to change the tense?

b ➤ **p.142 Grammar Bank 6A.** Learn more about the passive and practice it.

3 PRONUNCIATION sentence stress

a **3 32** Listen and write the stressed words in the large pink rectangles.

1 ___ *movie* ___ *based* ___ ___ *famous* *book*.
2 ___________________________________.
3 ___________________________________.
4 ___________________________________.
5 ___________________________________?
6 ___________________________________?

b Look at the stressed words and try to remember what the other (unstressed) words are. Then listen again to check and write them in.

4 VOCABULARY movies

a Look at some extracts from the texts in **1**. What do you think the highlighted phrases mean?

1 Cortlandt Alley has been used for almost all the alley scenes in movies and TV series that are set in New York.
2 These scenes are based on a real-life event.
3 Both the interior and exterior scenes were shot in and around the castle itself.

b ➤ **p.159 Vocabulary Bank** *Movies.*

c Explain the difference between these pairs of words and phrases.

1 a plot and a script
2 a horror movie and a thriller
3 a musical and a soundtrack
4 the main cast and the extras

5 SPEAKING

a Read the movie interview and think about your answers and reasons.

1 CAN YOU THINK OF A MOVIE THAT...?
- was incredibly funny
- had a very sad ending
- put you to sleep
- made you feel good
- you've seen several times
- made you buy the soundtrack

2 DO YOU PREFER...?
- seeing movies at home or in the movie theater
- seeing a) American movies
  b) other foreign movies
  c) movies from your country
- seeing foreign movies dubbed or with subtitles

3 TELL ME ABOUT A REALLY GOOD MOVIE YOU'VE SEEN THIS YEAR
- What kind of movie is it?
- Is it based on a book or on a real event?
- Where and when is it set?
- Who's in it? Who is it directed by?
- Does it have a good plot?
- Does it have a good soundtrack?
- Why did you like it?

b In pairs, interview each other. Ask for and give as much information as you can. Do you have similar tastes?

6 SPEAKING & LISTENING

a Look at the images from some famous movies. What kinds of movies are they? Have you seen any of them? What are they about? What do you think they have in common?

War Horse

Indiana Jones and the Temple of Doom

E.T. the Extra-Terrestrial

Minority Report

Catch Me If You Can

b Now look at some photos of Steven Spielberg and Dagmara Walkowicz, who worked as an interpreter on one of his movies. In pairs, answer the questions.

1. Where do you think they are?
2. Which Spielberg movie do you think was being made?
3. What do you think Dagmara is doing in the photo on the right?
4. Do you think Dagmara found Spielberg easy to work with?

c 3 36))) Listen to the first part of an interview with Dagmara and check your answers to **b** 1 and 2.

d Listen again and mark the sentences **T** (true) or **F** (false).

1. When the movie company came to Krakow, Dagmara was working as a teacher.
2. She got a part-time job doing translations for them.
3. There was party at the hotel to celebrate Spielberg's birthday.
4. When she arrived, she was asked to interpret Spielberg's speech, because the interpreter was late.
5. Spielberg was very happy with the way she had done her job.

e 3 37))) Now listen to the second part of the interview and check your answers to **b** 3 and 4.

f Listen again and make notes under the headings below.

What she had to do during the movie

go to the movie set every day, translate Spielberg's instructions

The worst thing about the job

One especially difficult scene

What it was like to work with Spielberg

Being an extra

What happened after the movie was finished

g Would you have liked to have done Dagmara's job? Do you think she made the right decision in the end?

7 WRITING

➤ **p.117 Writing** *A movie review.* Write a review of a movie.

G modals of deduction: *might, can't, must*
V the body
P diphthongs

She can't be his mother. She must be his sister.

No, she's his mother. She looks very young for her age.

6B Judging by appearances

1 READING & SPEAKING

a Answer the questions in pairs.

1. Do you have a profile photo of yourself that you use on social networking sites, or on your ID?
2. Why did you choose it?
3. What do you think the photo says about you?

b Look at the four profile photos. Why do you think the people have chosen these photos?

c Read the article and complete it with the headings below. Then look at the four photos again. Which of the 12 categories do you think they belong to?

A **Photo of you as a child**
B **Vacation photo**
C **Logo of your business or company**
D **Photo with a celebrity**
E **Photo with a partner**
F **Photo with your baby or child**

d Read the article again. Look at the highlighted phrases. With a partner, try to figure out their meaning.

e Think about the profile photos or ID card photos of your family and friends. Which categories do they fit in? Do you agree with the text? Has the article made you want to change your profile picture? Why (not)?

What does your profile picture say about you?

Whether it's a photo of you on a night out or of you with your newborn baby, the image you choose to represent you on social networking sites says a lot about you.

Profile pictures on Facebook and similar sites are the visual projection to friends and family of who you are and what you are like. On Twitter, where people follow both friends and strangers, profile pictures are smaller and perhaps more significant. They are often the first and only visual introduction people have to each other. So what does *your* profile photo say about you?

According to communications consultant Terry Prone, there are 12 categories that cover most types of profile pictures.

1 **The professionally taken photo**
You use social media mainly for business or career purposes.

2 ______________________
You want to show what you have achieved in your family life and are generally more interested in a response from women than from men.

3 ______________________
You see your other half as the most important thing in your life, and you see yourself as one half of a couple.

4 **Having fun with friends**
Generally young and carefree, you want to project an image of being fun and popular.

5 ______________________
You are a bit of an escapist and eager to show a different side of yourself from what you do on a day-to-day basis.

6 ______________________
This kind of image says that you don't really want to grow up and face the future. You are nostalgic for your childhood.

7 **Caricature**
Using a caricature is a way of saying that your image isn't rigid and that you don't take yourself too seriously.

8 **Photo related to your name, but not actually you (a shop sign or product label for example)**
You want to be identifiable, but you feel your name is more important than what you look like.

9 **Photo related to your political beliefs or a team that you support**
You think that your beliefs and interests are more important than your personality.

10 ______________________
You think that showing yourself with a well-known person will make you seem more important.

11 **Self-portrait taken with webcam / camera phone**
Functional. It says, "Look, I don't dress up; take me as I am."

12 ______________________
You only use social media in a professional capacity, and you identify more with your work role than with your private life.

Adapted from The Irish Times

2 VOCABULARY the body

a 3 38 Look at the four pictures and listen. Which one is the thief? Describe the four pictures with a partner.

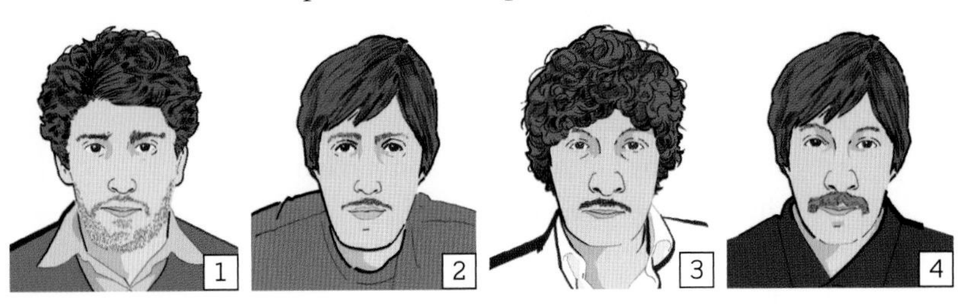

b ➤ **p.160 Vocabulary Bank** *The body.*

3 PRONUNCIATION diphthongs

a 3 41 Read the information about diphthongs. Then listen and repeat the five words and sounds.

Diphthongs
Diphthongs are a combination of two vowel sounds or vowel letters, for example the sounds /ɔɪ/ in voice.

b Write these words in the correct columns.

bite eyes face mouth nose outgoing pointy shoulders smile taste throw toes voice

c 3 42 Listen and check. Then practice saying the phrases below.

a loud voice | narrow shoulders | a wide mouth
brown eyes | a Roman nose | a round face

d Take the quiz with a partner. Answer with *my* / *your* / *their* + a part of the body.

WHICH PART(S) OF THE BODY...?

1 do you wear | a ring / gloves / socks / a cap | on
2 do ballet dancers stand on
3 do soccer players often injure
4 do women put makeup on
5 do people brush
6 do people carry a backpack on

4 3 43 SONG *I Got Life* ♫

5 GRAMMAR modals of deduction

a Look at the photos of three people. Then in two minutes, match three sentences with each person.

- ☐ He / she might be a criminal.
- ☐ He / she might not know how to use the Internet.
- ☐ He / she could be a model.
- ☐ He / she could be German or Scandinavian.
- ☐ He / she may not have a job.
- ☐ He / she may be a millionaire.
- ☐ His / her hair must be dyed.
- ☐ He / she must be retired.
- ☐ He / she can't be a business person.

b Compare with a partner. *I think he could be a model.*

c ➤ **Communication** *Judging by appearances p.106.* Find out about the three people. Did you guess correctly?

d Look at the sentences in **a** and answer the questions.

1 Which modal verbs mean *it's possible*?
might ________ ________ ________

2 Which modal verb means *it's very likely to happen?* ________

3 Which modal verb means *it's impossible*? ________

e ➤ **p.143 Grammar Bank 6B.** Learn more about modals of deduction and practice them.

6 LISTENING & READING

a In pairs, look at the man in the photo. Make sentences about him using *might / may / could (not) be*, *must be*, or *can't be* and words from the list.

American British
very famous homeless
funny dangerous

b **3 47** Listen to a woman talking about the man in **a** and answer the questions.

1 Where were the speaker and her friend, Ny?
2 What were they doing when they saw the man?
3 What did he look like?
4 What did Ny want to do?
5 What did the speaker do?

c **3 48** Why do you think the speaker stopped Ny? Listen and find out. Who was the man?

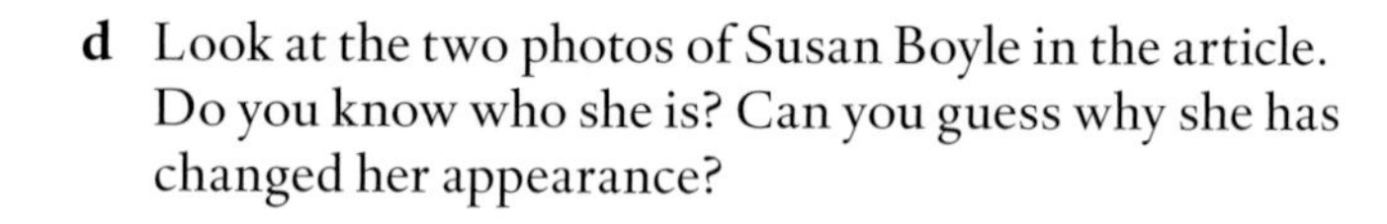

d Look at the two photos of Susan Boyle in the article. Do you know who she is? Can you guess why she has changed her appearance?

e Read the article once and choose the best summary.

1 We now realize that it is wrong to judge people by their appearance.
2 Judging people by appearance can be useful and is often right.
3 If you try to judge people by their appearance, you will usually be wrong about them.

f Read the article again and mark the sentences **T** (true) or **F** (false). Say why the **F** ones are false.

1 Most people predicted that Susan Boyle would be successful as a singer.
2 After her appearance on TV, people started saying that we shouldn't judge people by their appearance.
3 Scientists think that judging by appearance is an important skill.
4 It is more important to be able to make quick judgements about people than it used to be.
5 When we judge people by their appearance, we are usually wrong.
6 Susan Boyle has probably realized that people will never stop judging her by her appearance.

Yes, appearance matters.

When Susan Boyle first walked onto the stage of the *Britain's Got Talent* TV show, people immediately thought that she looked like a 47-year-old single woman who lived alone with her cat (which in fact she was). Nobody thought for a minute that she had a chance of doing well on the show, or could ever become a star. But when she opened her mouth and started singing *I Dreamed a Dream*, from the musical *Les Misérables*, everybody was amazed. After the video of her performance went viral, journalists started talking about how wrong it is to stereotype people into categories, and how we should learn, once and for all, "not to judge a book by its cover."

But social scientists say that there are reasons why we judge people based on how they look. On a very basic level, judging people by their appearance means putting them quickly into categories. In the past, being able to do this was vitally important, and humans developed the ability to judge other people in seconds. Susan Fiske, a professor of psychology and neuroscience at Princeton University, said that traditionally, most stereotypes are linked to judging whether a person looks dangerous or not. "In prehistoric times, it was important to stay away from people who looked aggressive and dominant," she said.

One reason why our brains persist in using stereotypes, experts say, is that often they give us generally accurate information, even if all the details aren't right. Ms. Boyle's appearance, for example, accurately told us a lot about her, including her socioeconomic level and lack of worldly experience.

People's enthusiasm for Susan Boyle, and for other underdogs who end up winning, is unlikely to stop us from stereotyping people. This may be one of the reasons why, although Ms. Boyle expressed the hope that "maybe this could teach them a lesson, or set an example," she did begin to change her appearance, wearing makeup, dying her gray hair, and appearing in more stylish clothing.

Adapted from The New York Times

g Find a word or phrase in the article for the definitions.

Paragraph 1

1 __________ __________ was sent all over the Internet

2 __________ *a* __________ *by* __________ __________ judge a person by his / her appearance

Paragraph 2

3 __________ __________ absolutely essential

Paragraph 3

4 __________ __________ what social class she is and how much money she has

Paragraph 4

5 __________ people who are not expected to succeed

h Talk to a partner.

1 Do you think people in your country tend to judge other people by their appearance? In what way?

2 How important do you think appearance is for the following people?
- politicians
- TV hosts
- business people
- singers
- doctors

Do you think it is right that their appearance matters?

3 On what occasions might *you* judge someone by their appearance?

5&6 Review and Check

GRAMMAR

Circle a, b, or c.

1 Elliot served, but the ball ______ into the net.
a went b was going c had gone

2 The athlete fell at the end of the race when she ______ toward the finishing line.
a run b was running c had run

3 I didn't realize that you two ______ before.
a didn't meet b weren't meeting c hadn't met

4 **A** I can't find my glasses anywhere.
B ______ them when you left home this morning?
a Did you wear b Were you wearing c Had you worn

5 ______ walk to work, or do you drive?
a Do you use to b Do you usually c Use you to

6 When I was a child I ______ like vegetables.
a don't used to b didn't used to c didn't use to

7 ______ play any sports when you were in college?
a Did you use to b Use you to c Did you used to

8 A lot of famous movies ______ in Cortlandt Alley.
a have shot b have been shot c has been shot

9 He's an actor who hates ______ about his private life.
a asking b being asking c being asked

10 Why ______ in New Zealand?
a is the movie being made b is the movie making
c is making the movie

11 Many people believe that Columbus ______ America.
a didn't really discover b wasn't really discovered
c weren't really discovered

12 **A** I've just rung the doorbell, but there's no answer.
B They ______ in the yard. Take a look.
a can't be b might be c can be

13 He's a little older than me, so he ______ in his 30s now.
a must be b may be c can't be

14 **A** Did you know Ann and David broke up?
B That ______ true! I saw them together just now.
a must not be b might be c can't be

15 **A** Does your sister know Travis?
B She ______ him. I'm not sure.
a can't know b may know c can know

VOCABULARY

a Write the parts of the body that you use to do these actions.

1 kiss ________ 3 smell ________ 5 bite ________
2 stare ________ 4 clap ________

b Circle the right verb or phrase.

1 The Nets *won* / *beat* the Nuggets 108–102.
2 Can you book a tennis *course* / *court* on Friday?
3 Sports players are usually very careful not to *get injured* / *get in shape* before important events.
4 Real Madrid *scored* / *kicked* a goal just before half-time.
5 I *do* / *go* swimming every morning during the week.

c Complete the words.

1 Luke is a very **cl**______ friend. I've known him all my life.
2 My wife and I have a lot in **c**______.
3 Gina and I lost **t**______ after we both changed jobs.
4 We met in our first class in college, and we **g**______ to know each other very quickly.
5 Linda is getting married next month. Her **f**______ is Canadian. He's very nice.

d Write words beginning with ***s*** for the definitions.

1 ________ the music of a movie
2 ________ the translation of the dialogue of a movie
3 ________ ________ images often created by computer
4 ________ the most important actor in a movie
5 ________ one part of a movie that happens in one place

e Complete the sentences with one word.

1 I love working ______ at the gym. I go every evening.
2 Please don't laugh ______ Greg—he's trying to do his best.
3 My sister and her boyfriend have broken ______.
4 I wish you could be more excited ______ the opera tickets I got for tonight. They were really expensive.
5 Is there anything good ______ TV tonight?

PRONUNCIATION

a Circle the word with a different sound.

1	score	warm up	court	couple
2	taste	lose	propose	nose
3	face	eyes	audience	course
4	throw	shoulder	doctor	toe
5	noisy	enjoy	shoe	voice

b Underline the stressed syllable.

1 re|fe|ree 3 spec|ta|tors 5 co|lleague
2 re|view 4 di|rec|tor

CAN YOU UNDERSTAND THIS TEXT?

a Read the text. Do you know of any similar theatrical superstitions in your country? What are they?

b Read the text again and choose a, b, or c.

1 Before a performance, actors often...
   a wish each other good luck
   b wish each other bad luck
   c touch each others' legs.

2 Whistling in a theater is considered unlucky because...
   a it used to cause problems for the scene changers
   b it was associated with being out of work
   c it confused the actors

3 It is bad luck to...
   a rehearse any part of a play without an audience
   b rehearse a play in front of family members
   c get to the end of a play when nobody is watching

c Choose five new words or phrases from the text. Check their meaning and pronunciation and try to learn them.

THEATRICAL SUPERSTITIONS

Along with sports players, theater professionals are considered some of the most superstitious people around. These are some of their more common beliefs and practices.

NOT WISHING "GOOD LUCK"

Generally, it is considered bad luck to wish someone "good luck" in a theater. Before a performance, it is traditional for the cast to get together and prevent bad luck by wishing each other bad luck. English actors used to say to each other "I hope you break a leg," and even today actors and musicians often say "break a leg" to each other instead of "good luck" before they go on stage.

WHISTLING

It is considered bad luck for an actor to whistle on or off stage. Original stage crews were often hired from ships that were in port, and whose sailors were temporarily unemployed. These sailors, as they did on ships, often used special whistles to communicate scene changes to each other. If an actor whistled, this could confuse the sailors into changing the set or scenery at the wrong time.

NOT WITHOUT AN AUDIENCE

It is considered bad luck to complete a performance of a play when there is no audience. For this reason actors never say the last line of a play during rehearsals, or some production companies allow a limited number of people (usually friends, family, and reviewers) to attend the dress rehearsals.

VIDEO CAN YOU UNDERSTAND THESE PEOPLE?

3 49))) **On the street** Watch or listen to five people and answer the questions.

Andrew

Adrian

Ryder

Helen

Rebekah

1 Andrew ____.
   a prefers watching sports to playing sports
   b plays at least five sports
   c thinks basketball and lacrosse are interesting team sports

2 An old friend of Adrian's who was using online dating ____.
   a thought the person looked less attractive in real life
   b thought the person looked younger on the Internet
   c married the person they met on the Internet

3 Ryder hasn't cheated by ____.
   a using his phone
   b bringing a book to an exam
   c looking at another student's exam

4 Helen likes *Dirty Dancing* because ____.
   a she loves the soundtrack
   b some of the actors in it are attractive
   c it makes her laugh

5 Rebekah chose her profile picture because she and her siblings look ____ in it.
   a young   b funny   c dressed up

CAN YOU SAY THIS IN ENGLISH?

Do the tasks with a partner. Check (✓) the box if you can do them.

Can you...?

1 ☐ tell an anecdote about something that happened to you using the simple past, past continuous, and past perfect

2 ☐ talk about three past and three present habits of yours

3 ☐ describe a movie, saying where is was set, what it is based on, who it was directed by, and what you thought of it

4 ☐ make deductions about a famous person using *might be*, *must be*, and *can't be*

VIDEO **Short movies** Iconic movie locations
Watch and enjoy the movie.

G first conditional and future time clauses + *when, until*, etc.
V education
P the letter *u*

What will you do if you don't pass your exams?

I'll probably retake them.

7A Extraordinary school for boys

1 VOCABULARY education

a You have two minutes. Answer as many of questions 1–8 as you can in **one** minute. How many did you get right?

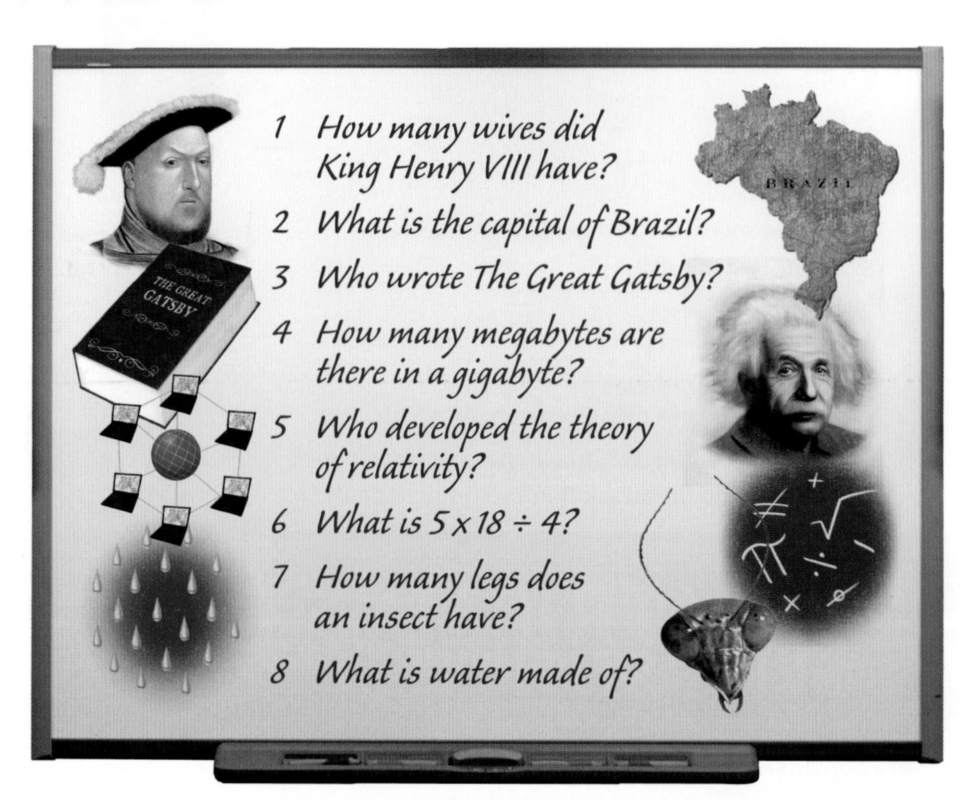

b 4 2))) Now match the questions with these school subjects. Then listen and check.

- [ ] biology
- [ ] chemistry
- [ ] geography
- [ ] history
- [ ] information technology
- [ ] literature
- [ ] math
- [ ] physics

c ➤ **p.161 Vocabulary Bank** *Education.*

2 PRONUNCIATION & SPEAKING the letter *u*

The letter *u*
The letter *u* is usually pronounced /yu/, e.g., *usually* or /ʌ/, e.g., *lunch* and sometimes /u/, e.g., *true*, or /ʊ/, e.g., *put*.

a Put the words in the correct column.

full future lunch music nun put rude rules student study subject true uniform university

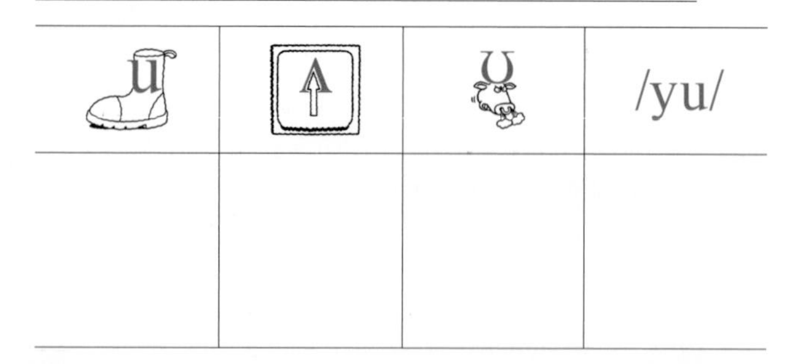

			/yu/

b 4 6))) Listen and check. Practice saying the words. Why do we say *a university* but *an umbrella*?

c 4 7))) Listen and write four sentences.

d Interview your partner using the questionnaire. Ask for more information.

YOUR EDUCATION

- What kind of high school / you go to?
- / you like it?
- How many students / there in each class? Do you think it / the right number?
- How much homework / you usually have?
- / you think it / too much?
- / you have to wear a uniform? / you like it? Why (not)?
- / your teachers too strict or not strict enough? Why? What kind of discipline / they use?
- / students behave well?
- Which subjects / you good and bad at?
- Which / your best and worst subject?

What kind of high school did (do) you go to?

3 LISTENING

Gareth Malone first made his name on TV as a choirmaster in *The Choir*, a series in which he brought together all kinds of different people who had never sung before and turned them into accomplished singers.

Last April, Gareth took on what was maybe an even bigger challenge. He became an elementary school teacher for a quarter. His mission was to teach a group of 11-year-old boys from a mixed elementary school. Many of the boys weren't doing very well at school and, like many other boys, they were a long way behind the girls in reading and writing. The result is *Gareth Malone's Extraordinary School for Boys* – a three-part TV series...

GARETH MALONE'S EXTRAORDINARY SCHOOL FOR BOYS

a Look at the photos above. What can you see? Now read about Gareth Malone's *Extraordinary School for Boys*. In your country, are boys usually behind girls in reading and writing?

b 4 8))) Listen to **Part 1** of a radio program about the experiment and answer the questions.

1 How long did Gareth have to teach the boys?
2 What was his aim?
3 What three things did he believe were important?

c 4 9))) Listen to **Part 2**. Complete the chart.

Gareth made some general changes, for example:	1
	2
To improve their language skills, he organized:	1 A ________________ competition
	2 A ________________ "World Cup"
	3 A ________________, that the boys (and girls) had to both write and perform

d Listen again. How successful were the three activities?

e 4 10))) Now listen to **Part 3** to find out what the result of the experiment was. Did the boys' reading improve?

f What do you think of Gareth's ideas? Do you think they are appropriate for girls? Are any of them used in your country?

4 SPEAKING

a In groups of three, each choose one (different) topic from the list below. Decide if you agree or disagree and write down at least three reasons.

- Boys and girls both learn better in single-sex schools.
- Schools should let children wear whatever they want at school.
- Cooking and housework should be taught at school.
- Schools don't teach children the important things they need to know to be an adult.
- Physical education should be optional.
- School summer vacations should be shorter.
- Children spend too much time at school on math and IT and not enough on things like music, art, and drama.
- Private schools are usually better than public schools.

Debating a topic: organizing your ideas

- The topic I've chosen is...
- I | completely agree / partly agree / completely disagree | that...
- First of all, (I think that...)
- My second point is that...
- Another important point is that...
- Finally,...

b Explain to the rest of your group what you think about your topic. The others in the group should listen. At the end, they can vote for whether they agree or disagree with you and say why.

5 GRAMMAR first conditional and future time clauses + *when, until,* etc.

a In pairs, answer the questions.

1 When was the last time you took an exam? Did you pass or fail?
2 What's the next exam you are going to take? How do you feel about it?
3 How do you usually feel before you take an exam?
4 What do you usually do the night before an exam?
5 Have you ever failed an important exam you thought you had passed (or vice versa)?

b 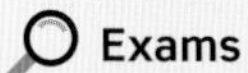 **4 11, 12** Listen to Olivia and Woo-sung, who are waiting for their exam scores, and answer the questions.

1 Do they think they did well on the tests?
2 When and how will they get the test results?
3 How will they celebrate if they get good scores?
4 What do they want to do if they get good scores?
5 What will they do if they fail, or if they don't get the scores that they need?

> **Exams**
> Exam scores can be given as **numbers** (usually out of 10 or 100) or as **letters** (A, B, C, etc.). College grades are usually given in numbers (out of 100). High school grades are usually given in letter (A+, A, A–, etc.)

c **4 13** Listen and complete the sentences.

1 They probably won't admit me **unless** ______________.
2 **As soon as** ______________ I'll look up my scores.
3 I don't want to plan any celebrations **until** ______________.
4 **If** I don't get into a good college, ______________.
5 **When** ______________, they'll mail the results.

d **4 14** Listen to Olivia and Woo-sung. What scores did they get? What are they going to do?

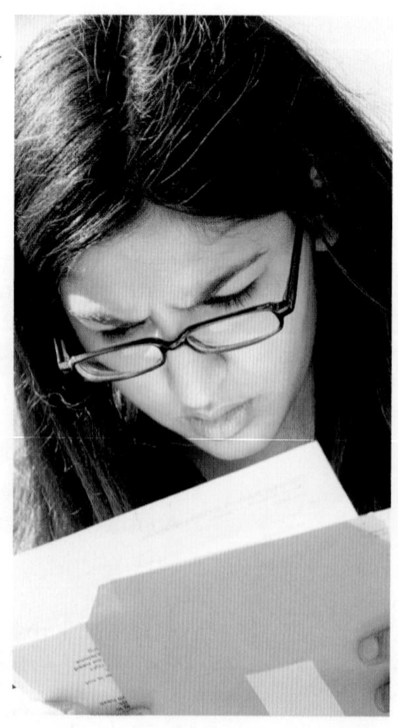

e ➤ **p.144 Grammar Bank 7A.** Learn more about first conditionals and future time clauses, and practice them.

f Ask and answer with a partner. Make full sentences.

What will you do...?
- as soon as you get home
- if you don't pass your English exam
- when this class ends
- if it rains on the weekend

g ➤ **Communication** *Three in a row p.106.*

6 READING & SPEAKING

a Read the article once. What is a "tiger mother?"

Your 12-year-old daughter is delighted. She got an A-minus in math, second place in a history competition, and top scores on her piano exam. Do you a) say *Good job!*, give her a hug, and tell her she doesn't need to practice the piano today, and can go to a friend's house, or b) [1] ask why she didn't get an A in math, why she didn't get first place on the history exam, and tell her she'll be punished if she doesn't practice the piano?

If you chose a), you are definitely not Amy Chua.

A lot of people wonder why so many Chinese children are math geniuses and musical prodigies. Amy Chua explains why in her book *Battle Hymn of the Tiger Mother.* It is a book that caused great controversy among parents when it was first published. [2] ______________, Chua married a man who she met at Harvard University, and when their two daughters were born she was determined that they would be as successful as she was.

Her system had strict rules. Her two daughters were expected to be number one in every subject (except gym and drama) and [3] ______________. Playing with friends and TV was forbidden. Music was required.

The system seemed at first to be working. From a very early age her daughters Sophia and Lulu were outstanding students and musical prodigies.

Do you want to practice for five hours or six?

Amy Chua brought up her daughters the Chinese way...

At 13 Sophia played a piano solo at Carnegie Hall in New York City, and at 12, Lulu a violinist, was the leader of a prestigious orchestra for young people. Chua chose math and music for her daughters, but it seems that they could have excelled in anything. 4________________________.

Eventually Chua realized that she was pushing her daughters too hard. Lulu had always rebelled the most, and when she was 13 she refused to cooperate at all. After a series of violent arguments, Chua decided to give her daughters a little more freedom, and Lulu immediately gave up violin lessons and took up tennis. 5____________________.

Many people have been shocked by the book. 6____________________. She once sent her daughter Lulu, aged three, into the yard without her coat when it was 21°F because she had behaved badly at her first piano lesson.

However, the girls do not seem to resent their mother. Sophia said that she herself chose to accept the system, and after the book was published, she wrote an article defending her mother. Lulu says that although she no longer wants to be a violinist, she still loves playing the violin. 7____________________. Sophia is now studying law at Harvard, and Lulu is doing well in high school and winning tennis trophies.

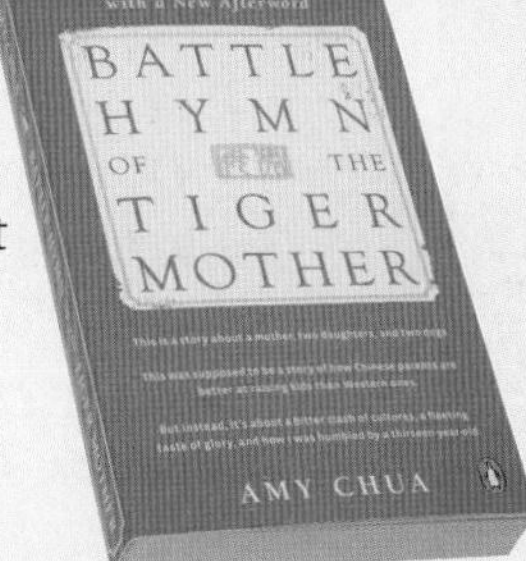

Interestingly Chua, who was brought up in a family of four girls, has no idea whether she could apply her Chinese parenting system to boys. 8____________________.

Adapted from The Times

b Read the article again and put the phrases **A–H** in the correct places.

A "They are a mystery to me," she says
B Later Sophia was even allowed to go to a rap concert
C ~~ask why she didn't get an A in math~~
D Chua spent much of her daughters' childhood shouting at them and criticizing every mistake they made
E Born in the Unites States to Chinese immigrant parents
F In fact, she is glad her mother made her learn
G to be at least two years ahead of their classmates in math
H "There's no musical talent in my family," she says, "it's just hard work"

c In pairs, look at the highlighted words and phrases and figure out their meaning from the context.

d Read three responses that were posted after the article was published. Do you agree with any of them?

Wow, what a different way of looking at how to learn! Amy Chua certainly shows that strict discipline works. But personally I think that being positive and encouraging children is better than being so strict.

I disagree with the idea that children on their own never want to work. My son was motivated by himself to succeed in music. If having strict and pushy parents is what it takes to be a child prodigy, then I feel sorry for the child. Yes, they might be very successful, but at what cost? What is the rest of their life going to be like?

I agree that no matter what we do in life, hard work is required to be successful. That's a great lesson to learn. BUT, it should be accompanied by love and respect for the child.

e Talk to a partner.

1 What do **you** think of Amy Chua's system?
2 Were (are) your parents strict about your education?
3 Did they (do they)...?
- help you with your homework
- make you study a certain number of hours every day
- punish you if you didn't (don't) pass exams
- let you go out with friends during the week
- let you choose your extra activities
- make you do extra activities that you didn't (don't) really want to do

make* and *let
After *make* and *let* we use the base form of a verb.
My parents made me work very hard.
They didn't let me go out during the week.

G second conditional
V houses
P sentence stress

If I could afford it, I'd move out tomorrow.

I wouldn't. I like living with my parents.

7B Ideal home

1 GRAMMAR second conditional

a Work with a partner. Describe the two photos, and then answer the questions.

1. Which of the two houses would you prefer to live in? Why?
2. Who do you live with? Do you get along well? Do you argue about anything? What?

b Read the article. How many of the people would like to leave home?

Still living at home?

More and more young people in their 20s all over the world are living with their parents because it is too expensive for them to rent or buy a place of their own. Are you living at home? Are you happy with it? Post a comment at #stilllivingathome

c Read the article again. Who...?

1. is not happy living at home because of family conflict
2. thinks his / her parents think of him / her as still being a teenager
3. thinks that the advantage of living at home is not having to do any work
4. would like to be able to decorate his / her home in his / her own taste

d Look at the article again, and answer the questions.

1. In the highlighted phrases, what tense is the verb after *if*?
2. What tense is the other verb?
3. Do the phrases refer to a) a situation they are imagining or b) a situation that will probably happen soon?

e ➤ **p.145 Grammar Bank 7B.** Learn more about the second conditional and practice it.

Comments

Vivienne @Montreal, Canada
If I had the money, I would move out immediately. All I want is somewhere that's my own, where I can do what I want, where I can have my own furniture and pictures, where no one can tell me what to do. If it were my place, I'd be happy to do the cleaning and things like that. I would take care of it. But right now it's just a dream, because I can't find a job.

Mauro @Recife, Brazil
I'm perfectly happy living at home. If I lived on my own, I'd have to pay rent, do the housework, and the cooking. Here my mother does my laundry, she cleans my room, and of course she cooks, and her food is wonderful. I have a nice room. I have my computer where I can watch TV... Why would I want to leave? Even if I could afford it, I wouldn't move out. Not until I get married...

Andrea @Melbourne, Australia
It isn't that my parents aren't good to me – they are. If they weren't, I wouldn't live with them. But I just don't feel independent. I'm 29, but I sometimes worry that if I come back late after a night out, I'll find them still awake waiting up for me. It's never happened, but it still makes me want to move out.

Carlos @San Antonio, Texas
I'd love to move out. I get along well with my parents, but I think I'd get along with them even better if I didn't live at home. My mother drives me crazy – it isn't her fault, but she does. And I'd really like to have a dog, but my mother is allergic to them.

2 PRONUNCIATION & SPEAKING
sentence stress

a 4 18 Listen and repeat the sentences. Copy the rhythm.

1. If I **lived** on my **own**, I'd **have** to **pay rent**.
2. **Would** you **leave home** if you **got** a **job**?
3. **Even** if I **could afford** it, I **wouldn't move out**.
4. If it were **my apartment**, I'd be **happy** to **do** the **cleaning**.
5. I'd **get** along **better** with my **parents** if I **didn't live** at **home**.

b ➤ **Communication** *Guess the sentence* **A** *p.107* **B** *p.109.*

c Choose three of the sentence beginnings below and complete them in a way that is true for you.

If I
...could live anywhere in my town or city, I'd live...
...won a "dream vacation" in a competition, I'd go...
...could choose any car I liked, I'd have a...
...could choose my ideal job, I'd be...
...had more time, I'd learn...
...had to go abroad to work, I'd go to...

d Work with a partner. **A** say your first sentence. Try to get the right rhythm. **B** ask for more information. Then say your first sentence.

If I could live anywhere in my city, I'd live downtown.
Why downtown?

3 VOCABULARY houses

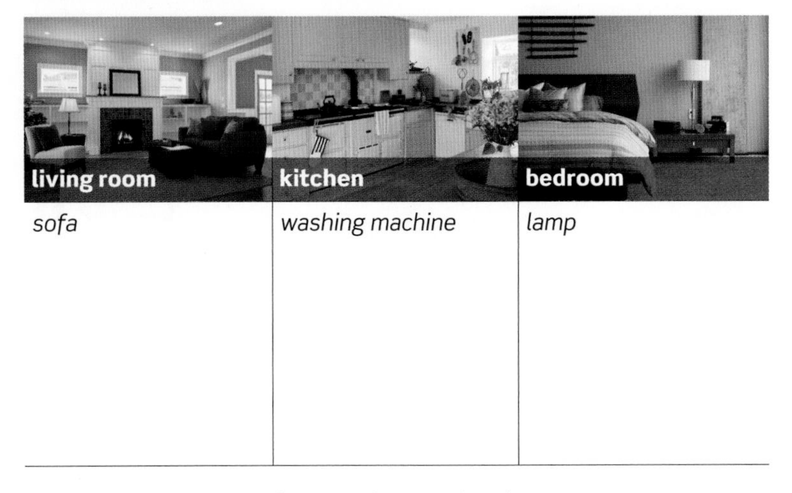

living room	kitchen	bedroom
sofa	*washing machine*	*lamp*

a With a partner, write five words in each column.

b ➤ **p.162 Vocabulary Bank** *Houses.*

c Answer the questions with a partner.

What's the difference between...?

1. the outskirts and the suburbs
2. a village and a town
3. a roof and a ceiling
4. a balcony and a deck
5. a chimney and a fireplace
6. the basement and the first floor
7. wood and wooden

4 READING

a Do you know where Tchaikovsky was from and what he did?

b Look at the photos of Tchaikovsky's house. Which do you think shows...?

a the place where he composed
b the place where he wrote letters
c his favorite place

c 4 22 Read and listen to the audio guide once to check.

d Read the guide again. What is the connection between these things and Tchaikovsky's house?

1 Maidanovo
2 The *Pathétique* symphony
3 Alexei
4 Lilies of the valley
5 Doroshenko
6 The International Tchaikovsky Competition

e Look at the highlighted words and first try to figure out their meaning from context. Then match them with definitions 1–8.

1 ________________ in good order
2 ________________ stay or continue
3 ________________ having a view of
4 ________________ fixed to a wall with a cord
5 ________________ make something become
6 ________________ without a pattern or decoration
7 ________________ something that is owned (by someone)
8 ________________ a piece of furniture with shelves to keep books in

f Have you ever visited the house where a famous person was born or lived? Where was it? What do you remember most about it?

1

2

3
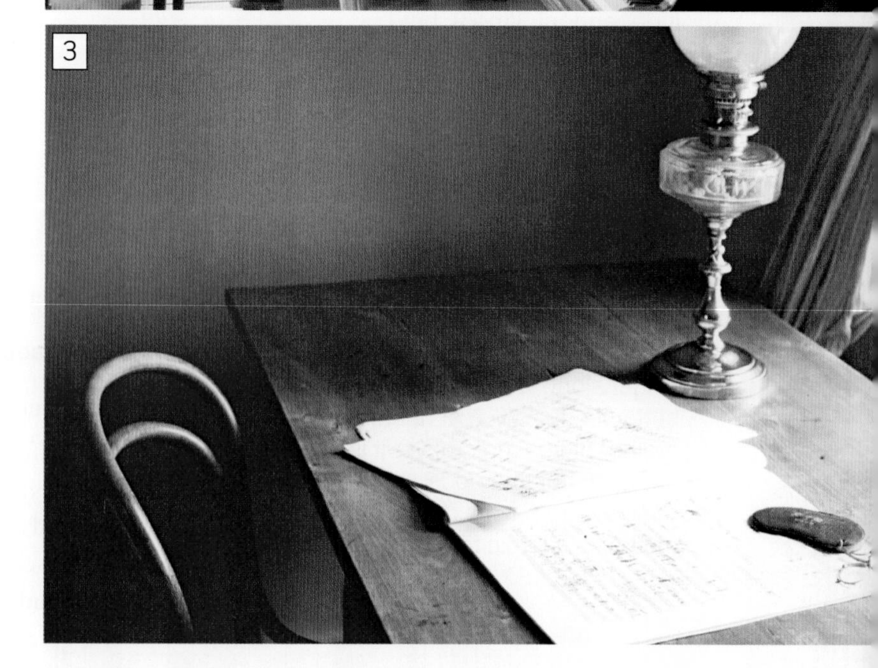

Tchaikovsky's house

In 1885 Tchaikovsky wrote to a friend,

"These days I dream of settling in a village not far from Moscow where I can feel at home."

First he rented a small house in the village of Maidanovo. But Maidanovo was too full of tourists in the summer, and Tchaikovsky had too many visitors, when what he wanted was peace and quiet. Eventually he found the perfect house, in the small town of Klin. It was 52 miles northwest of Moscow, and he lived there until his death on November 6, 1893. It is the place where he wrote his last major work, *Symphony No. 6*, or the *Pathétique* as it's sometimes called.

It's a gray wooden house with a green roof. Tchaikovsky's servant Alexei lived on the first floor, and the kitchen and dining room were on the second floor. Tchaikovsky himself lived on the third floor. The living room and study, where his piano is located, is the largest room in the house, and there is a fireplace and a bookcase with his music books. His writing desk, where he wrote letters every morning after breakfast, is at the end of the room. But the place where he composed music was in his bedroom, on a plain, unpainted table overlooking the yard.

In his final years, Tchaikovsky's great love was his yard. It was not a neat English-style garden, but more like a forest. He adored flowers, particularly lilies of the valley, and after his death, his brother Modest, who had decided to turn the house into a museum, planted thousands of lilies of the valley around the yard.

In 1917, after the Bolshevik revolution, an anarchist named Doroshenko lived there with his family. People say that he fired shots at the portrait of Pope Innocent hanging in one of the bedrooms. He was finally arrested in April, and the house became the property of the state.

Since 1958, the winners of the annual International Tchaikovsky Competition have all been invited to come to Klin to play his piano, and there is a tradition that each musician plants a tree in his yard in the hope that, like his music, it will remain beautiful forever.

5 LISTENING & SPEAKING

a 4 23 Listen to four architecture students describing their "dream house." Which speaker's house is...?

- ☐ the most hi-tech
- ☐ the most luxurious
- ☐ the most eco-friendly
- ☐ the most romantic

b Listen again and make notes about the location and special features of each house.

Speaker 1

Speaker 2

Speaker 3

Speaker 4

c 4 24 Now listen to four sentences the students said. Why do the speakers use *would*?

d Think for a few minutes about what your dream house or apartment would be like and make brief notes. Use ➤ **p.162 Vocabulary Bank** *Houses* to help you.

Where would it be?
What kind of house or apartment would it be?
What special features would it have?

e In groups, describe your dream houses. Try to describe your house in as much detail as possible. Whose do you like best?

6 WRITING

➤ **p.118 Writing** *Describing a house or apartment.* Write a description of your house or apartment for a house rental website.

7 4 25 SONG *If I Could Build My Whole World Around You* ♫

Practical English Boys' night out

EPISODE 4

1 VIDEO ROB AND PAUL CATCH UP

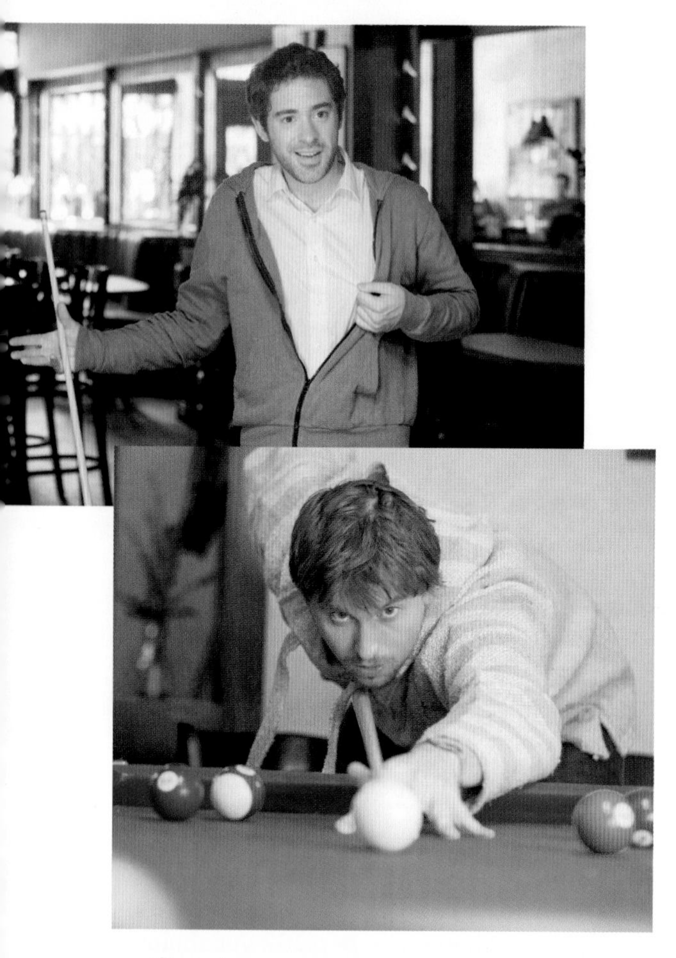

a 4 26 Watch or listen to Rob and Paul. What does Paul think of Jenny?

b Watch or listen again. Mark the sentences **T** (true) or **F** (false). Correct the **F** sentences.

1 Rob used to play pool when he was younger.
2 Rob has a lot of free time.
3 Rob had light hair the last time Paul saw him.
4 Paul thinks Rob has changed a lot.
5 Jenny's parents gave Rob the shirt he's wearing.
6 Rob doesn't want to keep Jenny waiting.

2 VIDEO MAKING SUGGESTIONS

a 4 27 Watch or listen to Paul, Rob, and Jenny talking about what to do after dinner. What do Paul and Rob decide to do? What excuse does Jenny give? What does she do in the end?

b Watch or listen again. Answer with **P**aul, **R**ob, or **J**enny.

Who suggests...?

1 ☐ going dancing
2 ☐ exercising
3 ☐ going to a club
4 ☐ going to an art museum
5 ☐ staying at home
6 ☐ going to a gig
7 ☐ meeting Kerri

c 4 28 Look at some extracts from the conversation. Can you remember any of the missing words? Watch or listen and check.

1 **Paul** What shall we ________ now?
Rob What do you want to do?
Paul Well... I haven't been on a dance floor for weeks now. I've got to move my body. ________ go dancing!

2 **Jenny** I'm going running in the morning. Why ________ you join me?
Paul No, thanks. I'm not ________ keen on running. But I've read about this place called Deep Space, where they play great music. We ________ go there.

3 **Jenny** ________ about going to the late show at MOMA?
Paul MOMA? What's that?

4 **Jenny** ________ about staying in and watching a movie on TV?
Paul I'm in New York. I can watch TV anywhere.

5 **Paul** I didn't think so. So shall we ________ there?
Rob ________ not?

6 **Rob** We ________ meet her outside and go together.
Paul That's a great ________!

Verb forms
Remember to use the base form of the verb after:
Shall we... We could... Why don't you / we... Let's...
Remember to use the gerund after:
What about...? How about...?

d Look at the highlighted expressions for making and responding to suggestions. Which of the ways of making suggestions do you think is the most emphatic?

e 4 29 Watch or listen and repeat the highlighted phrases. Copy the rhythm and intonation.

f Practice the dialogues in **c** with a partner.

g In small groups, practice making suggestions and responding.

You are going to have an end-of-semester class party. You need to decide:

- When to have it
- Where to have it
- What time to have it
- What foods and drinks to have

3 VIDEO THE MORNING AFTER THE NIGHT BEFORE

a 4 30 Watch or listen to Rob and Jenny talking on the phone. What's the problem?

b Watch or listen again. Complete the sentences with 1–3 words.

1 Rob says that he's feeling ________.
2 Kerri invited Rob and Paul to ________.
3 Rob says that he can't make ________.
4 Jenny is upset because it's an ________.
5 Rob promises that ________ again.
6 Rob also says that Paul ________ that afternoon.
7 Jenny tells Don that Rob is such ________.

c Look at the **Social English phrases**. Can you remember any of the missing words?

Social English phrases

Jenny Where are you ________?
Rob That's ________ I'm calling. I'm not going to make it.
Rob It won't ________ again.
Rob He's ________ to Boston this afternoon.
Jenny I mean, ________ not that I don't like Paul, but...
Don I wanted to have a ________ with him before the meeting.
Jenny He's ________ a professional.

d 4 31 Watch or listen and complete the phrases.

e Watch or listen again and repeat the phrases. How do you say them in your language?

Can you...?
☐ use different ways of making suggestions
☐ respond to suggestions
☐ apologize and make an excuse

G reported speech: sentences and questions
V shopping, making nouns from verbs
P the letters *ai*

8A Sell and tell

She said that she was going to complain.

Did they give her a refund?

1 GRAMMAR reported speech: sentences and questions

a Look at the home page of a new website. What do you think you can sell or buy there?

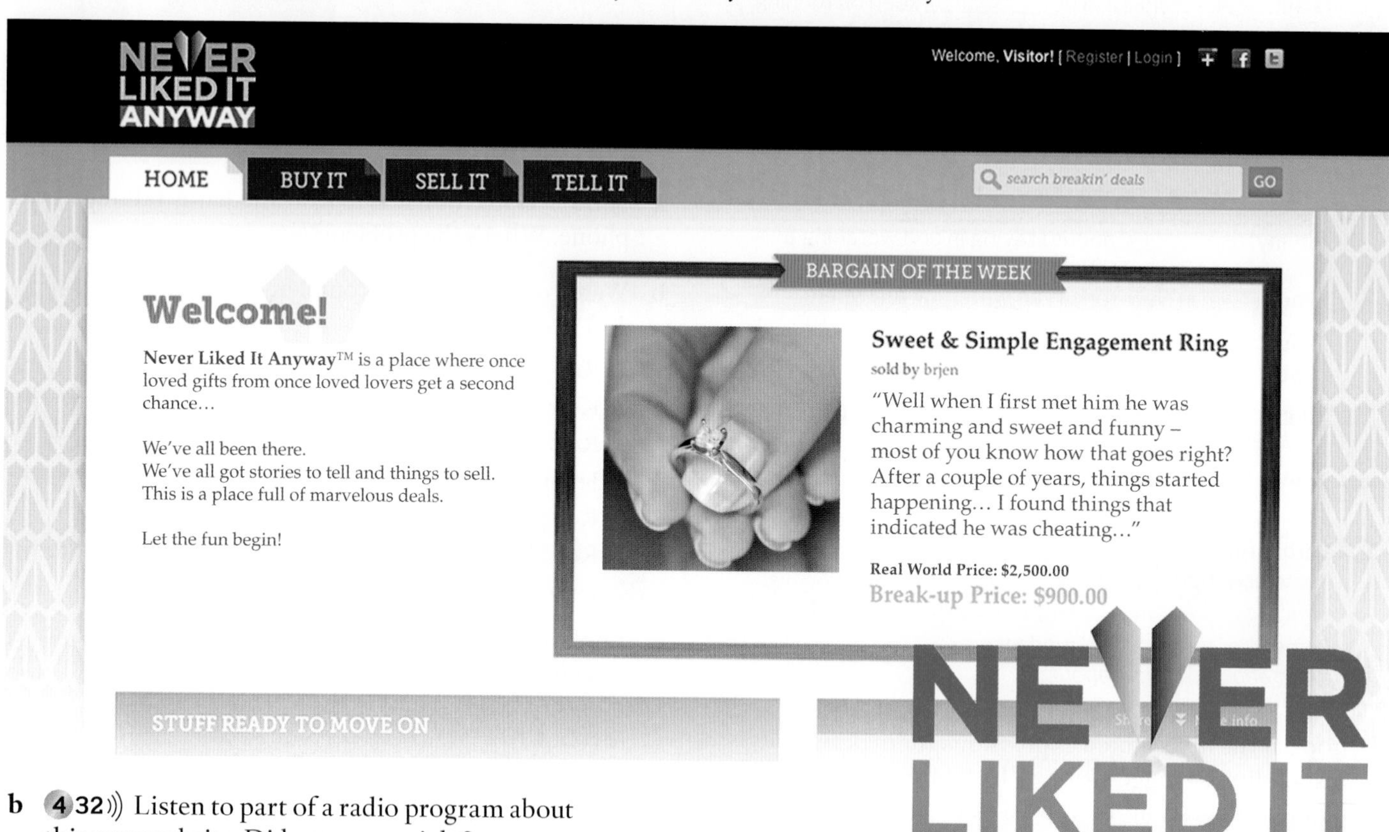

b 4 32 Listen to part of a radio program about this new website. Did you guess right?

c Listen again and answer the questions.

1 Why did Annabel Acton set it up?
2 What kinds of things do people sell on it?
3 What else do they do apart from selling things?

d Now look at three things from the website and answer the questions with a partner.

1 Would you like to buy any of them?
2 Which breakup do you think was the worst?
3 Do you have anything you would like to sell on the website?

e Look at four sentences from the website. What do you think were the actual words that the people used when they said these things?

1 My fiancé told me that he was in love with another woman.
2 She said that she'd come and pick it up.
3 I asked if it was new.
4 I asked her who had given it to her.

1 *"I'm in love with another woman."*

f ➤ **p.146 Grammar Bank 8A.** Learn more about reported sentences and questions, and practice them.

g 4 35 Imagine you were stopped in a shopping mall last Saturday by a woman taking a survey. Listen and write down the questions she asked. Then write your answers.

h Work in pairs. Take turns telling your partner about the survey, what the woman asked you, and what you said.

Last Saturday I was in a shopping mall, and a woman who was taking a survey stopped me. She asked me if I usually...

Wedding dress

sold by Marianne

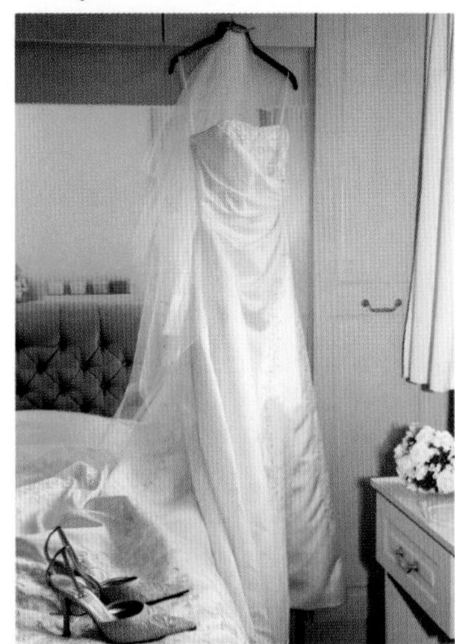

Real World Price: $1,200.00
Break-up price: $500.00

The Product:
Never worn, still has price tags. Selling matching veil and other extras.

The Story:
Two weeks before our wedding was supposed to take place, my fiancé called and told me that he was in love with another woman. I'm over it now, but selling the dress will help me to move on.

BUY IT

Apple MacBook Pro

sold by Carl

Real World Price: $850
Break-up price: $250

The Product:
Everything works fine. A few scratches.

The Story:
My ex-girlfriend left it here when she walked out. She said that she'd come and pick it up, but she never did. Her new guy must have a lot of money!

BUY IT

Tiffany™ heart necklace

sold by Ellie

Real World Price: $1,400.00
Break-up price: $650.00

The Story:
I got this very beautiful necklace as a Christmas present from my boyfriend, Andy. A year later I went to a party at his office, and I saw a girl wearing the exact same necklace. I asked if it was new, and she said yes, it was a present, so I asked her who had given it to her, and she said Andy. I dumped him the next day.

BUY IT

2 VOCABULARY & SPEAKING
shopping

a In pairs, say if you think these are the same or different. Then check with your teacher.

1 *buy something online* and *buy something on the Internet*
2 *a drug store* and *a pharmacy*
3 *an outlet store* and *a department store*
4 *a shopping center* and *a shopping mall*
5 *a library* and *a book store*
6 *put on a shirt* and *try on a shirt*
7 *It fits you.* and *It suits you.*
8 *for sale* and *on sale*

b With your partner, explain the meaning of the words in the list.

a bargain a discount a price tag
a receipt a refund take something back

c Work with a different partner. Interview him / her with the questionnaire below. Ask for and give as many details as you can.

Shopping – in town or online?

1 What's your favorite store or website to buy...?
- ○ a clothes
- ○ b shoes
- ○ c books and music
- ○ d presents
- ○ e food

2 Do you ever shop...? What do you buy?
- ○ a in street markets
- ○ b in supermarkets
- ○ c in shopping centers or malls
- ○ d online

3 What do you...?
- ○ a enjoy buying
- ○ b hate buying

4 Do you prefer shopping for clothes...?
- ○ a by yourself or with somebody
- ○ b at the beginning of the season or when stores have sales

5 What do you think are the advantages and disadvantages of buying clothes online?

Email address | Submit

3 READING

a In your country, if people have a problem with something they've bought, or with the service in a store or restaurant, do they usually complain? If not, why not?

b Read the article *The King of Complainers*. Which of these adjectives (or any others) would you use to describe Clive? Why?

admirable cheap crazy eccentric obsessive smart

c What does Clive think is the best way to complain? What did he get as a result of complaining about…?

1 the smell of cookies
2 a friend's faulty car
3 his wife's fall during a vacation
4 some old strawberries

d Now read *Clive's top tips*. Complete the tips with a heading from the list.

DON'T BE TOO SPECIFIC
DON'T LOSE YOUR TEMPER
KNOW WHO YOU ARE WRITING TO
THREATEN ACTION
WRITE A LETTER
USE FLATTERY

e Now look at the highlighted verbs and verb phrases. With a partner, try to figure out their meaning from the context.

f Which two tips do you think are the most important?

The **King** of Complainers

Clive Zietman loves complaining – but not shouting in hotel lobbies, or angrily telling a salesperson to call the manager, or making a waitress cry. He loves complaining properly and in writing. Over the last 20 years, he has written over 5,000 letters of complaint. His successes include refunded vacations, countless free meals, and complimentary theater tickets.

So how has he achieved this? "Screaming and shouting is a complete waste of time and is usually directed at a person who is not in a position to do anything," he says. "I like to write a polite letter to the company. People won't want to help you if you are aggressive. They respond much better to good manners."

It all started many years ago, on a boring train trip home to West London. The train passed by a cookie factory, and the smell of the cookies made Clive feel hungry. He wrote a letter to the managing director to complain, in a humorous way, about the fumes coming through the train window. The result? Some free packages of cookies. But since then there have been more serious victories as well. On one occasion he managed to get a Volkswagen Golf GTI within 24 hours for a friend who had been complaining for almost a year (without any success) about his faulty vehicle. On another occasion he got a travel agent to refund the cost of a vacation after Clive's wife Bettina broke her leg when she slipped in a puddle of water in their vacation apartment in Spain.

These days, there is almost nothing he won't complain about. After Clive was served moldy strawberries on a British Airways flight, he used a courier service to send the fruit to the airline's chief executive. To compensate, BA invited his daughters, Nina and Zoë, to Heathrow to personally inspect the airline's catering facilities. "I just can't bear bad service," says Clive. "We have a right to good service, and should expect it and demand it. In fact, what irritates me more than anything is that, unlike Americans, we British are hopeless at complaining."

So how do Bettina, his wife, and daughters Nina, 22, Zoë, 18, and 12-year-old son Joe cope with living with one of the world's biggest complainer? Surely he must be a nightmare to live with? Has he ever asked Bettina to explain why a meal she made is badly cooked? "Oh, no, of course not," says Clive. It seems there are some things even he knows you should never complain about!

Adapted from the Daily Mail *website*

How to complain successfully: Clive's top tips

1 ______

Never shout and swear – it achieves nothing. Don't spoil your meal or your vacation by getting into an argument with a waiter or customer service call center operator. Make a mental note of the circumstances and write a letter later.

2 ______

Don't send emails, or standard, printed-out complaints forms. Companies may not read these, but they probably will read a letter. And unless you are particularly fond of Vivaldi, don't waste your time calling a customer complaint line! Your letter should be short and to the point, and should fit on one side of an 8 1/2″ by 11″ sheet of paper. And type it. Reading other people's handwriting is hard work.

3 ______

Write to the company's marketing director or finance director because they're probably the least busy. Find his or her name on the Internet or by calling. Writing *Dear Sir / Madam* is lazy. Taking the time to find a person's name and title shows initiative.

4 ______

If your complaint is serious enough, make it clear you will not hesitate to change to another bank / cell phone company. Smart companies know that changing an angry customer into a satisfied one will make the customer more loyal.

5 ______

Don't say exactly what you expect to receive as compensation. Leave it to the company.

6 ______

Use phrases like "I can only imagine this is an unusual departure from your usual high standards," and "I would love to shop with you again if you can demonstrate to me that you are still as good as I know you used to be."

Glossary
lose your temper become angry
threaten *verb* warn that you may punish somebody if he or she does not do what you want
flattery *noun* saying good things about somebody that you may not mean

4 PRONUNCIATION the letters *ai*

a Say the words aloud, and then write them in the correct column.

airline bargain captain complain email fair obtain hairdresser paid painting repair villain

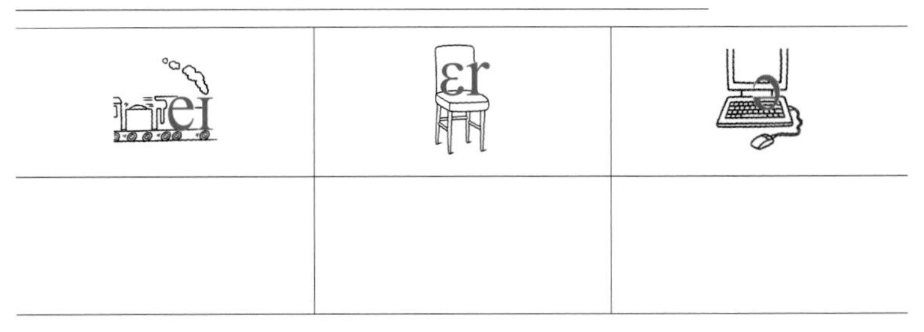

b 4 36 Listen and check, and then answer the questions.

1 What is the pronunciation of *ai* when it is a) stressed b) unstressed?
2 How is *air* usually pronounced?
3 Is *said* pronounced /seɪd/ or /sɛd/?

c 4 37 Listen and write four sentences. Practice saying them.

5 VOCABULARY making nouns from verbs

a Look at some nouns from the article. What verbs do they come from?

complaint argument compensation

b ➤ p.163 **Vocabulary Bank** *Word building*. Do Part 1.

6 LISTENING & SPEAKING

a 4 40 Listen to part of a radio consumer program where people are talking about bad service. What did the people complain about...?

1 in the taxi 2 in the hotel 3 in the restaurant

b Listen again and answer the questions.

1 Who did each person complain to?
2 What did the people they complained to do as a result?

c Talk to a partner.

1 Who's best at complaining in your family? Give examples.
2 Can you remember a time when you (or someone in your family) complained...?
- to a taxi driver
- to a hotel receptionist
- to a waiter
- to someone else

Why did you complain? What did you say? What happened?

d ➤ **Communication** *I want to speak to the manager* **A** *p.107* **B** *p.109.* Role-play a customer complaining to a salesperson and a restaurant manager.

7 WRITING

➤ **p.119 Writing** *A letter of complaint.* Write a letter to complain about something you bought online.

G gerunds and infinitives
V work
P word stress

Do you like your job?

Yes. I'm an accountant – I enjoy working with numbers.

8B What's the right job for you?

1 VOCABULARY work

a Look at the picture story. Match sentences A–I with pictures 1–9.

A ☐ She decided to **set up** an online business selling birthday cakes.
B ☐ Her business is **doing very well**. Clare is a success!
C ☐ She was **unemployed** and had to **look for a job**.
D ☐ They had an argument, and Clare **was fired**.
E *1* Clare **worked for** a marketing company.
F ☐ She **applied for** a lot of jobs, and **sent in résumés**.
G ☐ She made a **good salary**, but she didn't like **her boss**.
H ☐ She had some interviews, but didn't **get the jobs**.
I ☐ She had to work very hard and **work overtime**.

b 4 41))) Listen and check. Then cover the sentences and look at the pictures. Tell the story from memory.

c ➤ **p.164 Vocabulary Bank** *Work*.

2 PRONUNCIATION & SPEAKING word stress

a Underline the stressed syllable in each word. Use the phonetics to help you.

1 a|pply /ə'plaɪ/
2 sa|la|ry /'sæləri/
3 down|size /'daʊnsaɪz/
4 ex|per|i|ence /ɪk'spɪriəns/
5 o|ver|time /'oʊvərtaɪm/
6 per|ma|nent /'pərmənənt/
7 qua|li|fi|ca|tions /kwɑləfə'keɪʃnz/
8 re|sign /rɪ'zaɪn/
9 re|tire /rɪ'taɪər/
10 tem|po|rar|y /'tɛmpərɛri/

b 4 45))) Listen and check. Practice saying the words.

c Do you know anybody who…

– is applying for a job? What kind of job?
– is doing a temporary job? What?
– has a part-time job? What hours does he / she work?
– is self-employed? What does he / she do?
– has been promoted recently? What to?
– was fired from his / her job, or was downsized? Why?
– has just retired? How old is he / she?

d Think of someone you know who has a job. Prepare your answers to the questions below.

- What / do?
- Where / work (in an office, at home, etc.)?
- What qualifications / have?
- What hours / work?
- / have to work overtime?
- / make a good salary?
- / like the job? Why (not)?
- Would *you* like to do his / her job? Why (not)?

e Work in pairs. **A** interview **B** about their person's job. Ask more questions if you can. Then switch.

I'm going to tell you about my cousin. Her name's Corinne.

What does she do?

She's a journalist. She works for a local newspaper...

3 GRAMMAR gerunds and infinitives

a Complete *The right job for you* questionnaire by putting the verbs in the correct form, the gerund (e.g., *working*) or infinitive (e.g., *to work*).

b Read the questionnaire and check (✓) only the sentences that you strongly agree with. Discuss your answers with another student.

c Now see in which group(s) you have the most check marks, and go to ➤ **Communication** *The right job for you p.107.* Do you agree with the results?

d Look at the sentences in the questionnaire. Complete the rules with **the gerund** or **the infinitive**.

1 After some verbs, e.g., *enjoy, don't mind* use... ______
2 After some verbs, e.g., *would like* use... ______
3 After adjectives use... ______
4 After prepositions use... ______
5 As the subject of a phrase or sentence use... ______

e ➤ **p.147 Grammar Bank 8B.** Learn more about gerunds and infinitives, and practice them.

f Choose *five* of the circles below and write something in them.

somebody you find very **easy to talk** to

something you are **planning to do** in the summer

something you **enjoy doing** on Sunday mornings

a job you **hate doing** in the house

a country **you'd like to visit** in the future

a sport, activity, or hobby you **love playing or doing**, but never have time for

something you're **afraid of doing**

somebody you **wouldn't like to go** on vacation with

a job **you'd love to do**

g Work in groups. Tell the others about what you put in your circles, and answer their questions.

I'm going to tell you about someone I find really easy to talk to. It's my uncle...

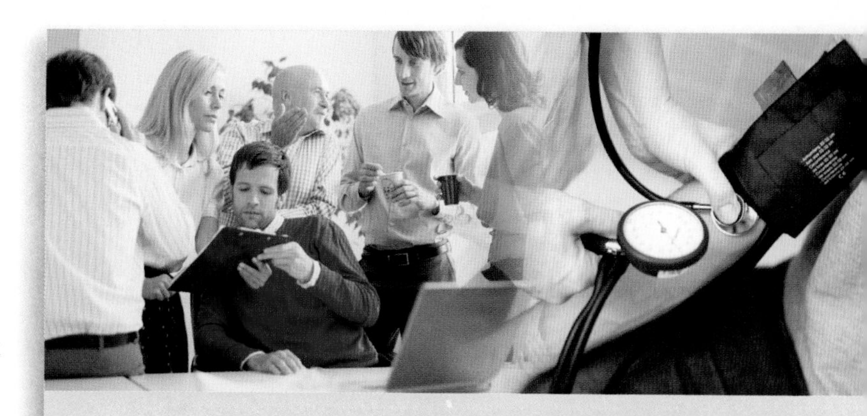

The right job for you –
MATCH YOUR PERSONALITY TO THE JOB

1 I'd like *to work* as part of a team.	work
2 I enjoy ______ people with their problems.	help
3 I don't mind ______ a very large salary.	not earn
4 I'm good at ______ to people.	listen

5 I'm good at ______ quick decisions.	make
6 ______ risks doesn't worry me.	take
7 I'm happy ______ by myself.	work
8 I'm not afraid of ______ large amounts of money.	manage

9 I'm good at ______ myself.	express
10 I always try ______ my instincts.	follow
11 It's important for me ______ creative.	be
12 I enjoy ______.	improvise

13 ______ complex calculations is not difficult for me.	do
14 I enjoy ______ logical problems.	solve
15 I find it easy ______ theoretical principles.	understand
16 I am able ______ space and distance.	calculate

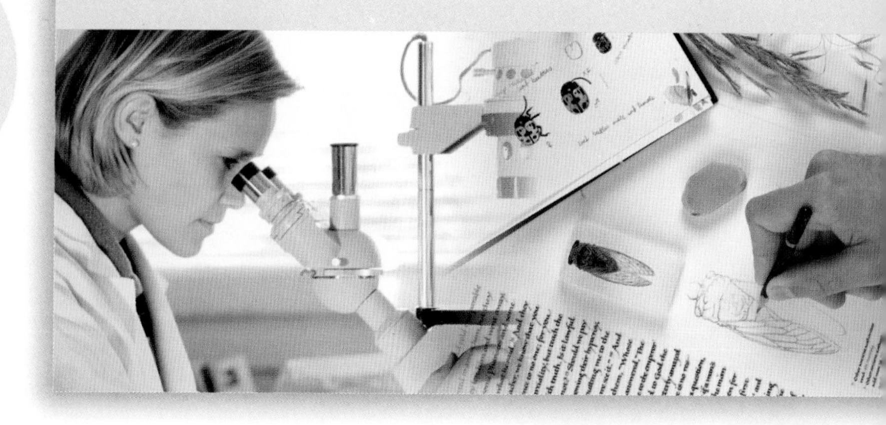

4 READING

a Read the first paragraph of an article about the TV show *Shark Tank*. Answer the questions.

1 Who are the "Sharks?"
2 What is their "Tank?"
3 How does the show work?
4 Is there a similar TV show in your country? How does it work?

b Look at the photos and read about three products that were presented on the show, a device for a guitar (**A**), baby bibs (**B**), and shrimp burgers (**C**). Which product...?

1 has been very successful although the Sharks didn't invest in it
2 was presented by a musician
3 was presented by a female
4 has a celebrity representing the product
5 is practical for moms and kids
6 is now sold in many US states

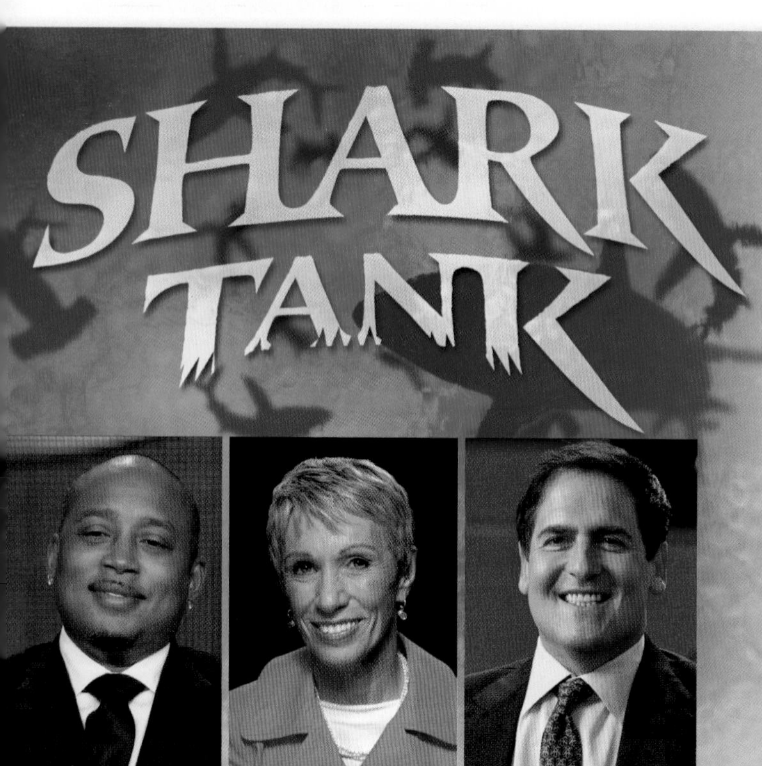

Daymond John and Barbara Corcoran have been Sharks on the show since it started. Mark Cuban appeared on the show since the beginning, but became a regular Shark in 2012.

Shark Tank is a US TV show, with similar versions in many different countries. On the US show, contestants have about ten minutes to present their business ideas to five very successful businesspeople. These people are nicknamed the "Sharks," and the intimidating room where they meet the contestants is the "Tank" (the sharks' home). The Sharks, who are often multimillionaires, are prepared to invest money in any business that they believe might be a success. In return, they take a share of the profits. The contestants are usually entrepreneurs, product designers, or people with a new idea for a service. After the contestants have made their presentations, the Sharks ask them questions about the product and its possible market, and then say if they are prepared to invest or not. If they are not convinced by the presentation, they say the dreaded words "I'm out."

So far, the Sharks have agreed to invest over $6.2 million in products, companies, and ideas presented on *Shark Tank*. They were very happy with their investment in Travis Perry, a guitar player from Alabama who had the idea for Chord Buddy – a device that helps people learn to play the guitar. He came into the Tank with some guitars that had the device attached to them. Shark, Robert Herjavec immediately sensed an opportunity in the charismatic Travis and agreed to invest $125,000 in his product. A year later, Chord Buddy has made over $1.5 million in sales and has John Rich – a famous country singer – representing the product. Travis is now running an impressive and profitable company.

Susie Taylor wanted the Sharks to invest in her high-tech baby bib company. The bibs are made from high-quality materials that don't stain. Nobody was enthusiastic, and the Sharks rejected her idea. But Susie hasn't given up. Since appearing on the TV show, orders for Susie's bibs increased and she has been contacted by other investors. And that is what makes a real entrepreneur—he or she never gives up. If the Sharks invest in him or her, there is a chance he or she will be successful. But if they leave the Tank empty-handed, the determination to make it on their own is as great as ever.

And of course, the Sharks don't always get it right. Cook Shawn Davis's product, gourmet shrimp burgers, was rejected. One Shark said, "I'll buy the product, but I don't really know the food business well enough to make the product successful." Another Shark said, "I just don't like shrimp at all, so based on that, I'm out." A third shark said getting shrimp and keeping it cold makes the product too expensive for the public to buy. Today, Davis's company is worth $6 million, and his shrimp burgers are sold in supermarkets across the US!

c Which (if any) of the three products would you be interested / definitely not interested in buying? Why?

d Look at the highlighted words and phrases which are all related to business. Try to figure out their meaning from the context.

> **Words with different meanings**
> Sometimes the same word can have two completely different meanings, e.g., *I **work** in a store.* (= it's my job) and *My laptop **doesn't work**.* (= it's broken).

e With a partner, say what the difference in meaning is between the pairs of sentences.

1. He's **running** a business. *and*
   He's **running** a marathon.
2. Marion **was fired** last week. *and*
   When the man **fired** the gun, everyone screamed.
3. There's a **market** for this product. *and*
   There's a **market** where you can buy vegetables.
4. He's set up a **company**. *and*
   He's very good **company**.

5 LISTENING

a 4 49 Look at the photos of two more products that were presented on *Shark Tank*. Now listen and find out exactly what makes them special.

b Listen again. Do you think the Sharks invested in...? Why?

a both of them
b neither of them
c one of them (which?)

c 4 50 Now listen to what happened. Were you right? What influenced the Sharks' choice?

d Do you think either of these products would be successful in your country? Why (not)?

6 SPEAKING

a Work with a partner. Imagine you are going to appear on the program. You can choose one of the products below, or you can invent your own.

a watch a sandwich an app a chair
a dessert a pen a lamp a drink a gadget

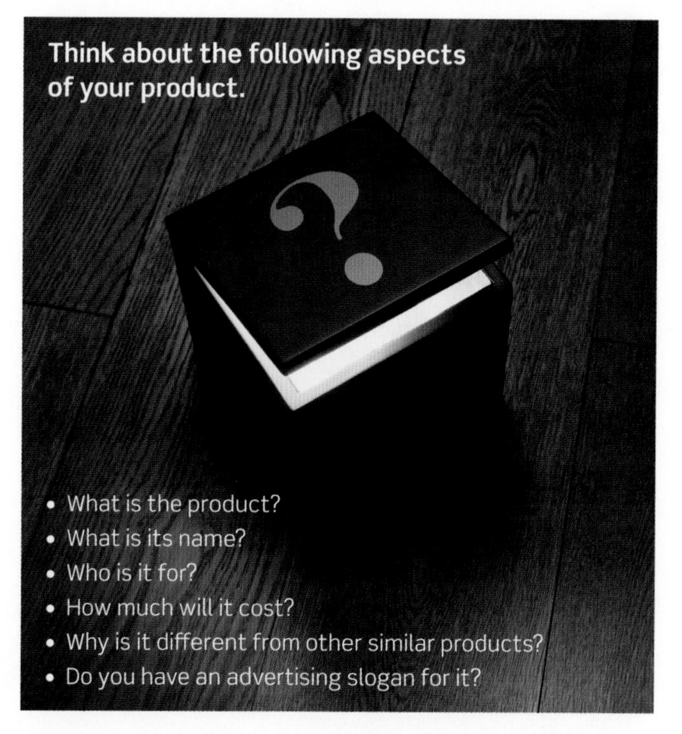

b Present your product to the class together. Spend a few minutes preparing your presentation. Take turns giving the information, and use language from the box to help you.

> **Presenting a product**
> Good morning. We're going to tell you about our new product.
> It's a... and it's called...
> We think it will be very popular with...
> It is completely different from / better than anything else on the market because...

c You also have money to invest in one of the products your classmates present, so listen to their presentations and decide which one to vote for.

7 WRITING

➤ **p.120 Writing** *A cover email with your résumé.*
Write an accompanying email to send with your résumé to apply for a job.

8 4 51 SONG *Piano Man* ♫

7&8 Review and Check

GRAMMAR

Circle a, b, or c.

1 We'll miss the train if we ______.
a don't hurry b won't hurry c didn't hurry

2 If you help me with the dishes, ______ in five minutes.
a we'll finish b we finish c we finished

3 I won't get into college unless ______ good scores on my aptitude tests.
a I'll get b I got c I get

4 If we bought a house, we ______ a dog.
a can have b could have c will have

5 I'd be sad if my brother and his wife ______.
a break up b 'll break up c broke up

6 If I had a job, I ______ live with my parents.
a won't b wouldn't c didn't

7 If I won a lot of money, ______ a big house.
a I'd buy b I'll buy c I buy

8 He said he ______ to his lawyer tomorrow.
a will speak b spoke c would speak

9 I asked Sally if ______ coming to the party.
a she is b she was c was she

10 The little girl ______ that she was lost.
a told b said us c told us

11 The police officer asked me where ______.
a did I live b I was live c I lived

12 Tom's really good at ______ problems.
a solve b solving c to solve

13 ______ clothes online saves a lot of time.
a Buying b To buy c Buy

14 I wouldn't ______ that car if I were you.
a get b getting c to get

15 It's really important ______ the receipt.
a keep b to keep c keeping

VOCABULARY

a Complete with one word.

1 The US school year has two ______.
2 Children under five can go to ______ school.
3 US schools are divided into ______ or age groups.
4 Children who ______ very badly at school may be suspended.
5 A school where parents have to pay for their children to attend is called a ______ school.

b Circle the right word.

1 We live in a residential area *in* / *on* the outskirts of Boston.
2 The *roof* / *ceiling* in our apartment is very low, so don't hit your head!
3 Close the *gate* / *door* or the dog might run out of the yard.
4 Our apartment is *in* / *on* the fifth floor of a large apartment building.
5 On the shelf above the *chimney* / *fireplace* there are some photos.

c Complete the sentences with a noun made from the **bold** word.

1 I don't like shopping in supermarkets because there is too much ______. **choose**
2 My roommates and I have an ______ about who does what in the house. **agree**
3 I'm sure the new company will be a ______. **succeed**
4 I made a ______ about the service in the hotel. **complain**
5 We went on a ______ to support the unemployed. **demonstrate**
6 The government is planning to raise the ______ age to 70. **retire**
7 If you want to get a job, you need good ______. **qualify**
8 My sister has been working as a ______ for the United Nations. **translate**
9 Some ______ say that drinking coffee may be good for us. **science**
10 I want an ______ for what happened yesterday. **explain**

d Complete the missing words.

1 I worked a lot of **ov**______ last week – two hours extra every day.
2 He works the night **sh**______ at the local factory.
3 It's only a **t**______ job, from March to September.
4 I'd like to **s**______ up a small business making children's clothes.
5 Lewis loves being **s**______-______ because it means he is his own boss and can choose the hours that he works.

PRONUNCIATION

a Circle the word with a different sound.

1	country	study	uniform	punished
2	choose	roof	wooden	school
3	kindergarten	fireplace	resign	private
4	paid	complain	sale	said
5	bargain	attach	entrance	educate

b Underline the stressed syllable.

1 se|mes|ter
2 un|em|ployed
3 de|li|ve|ry
4 a|pply
5 a|chieve|ment

CAN YOU UNDERSTAND THIS TEXT?

a Read the blog once. Complete the main message of the article in your own words.

It is better to do a job that ______________ than a job that you ______________, but that ______________.

The importance of doing what you love

When I was growing up, all I wanted to be was an artist. When I got to high school and could choose what classes to take, I took every art class that was available. Painting, drawing, photography, you name it – I took the class.

Then I took a chemistry class. I LOVED it. It was fun! And I was good at it. I started thinking: wouldn't I make more money if I went into the sciences instead of being a starving artist?

So I threw away the art school applications and went to study chemistry. College was fun, and when I graduated with my chemistry degree, I went to graduate school in Washington, D.C. to do a PhD program in chemistry! It was OK to start with, but after the first year, I was completely depressed. I hated the program. It was dry and boring. But I didn't know what to do about it.

So I quit. I spent the next month feeling bad about my failure, unsure what to do next. Finally, I went to an employment agency to get a job. Something – anything – that would pay money.

I got a temporary job filling envelopes at an NGO. One day they needed some graphic design and I volunteered. This was the major turning point in my career. Over the next few months, they gave me more and more design work. What began as a temporary job turned into a permanent job. I was finally doing something I loved, and I was making money doing it.

It's been difficult at times, but I really love my job. Believe me, it is FAR more important that you are happy and get to do what you are passionate about every day and get paid less for it, than to dread getting up in the morning because you dislike what you do.

Adapted from workawesome.com

b Read the blog again and mark the sentences **T** (true), **F** (false), or **DS** (doesn't say).

1. She used to get very good grades in art in high school.
2. She thought she would earn more money working as a chemist than being an artist.
3. She enjoyed graduate school but not college.
4. She lived at home after she quit graduate school.
5. She was very well-paid for filling envelopes at the NGO.
6. She feels passionate about design.

c Choose five new words or phrases from the text. Check their meaning and pronunciation and try to learn them.

CAN YOU UNDERSTAND THESE PEOPLE?

4 52 **On the street** Watch or listen to five people and answer the questions.

Amber

Max

Simon

Joe

Simone

1 Amber says ______ is mixed so a mixed school is better.
  a real interaction b the real world
  c the world of business
2 Max likes shopping online because ______.
  a there is more availability of products
  b he doesn't like looking at a variety of products
  c he is extroverted
3 Simon was ______ with what he sold on eBay.
  a satisfied b delighted c disappointed
4 Joe would like to ______.
  a paint the walls of his apartment
  b have more paintings in his apartment
  c invite more people to his house
5 Simone would like to have a job ______.
  a in banking b that's well paid c that's enjoyable

CAN YOU SAY THIS IN ENGLISH?

Do the tasks with a partner. Check (✓) the box if you can do them.

Can you...?

1 ☐ describe the schools you went to (or have been to) and say what you liked or didn't like about them
2 ☐ say what you will do a) if you don't pass your English exam at the end of the course and b) when you can speak English fluently
3 ☐ describe your ideal vacation house
4 ☐ say what you would do if a) you won a lot of money and b) you had more free time
5 ☐ report three questions that someone has asked you today and what you answered

VIDEO **Short movies** Trinity College, Dublin
Watch and enjoy the movie.

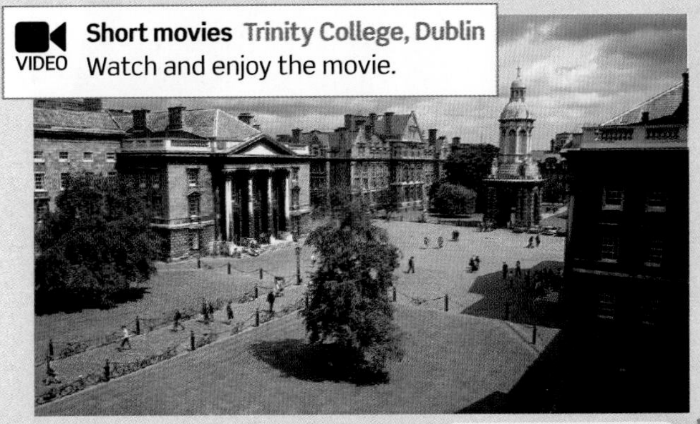

G third conditional
V making adjectives and adverbs
P sentence stress

You were really lucky!

Yes. If he hadn't helped me, I would have missed the train.

9A Lucky encounters

1 READING & SPEAKING

a Answer the questions with a partner. Say what you would do and why.

What would you do if...?

1. somebody on the street asked you for money on your way home tonight
2. you were driving home at night and you saw somebody who had run out of gas
3. you saw an old man being attacked on the street by a couple of teenagers
4. you were in a line at a bus station or airport and someone asked to go in front of you because he / she was in a hurry

b Read the beginning of a true story by the writer Bernard Hare, about something that happened to him when he was a student. Then in pairs, decide what you think happened next.

c 5 2))) Now listen to what happened. Were you right?

d Listen again and answer the questions.

1. What did Bernard have to do as soon as he got off the train?
2. How did Bernard react?
3. What did the ticket inspector then ask him to do?

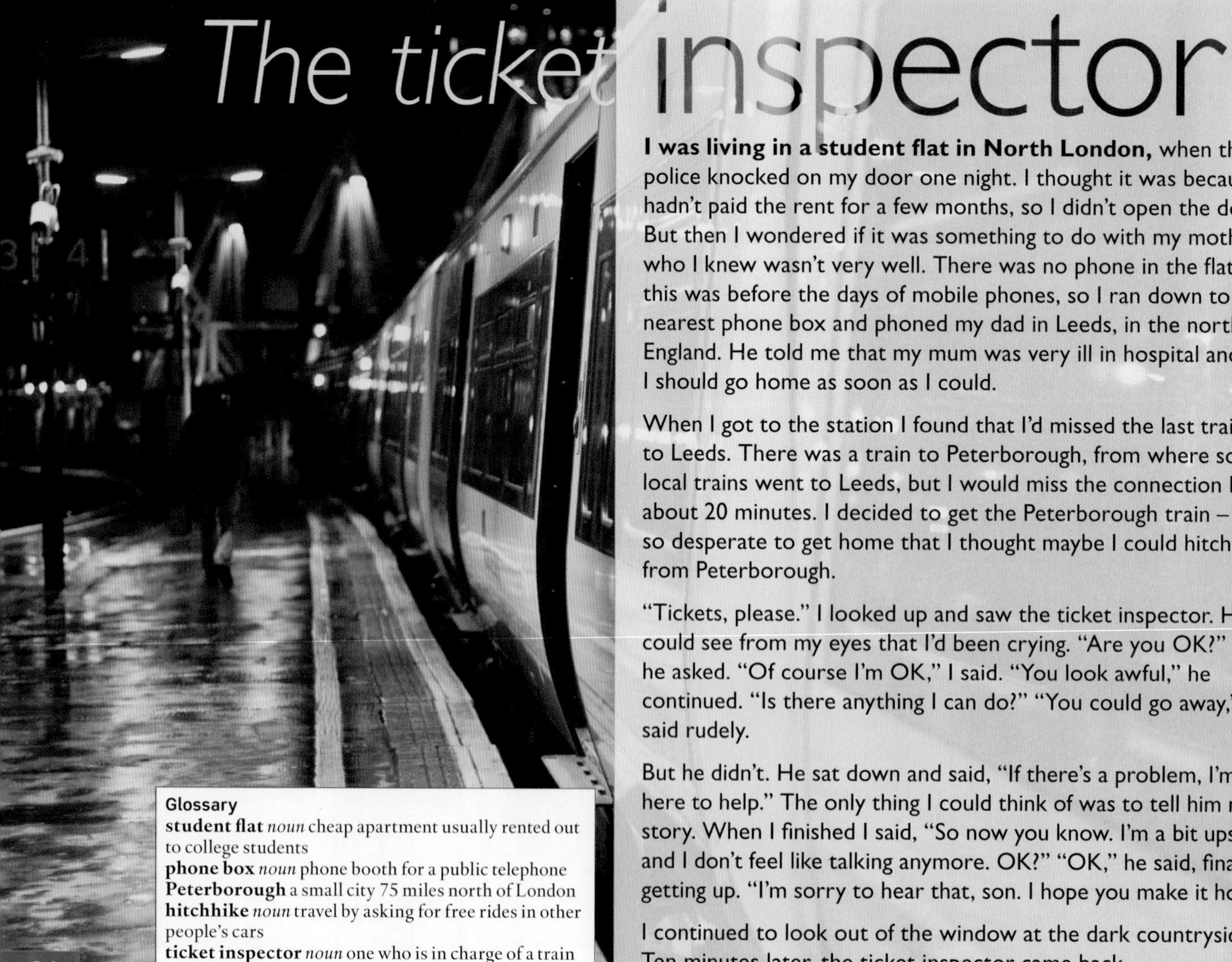

The ticket inspector

I was living in a student flat in North London, when the police knocked on my door one night. I thought it was because I hadn't paid the rent for a few months, so I didn't open the door. But then I wondered if it was something to do with my mother, who I knew wasn't very well. There was no phone in the flat and this was before the days of mobile phones, so I ran down to the nearest phone box and phoned my dad in Leeds, in the north of England. He told me that my mum was very ill in hospital and that I should go home as soon as I could.

When I got to the station I found that I'd missed the last train to Leeds. There was a train to Peterborough, from where some local trains went to Leeds, but I would miss the connection by about 20 minutes. I decided to get the Peterborough train – I was so desperate to get home that I thought maybe I could hitchhike from Peterborough.

"Tickets, please." I looked up and saw the ticket inspector. He could see from my eyes that I'd been crying. "Are you OK?" he asked. "Of course I'm OK," I said. "You look awful," he continued. "Is there anything I can do?" "You could go away," I said rudely.

But he didn't. He sat down and said, "If there's a problem, I'm here to help." The only thing I could think of was to tell him my story. When I finished I said, "So now you know. I'm a bit upset and I don't feel like talking anymore. OK?" "OK," he said, finally getting up. "I'm sorry to hear that, son. I hope you make it home."

I continued to look out of the window at the dark countryside. Ten minutes later, the ticket inspector came back.

Glossary
student flat *noun* cheap apartment usually rented out to college students
phone box *noun* phone booth for a public telephone
Peterborough a small city 75 miles north of London
hitchhike *noun* travel by asking for free rides in other people's cars
ticket inspector *noun* one who is in charge of a train and travels with it, but does not drive it

e After this story was on the news, several people wrote in with their stories about being helped by strangers. **A** read *The students*, **B** read *The angel*.

The students

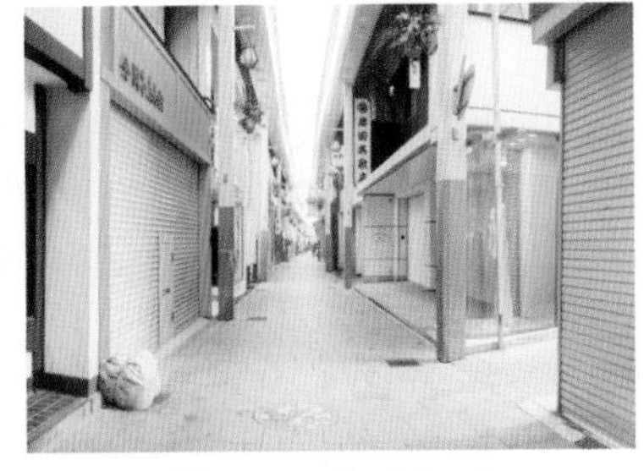

I was living in Korea at the time, teaching English. I had to leave the country and return again because of problems with my visa, so I booked a ferry to Fukuoka in Japan. I intended to change some South Korean money into Japanese yen when I got there, but when I arrived, I discovered it was a holiday in Japan and all the banks were closed. I didn't have a credit card, so I walked from the ferry terminal toward the town wondering what I was going to do without any Japanese money. I was feeling lonely and depressed when suddenly I heard a young couple speaking French. I asked them if they spoke any English, and they told me (in good English) that they were Belgian students. When I explained my problem, they immediately offered to take me around the city and look for somewhere where I could change money. They paid for my bus ticket, and they took me to several places, and in the end, we found a hotel where I was able to change my cash. They then invited me to join them and their friends for the evening. I had a fantastic night and have never forgotten how they changed all their plans just to help a stranger. – *Karina*

The angel

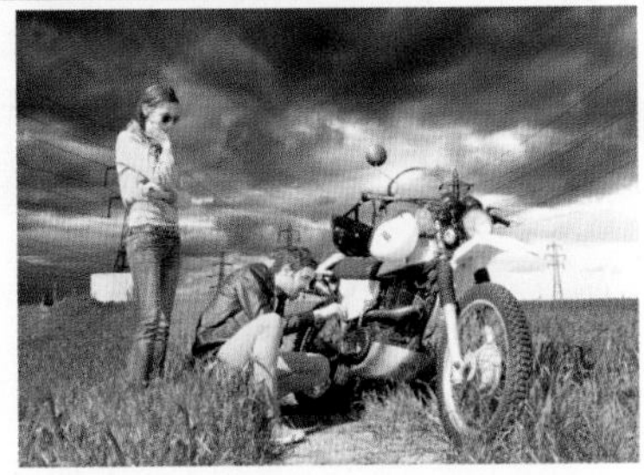

It was a cold Sunday evening in Manchester. I was a college student, and my girlfriend and I had been invited to dinner with our tutor at his house about 18 miles away. We decided to go on my motorcycle, but we hadn't realized how cold it was, so we hadn't dressed warmly enough, and after ten minutes on the bike we were absolutely freezing. When we were about half way there, the bike started to make a funny noise and then stopped. We had run out of gas. We stood at the side of the road, shivering with cold, and not sure what to do.

Suddenly a passing car stopped. The driver got out, opened the trunk of his car, and took out a can of gas. He walked up to my bike, opened the gas tank, and poured the gas in. He then closed the tank and got back into his car, without saying a single word, and drove away. We couldn't believe our luck. We sometimes wonder if the man who rescued us was an angel… – *Andy*

f In pairs, tell each other your story. Tell your partner:

Where it happened
What the problem was
What the stranger(s) did to help

g Which of the three stories do you think was a) the most surprising b) the most moving? Why?

h Have you ever helped a stranger, or been helped by a stranger? What happened?

2 GRAMMAR third conditional

a Match the sentence halves from the story.

1 ☐ If the inspector hadn't stopped the train to Leeds, …
2 ☐ If the couple hadn't helped Karina, …
3 ☐ If the man in the car hadn't stopped, …

A she would have been alone without any money.
B they would have had to walk for miles in the cold.
C he would have missed his connection.

b Now look at the sentences below. Which one describes what really happened? Which one describes how the situation might have been different?

1 If the inspector hadn't stopped the train, he would have missed his connection.
2 The inspector stopped the train, so he didn't miss his connection.

c ➤ **p.148 Grammar Bank 9A.** Learn more about the third conditional and practice it.

3 PRONUNCIATION sentence stress

a 5 4)) Listen and repeat the sentences. Copy the rhythm.

1 If I'd **known** you were **sick**, I would have **come** to **see** you.
2 If the **weather** had been **better**, we would have **stayed longer**.
3 If I **hadn't stopped** to **get gas**, I **wouldn't** have been **late**.
4 We would have **missed** our **flight** if it **hadn't** been **delayed**.

b 5 5)) Listen and write five third conditional sentences.

c ➤ **Communication** *Guess the conditional* **A** *p.106* **B** *p.108.*

4 SPEAKING

a Read the questions and think about your answers.

1 Look at some quotes about luck. Do you think they are true?

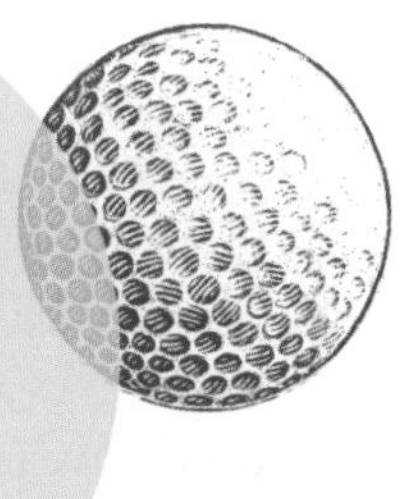

"The more I practice, the luckier I get."

Gary Player, golf player

"You've got to think lucky. If you fall into a mud hole, check your back pocket – you might have caught a fish."

Darrell Royal, American football coach

"You never know what worse luck your bad luck has saved you from."

Cormac McCarthy, writer

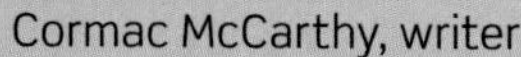

"If you have two friends in your lifetime, you're lucky. If you have one **good** friend, you're more than lucky."

Susan Hinton, writer

2 Do you consider yourself in general to be a lucky person? Why (not)?

3 Can you remember a time when you were either very lucky or very unlucky? What happened?

4 Do you know anyone who you think is particularly lucky or unlucky? Why?

b In groups of three or four, discuss your answers. Give as much detail as possible.

5 READING & LISTENING

a Think of some very successful people, e.g., business people, musicians, sports stars. Which of these three things do you think was probably most important in making them successful: a) talent b) hard work c) luck?

b Read the article *A question of luck?* about a book by Malcolm Gladwell, and answer the questions.

1 What three factors does he think being successful really depends on?

2 Why is it an advantage for sports players to be born in the first months of the year in some countries?

3 What is the 10,000 hours theory?

c 5 6))) Now listen to two other examples Gladwell mentions, The Beatles and Bill Gates. What two main reasons does he give for their extraordinary success?

d Listen again and answer the questions.

THE BEATLES

1 Where did they play and between which years?

2 Where did the club owner usually get bands from?

3 How much did they have to play?

4 How many times had they performed live by 1964?

BILL GATES

5 When did his school start a computer club?

6 Why was this unusual?

7 What did he and his friends do on weekends?

8 How many hours did he spend at the computer club every week?

e What do you think? Answer these questions with a partner.

1 Do you agree that luck and practice are just as important as talent? Is luck more important than practice or the other way around?

2 Think of something you are moderately good at or very good at. Were you lucky to be able to have the opportunity to start doing it? How many hours do you think you have spent practicing it? Do you think you have spent more hours doing it than other people you know?

A question of luck?

What is the question we always ask about successful people? We want to know what they're like – what kind of personalities they have, or how intelligent they are, or what kind of lifestyles they have, or what special talents they might have been born with. And we assume that it is those personal qualities that explain how that individual gets to the top of his or her profession.

But according to Malcolm Gladwell, in his book *Outliers*, we are asking the wrong questions. He thinks that while talent is obviously a factor, there are two other more important ones that make a person successful. The first of these factors is luck.

He begins with the example of sports players. In recent research done on various groups of elite ice hockey players from Canada and the Czech Republic, one fascinating fact came to light. In both countries, it was discovered that 40% of the players on the top teams were born between January and March, 30% between April and June, 20% between July and September, and only 10% between October and December. The explanation was simple. The school year in these countries runs from January to December. A boy who is ten on January 2nd will be in the same class as one whose 10th birthday is on December 30th. The chances are the first boy will be bigger, stronger, and more coordinated. He is much more likely than the other boy to be chosen to play on junior teams. He will then get better coaching than the others, and will play many more games, so will also get more practice. In the beginning, his advantage isn't so much that he is more talented, simply that he is older. He was lucky enough to be born in the first months of the year. But by the age of 13 or 14, with the extra coaching and practice, he really will be better than the others, and far more likely to be successful.

The extra practice is vital, because the second factor that Gladwell believes is of great importance in determining whether somebody is going to be successful or not is what he calls the "10,000 hours theory." This theory, based on studies in many different fields, says that in order to get to the very top you need to put in 10,000 hours of practice, whether it is playing an instrument or a sport, or programming a computer.

6 VOCABULARY making adjectives and adverbs

One of these is **luck**, for example being **lucky** enough to be in the right place at the right time.

a Look at the **bold** words in the sentence above. Which is a noun and which is an adjective? Using the word *luck*, can you make...?

1 a negative adjective
2 a positive adverb
3 a negative adverb

b ➤ **p.163 Vocabulary Bank** *Word building.* Do Part 2.

7 WRITING

a Read the rules for the sentence game.

The **sentence** game

1 You should write correct sentences with the exact number of words given (contractions count as one word).

2 The sentences must make sense.

3 You should include a form of the word given (e.g., if the word is *luck*, you can use *lucky*, *luckily*, etc.).

b Work in teams of three or four. Play the sentence game. You have five minutes to write the following sentences.

1 **fortune** (11 WORDS)
2 **comfort** (9 WORDS)
3 **luck** (7 WORDS)
4 **care** (6 WORDS)
5 **patience** (12 WORDS)

c Your teacher will tell you if your sentences are correct. The team with the most correct sentences is the winner.

8 5 9))) SONG *Karma* ♫

G quantifiers
V electronic devices, phrasal verbs
P *ough* and *augh*, linking

You look stressed!

Yes, I have too much work and not enough time to do it.

9B Too much information!

1 GRAMMAR quantifiers

a Look at the illustration. How many electronic devices can you see? Which ones do you have? What do you use them for?

b Circle the correct phrase in 1–6.

1. I used to have *a lot of* / *lot of* different gadgets, but now I use my phone for almost everything.
2. I'd like to buy a better computer, but I don't have *enough money* / *money enough* right now.
3. I spend *too much* / *too many* time every day online.
4. I only have *a little* / *a few* friends on Facebook, and *no* / *none* of them are close friends.
5. I never watch TV or movies on my phone because the screen isn't *enough big* / *big enough*.
6. I like downloading new apps to my phone, but I think some of them are *too* / *too much* difficult to use.

c ➤ **p.149 Grammar Bank 9B.** Learn more about quantifiers and practice them.

d Talk to a partner. Are the sentences in **b** true for you? Say why (not).

2 PRONUNCIATION *ough* and *augh*

ough* and *augh

Be careful with the letters ***ough*** and ***augh***. They can have different pronunciations.

Try to remember how to pronounce the most common words that have this combination of letters, e.g., *although*.

a Write the words in the list in the correct column.

although bought brought caught cough daughter enough laugh thought through tough

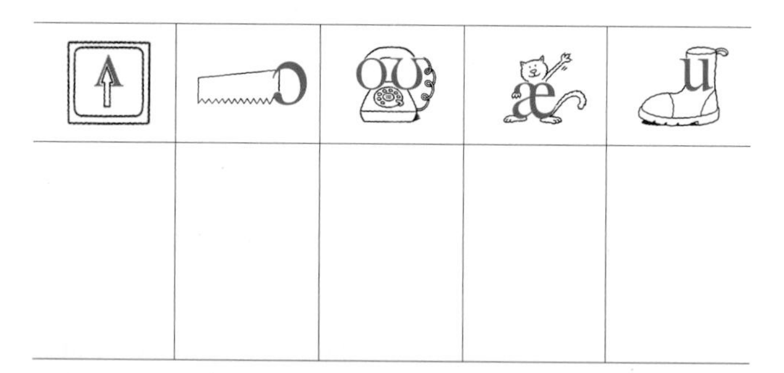

b 5 14)) Listen and check. Which is the most common sound? Which four words finish with the sound /f/?

c 5 15)) Listen to sentences 1–5 and practice saying them.

1. I thought I'd brought enough money with me.
2. My daughter caught a bad cold.
3. I bought it although it was very expensive.
4. We've been through some tough times.
5. I didn't laugh! It was a cough.

3 READING & SPEAKING

a Look at the title of the article. What do you think it means? Read the first paragraph to check.

b Now read the whole article. Choose a, b, or c.

1 Many of the managers surveyed think that as a result of information overload __.
   a they have to work harder
   b they enjoy their jobs less
   c they are sick more often

2 Scientists think that information overload makes people __.
   a more anxious but more productive
   b more productive but less creative
   c more stressed and less creative

3 One solution to information overload would be for people to spend less time __.
   a searching for information
   b using the Internet
   c talking on the phone

c Read the article again and figure out the meaning of the highlighted words and phrases related to the Internet and technology.

d Do you suffer from information overload in your own life? Talk to your partner about how information overload affects different parts of your life.

your work   your studies
your social life   your family life

Information overload

If you type the words "information overload" into Google, you will immediately get an information overload – more than 7 million hits in 0.05 seconds. Some of this information is interesting – for example, you learn that the phrase "information overload" was first used in 1970, before the Internet was invented. But much of the information is not relevant or useful: obscure companies and even more obscure bloggers.

Information overload is one of the biggest irritations in modern life. There are news and sports websites to watch, emails that need to be answered, people who want to chat with you online, and back in the real world, friends, family, and colleagues who also have things to tell you. At work, information overload is also causing problems. A recent survey has shown that many company managers believe that it has made their jobs less satisfying and has even affected their personal relationships outside work. Some of them also think that it is bad for their health.

Clearly there is a problem. It is not only the increase in the quantity of information, it is also the fact that it is everywhere, not just in the home and in the workplace. Many people today do not go anywhere without their smartphones. There is no escape from the Internet.

Scientists have highlighted three big worries. First, information overload can make people feel anxious: There is too much to do and not enough time to do it. People end up multitasking, which can make them even more stressed. Second, information overload can make people less creative. Research shows that people are more likely to be creative if they are allowed to focus on one thing for some time, without interruptions. Third, information overload can make people less productive. People who multitask take much longer and make many more mistakes than people who do the same tasks one after another.

What can be done about information overload? One solution is technological: There is now a computer program or app you can install called Freedom that disconnects you from the web at preset times. The second solution involves willpower. Turn off your cell phone and the Internet from time to time. The manager of an IT company puts "thinking time" into his schedule when all his electronic devices are turned off so that he isn't disturbed. This might sound like common sense. But nowadays, although we have more information than ever before, we do not always have enough common sense.

4 VOCABULARY & PRONUNCIATION electronic devices, phrasal verbs, linking

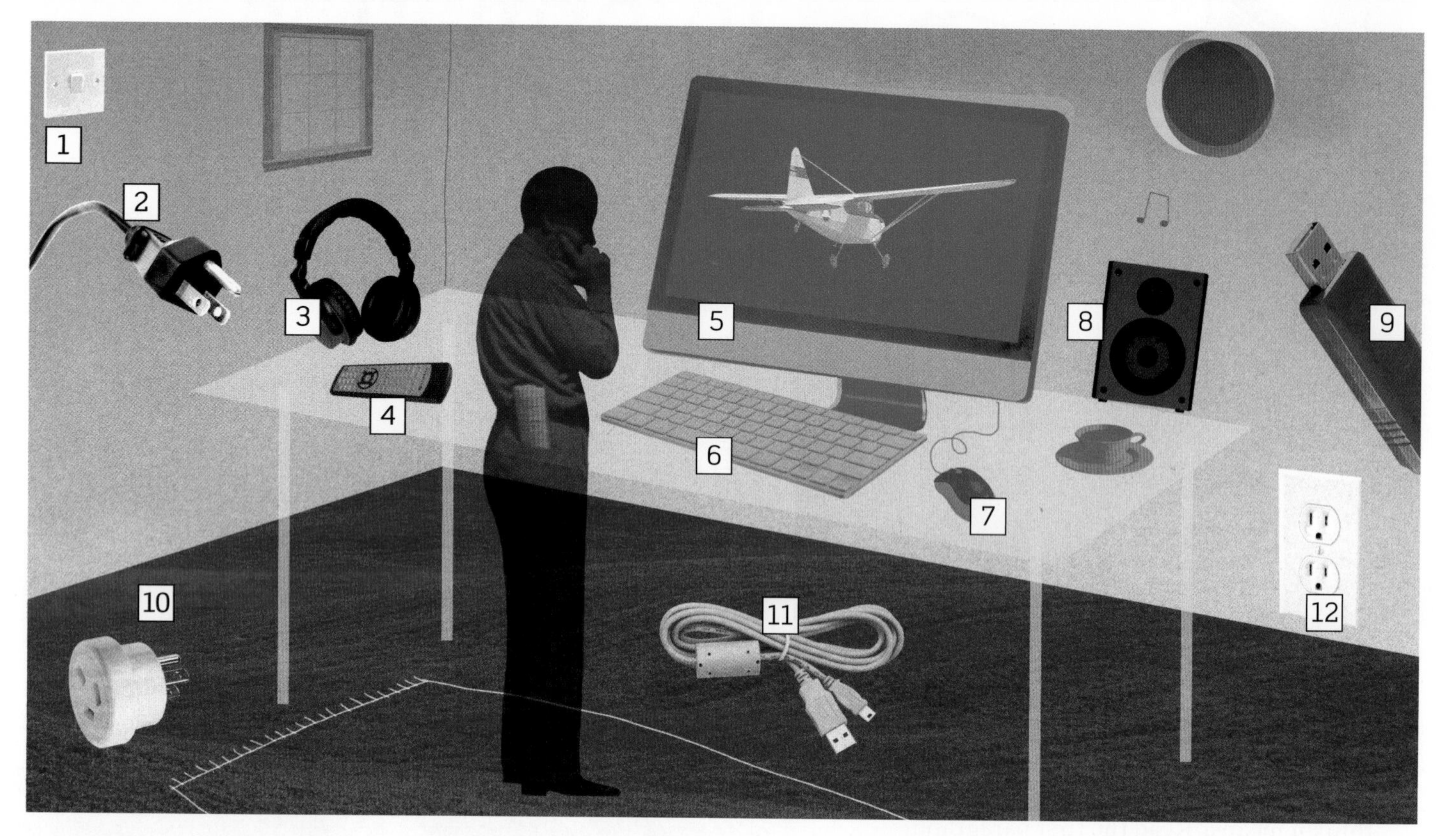

a Match the words and pictures.

☐ a mouse	☐ a flash drive	☐ an outlet
☐ a speaker	☐ a plug	1 a switch
☐ a USB cable	☐ a remote control	☐ an adaptor
☐ a keyboard	☐ a screen	☐ headphones

b 5 16))) Listen and check. Then test each other.

A What's 6? **B** (words covered) **It's a keyboard.**

c Match the sentences.

1 ☐ I changed the heat from 70° to 62°.
2 ☐ I disconnected my iPod from the computer.
3 ☐ I increased the volume on the TV.
4 ☐ I pressed the off button on the TV.
5 ☐ I programmed the alarm on my phone.
6 ☐ I put my phone charger into an outlet.
7 ☐ I pressed the on button on my laptop.

A I **switched** it **off**.
B I **switched** it **on**.
C I **turned** it **down**.
D I **turned** it **up**.
E I **plugged** it **in**.
F I **unplugged** it.
G I **set** it for 7:30.

d 5 17))) Listen and check.

e 5 18))) Listen and repeat A–G. Try to link the words. Now cover A–G and look at sentences 1–7. Say A–G from memory.

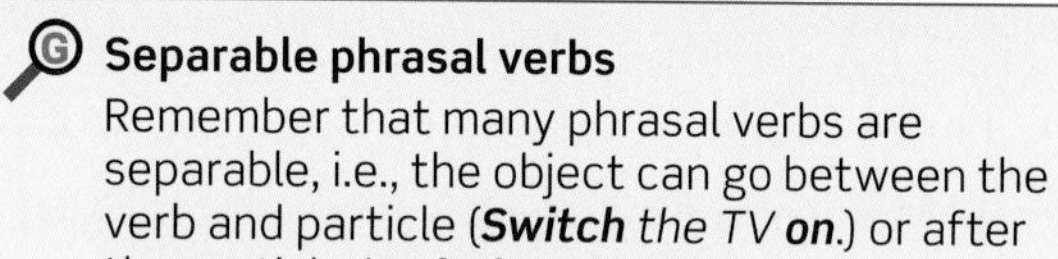

Separable phrasal verbs

Remember that many phrasal verbs are separable, i.e., the object can go between the verb and particle (***Switch** the TV **on**.*) or after the particle (***Switch on** the TV.*).
However, if the object is a pronoun, it must go between the verb and particle, e.g., *Switch it on*. NOT ~~*Switch on it*~~.

f Answer the questions with a partner. Give reasons for your answers.

1 How many devices do you have with screens? Which one do you use the most?
2 Do you prefer to use a keyboard with or without a mouse?
3 Do you usually listen to music with headphones or with speakers?
4 How many remote controls do you have? Do you think you have too many?
5 How many prongs do plugs in your country have? Do you need a travel adaptor if you go abroad?
6 In your house do you usually agree about what the temperature should be, or is someone always turning the heat or air conditioning up and down?

5 LISTENING & SPEAKING

a Look at the book cover and the book review information. What do you think the book is about? How do you think the three teenagers feel?

The wise and hilarious story of a family who discovered that having fewer tools to communicate with actually led them to communicate more.

When Susan Maushart first announced her intention to pull the plug on her family's entire collection of electronic gadgets for six months, her three kids didn't react at all. Says Maushart, "Looking back, I can understand why. They didn't hear me."

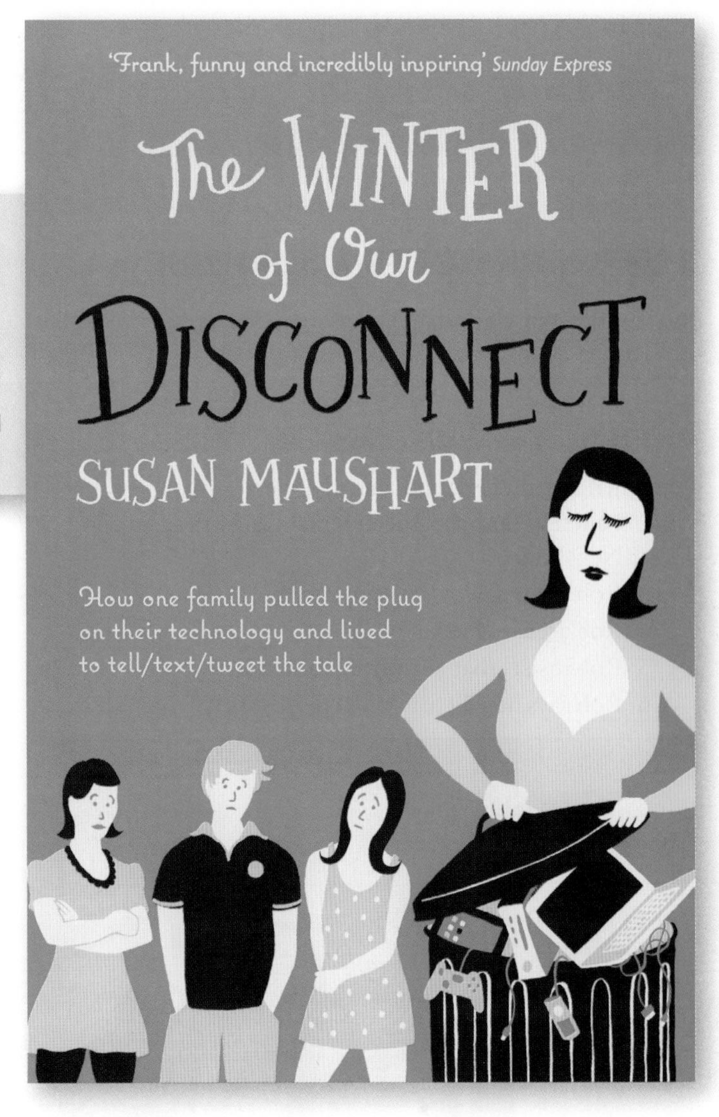

* The title is a play on words. Shakespeare's play *Richard III* opens with the famous phrase "Now is the winter of our discontent..."

b 5 19 Listen to **Part 1** of a radio breakfast show where the guests are discussing the book. Answer questions 1–6.

1 Why did Susan Maushart decide to do the experiment?
2 Was it just her children who were spending too much time using technology?
3 Who are "digital immigrants" and "digital natives"?
4 What gadgets did Susan Maushart's family have to switch off? Where?
5 What were they allowed to use?
6 How did she get the children to agree to the experiment?

c 5 20 Listen to **Part 2**. In general, was the experiment positive or negative? Why?

d Listen again and complete the sentences in your own words.

1 At the beginning the children complained that...
2 Later they started to...
3 Her son started to...
4 Their mother found it difficult to...
5 Another negative thing was that...
6 They now have new house rules; for example...

e 5 21 Now listen to **Part 3**. What does each guest say he / she would miss most if he / she had to do the experiment?

1 Sally	
2 Andrew	
3 Jeremy	
4 Chloe	

f Discuss the questions with a partner.

1 Have you ever had to live without the Internet for a few days or more, e.g., when you were on vacation somewhere? Did you miss it a lot? Why (not)?
2 Do you think Susan Maushart's experiment was a good idea? Why (not)?
3 If you had to do the experiment, what do you think you would miss the most? Why?

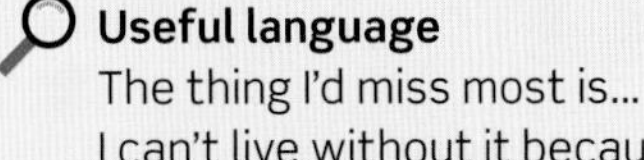

Useful language
The thing I'd miss most is...
I can't live without it because...
I need / use it (for)...
I'm addicted to it...
I depend on it (for)...

6 WRITING

➤ **p.120 Writing** *A magazine article – advantages and disadvantages.* Write an article about the advantages and disadvantages of smartphones.

Practical English Unexpected events EPISODE 5

1 VIDEO JENNY GETS A SURPRISE

a 5 22 Watch or listen. How do you think Jenny and Rob feel at the end?

b Watch or listen again. Mark the sentences **T** (true) or **F** (false). Correct the **F** sentences.

1 Jenny didn't expect Paul to be there.
2 Paul tells Jenny that Rob is planning to stay in New York.
3 Rob arrives with croissants for breakfast.
4 Rob accuses Paul of lying.
5 Rob insists that he's serious about Jenny.
6 Rob says he will drive Paul to Boston.

2 VIDEO INDIRECT QUESTIONS

a 5 23 Watch or listen to Rob and Jenny talking in the office. Do they resolve their problems?

b Watch or listen again and answer the questions.

1 What reason does Rob give for Paul being in his apartment?
2 How does Rob know that Paul is really leaving?
3 Why doesn't Jenny believe that Rob wants to stay in New York?
4 According to Jenny, how did Rob behave when he was with Paul?
5 What does Jenny think about their relationship?

c 5 24 Look at some extracts from the conversation. Can you remember any of the missing words? Watch or listen and check.

1 **Jenny** Could you _________ me why Paul is still in your apartment?
Rob Well, he couldn't get a ticket to Boston...

2 **Jenny** Do you _________ if he's got one now?
Rob I bought it! He's leaving this evening.

3 **Jenny** Look Rob, I'd _________ to know what you really want.
Rob What do you mean?

4 **Jenny** I _________ if you really want to be here. I wonder if...
Rob Jenny, what is it?

5 **Don** I need a word. _________ you tell me what you decided at the last meeting?
Jenny Right away, Don. Rob was just leaving.

d 5 25 Watch or listen and repeat the highlighted phrases. Copy the rhythm and intonation.

e Practice the dialogues in **c** with a partner.

f Read the information about indirect questions. Then make questions 1–5 more indirect by using the beginnings given.

> **Indirect questions**
> We often put *Can / Could you tell me...?, Do you know...?, I'd like to know..., I wonder...* before a question to make it less direct. When we do this, the direct question changes to an affirmative sentence, i.e., the word order is subject + verb, and we don't use *do / did* in the present and the past.
>
> Compare:
> ***Why is Paul** in your apartment?*
> Could you tell me why Paul is still in your apartment?
> ***Has he got** one now?*
> Do you know if (or whether) he's got one now?
> *What **do you really want**?*
> I'd like to know what you really want.
> ***Do you really want** to be here?*
> I wonder if (or whether) you really want to be here.
> ***What did you decide** at the last meeting?*
> Can you tell me what you decided at the last meeting?

1 *Where's the station?*
Excuse me, can you tell me ______________________ ?

2 *What did he say?*
I'd like to know ______________________ .

3 *Does she like me?*
I wonder ______________________ .

4 *Is your brother coming tonight?*
Do you know ______________________ ?

5 *What time does the store close?*
Could you tell me ______________________ ?

g **Communication** *Asking politely for information* **A** *p.106* **B** *p.109.*

3 VIDEO ROB GETS SERIOUS

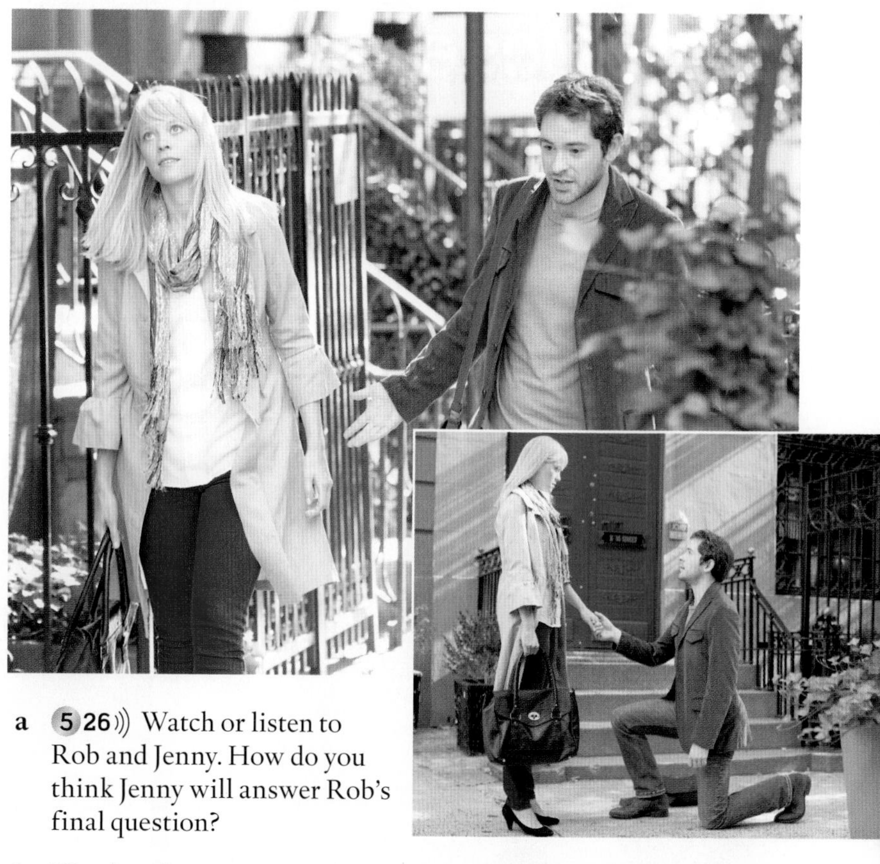

a 5 26 Watch or listen to Rob and Jenny. How do you think Jenny will answer Rob's final question?

b Watch or listen again and complete the sentences with 2–4 words.

1 Rob is trying to convince Jenny that he __________.
2 Jenny says that she's sure that Rob wants to __________.
3 Rob says that he loves his __________.
4 Jenny and Rob are going to visit __________.
5 Rob promises not to forget __________.
6 Rob asks Jenny to __________.

c Look at the **Social English phrases**. Can you remember any of the missing words?

Social English phrases	
Jenny	It's ________ you want to go back.
Rob	Of ________ I miss London, but I love my life here.
Rob	And I won't forget the chocolates this time ________.
Jenny	Well, that's a start, I ________.
Rob	________ if I proposed to you?
Jenny	Rob, ________ it. It's embarrassing.

d 5 27 Watch or listen and complete the phrases.

e Watch or listen again and repeat the phrases. How do you say them in your language?

> **Can you...?**
> ☐ make indirect questions, e.g., beginning with *Can you tell me...?*
> ☐ discuss a problem

G relative clauses: defining and nondefining
V compound nouns
P word stress

Is that the first Apple computer?

No, it's the one they made in 1990.

10A Modern icons

1 READING

a In pairs, take the quiz. Choose a, b, or c.

b 5 28))) Compare with another pair, and listen and check.

c Look at the photos and guess what the connection is between each of the things, people, or places and Steve Jobs.

What do you know about Steve Jobs?

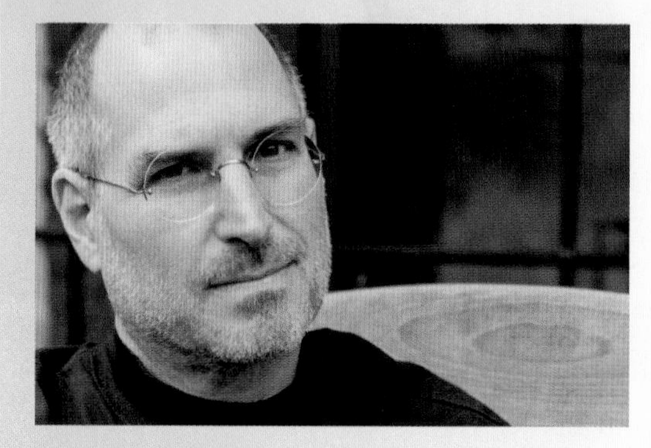

1 **He was born in...**
a New York
b San Francisco
c Texas

2 **In college...**
a he was a star student
b he dropped out
c he was asked to leave

3 **His first job was with a company that made...**
a video games b TVs c computers

4 **The Apple Macintosh was the first successful computer to use...**
a a mouse
b a keyboard
c a USB port

5 **In 1986 he cofounded...**
a Pixar
b HandMade Films
c DreamWorks

6 **Steve Jobs died of cancer in...**
a 2010 b 2011 c 2012

7 **He was ____ years old.**
a 46 b 56 c 66

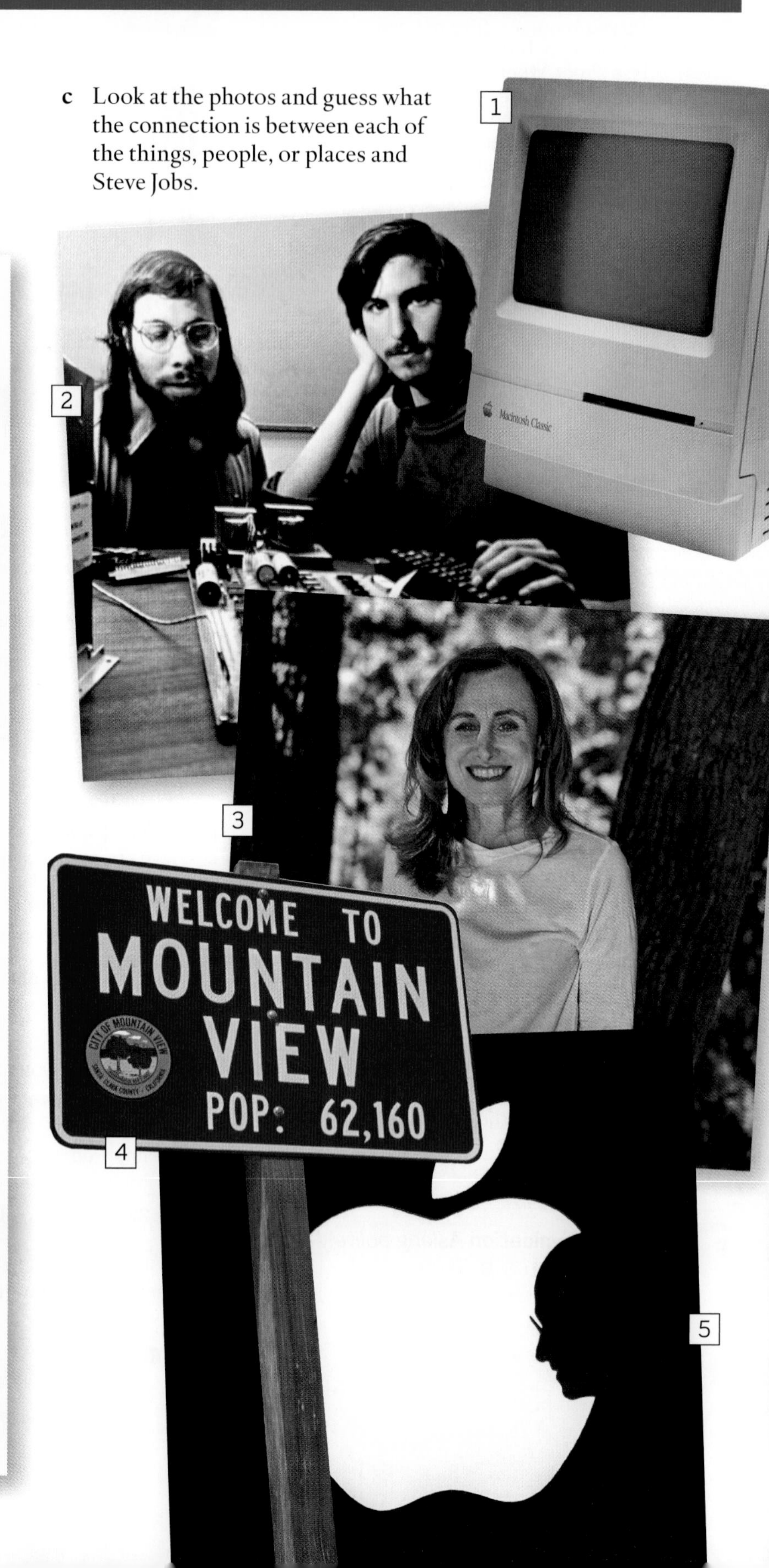

d Now read paragraphs 1–5 and check.

1 The Macintosh Classic was the personal computer that was made by Apple in 1990. It had a 9-inch monochrome screen and a 4 megabyte (MB) memory. It was cheaper than earlier Apple computers and very easy to use. It was their first commercially successful computer.

2 Stephen Wozniak is the American computer engineer and programmer whose computer designs became the original Apple I and Apple II computers. He and Steve Jobs became friends when they were both working at Hewlett Packard. They started making computers in Jobs's parents' garage, and together they founded Apple Computers (now Apple Inc.) in 1976.

3 Mona Simpson is Steve Jobs's sister. Jobs was adopted when he was born, but in the 1980s he found his biological mother, who told him that he had a sister. Mona and Steve met for the first time in 1985 (when she was 25 and he was 30) and they became very close. They kept their relationship secret for a year until Mona introduced Steve as her brother at the party that she gave to celebrate the publication of her first novel, *Anywhere But Here*.

4 Mountain View is the city in California where Steve Jobs grew up. He was born in San Francisco and was adopted by Paul and Clara Jobs. When he was six years old the family moved to Mountain View, which was becoming a center for electronics. People began to call the area "Silicon Valley" because silicon is used to manufacture electronic parts.

5 This is the logo that was designed by Jonathan Mak, a Chinese design student from Hong Kong, as a tribute to Steve Jobs when he died. The design, which used Jobs's silhouette incorporated into the "bite" of a white Apple logo, became a worldwide Internet sensation. The teenager said that Jobs had inspired him to become a designer.

2 GRAMMAR relative clauses

a Cover the text. Complete the sentences with *who*, *whose*, *which*, *that*, or *where*. In some cases, two answers are possible.

1 The Macintosh Classic was the personal computer ________ was made by Apple in 1990.

2 Stephen Wozniak is the American computer engineer ________ founded Apple Computers with Steve Jobs and ________ computer designs became the original Apple I and Apple II computers.

3 Mona introduced Steve as her brother at the party ________ she gave to celebrate the publication of her first novel.

4 Mountain View is the area in California ________ Steve Jobs grew up.

5 Jonathan Mak's design, ________ used Jobs's silhouette incorporated into the "bite" of a white Apple logo, became a worldwide Internet sensation.

b Answer the questions in pairs.

1 In which phrase is the relative pronoun (*who, that*, etc.) not necessary?

2 In which sentence could you leave out the relative clause, but the sentence would still make sense?

c ➤ **p.150 Grammar Bank 10A.** Learn more about defining and nondefining relative clauses, and practice them.

d Cover the text and look at the photos. Can you remember the connections with Steve Jobs? Try to use a relative clause.

3 WRITING

a ➤ **p.121 Writing** *A biography*. Write a biography of an interesting or successful person you know about.

b ➤ **Communication** *Relatives quiz* **A** *p.108* **B** *p.112*. Write quiz questions to ask a partner.

GREAT AMERICAN DESIGN ICONS

Some of the things that are considered the best in American design.

4 LISTENING

a Look at the photos that show four famous examples of American design. What are they? What do you know about them?

b 5 31 Now listen to a professor talk about them. Complete sentences 1–4.

1. Ruth Handler was the woman who…
2. William Van Alen was the man who…
3. Robert Indiana is the man who…
4. Peter Moore and Tinker Hatfield are the men who…

c Listen again and answer the questions.

Which icon…?

1. is the most recent
2. is the oldest
3. has been used in many different products
4. was named after a family member
5. didn't make its designer much money
6. had more than one designer
7. was the result of a trip to Europe
8. used car parts as inspiration for decorations

d Which of the four do you find the most attractive design? What would you consider to be examples of iconic design in your country?

5 SPEAKING

a Write the names of people, things, or places in as many of the circles as you can.

b In groups, talk about your people, things, and places. Explain why you admire them.

a famous dead person (who) you admire

a famous living person (that) you admire

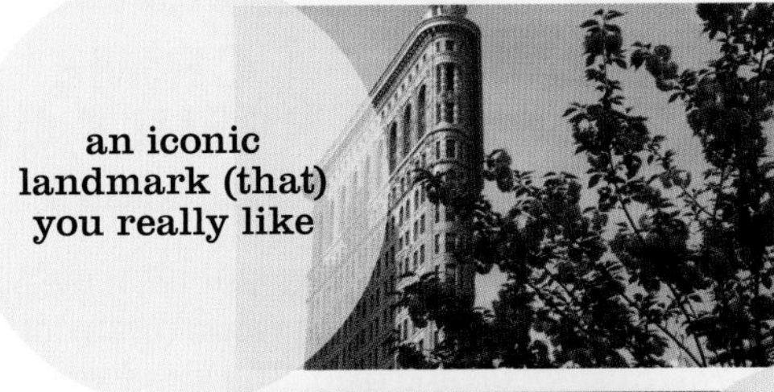

an iconic landmark (that) you really like

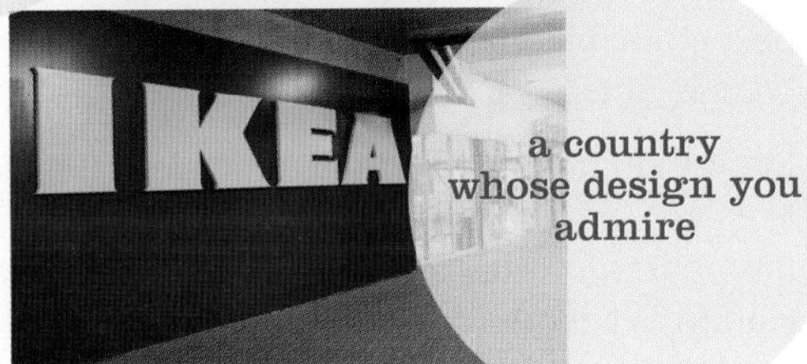

a country whose design you admire

an everyday object (that) you own that you think has a beautiful design

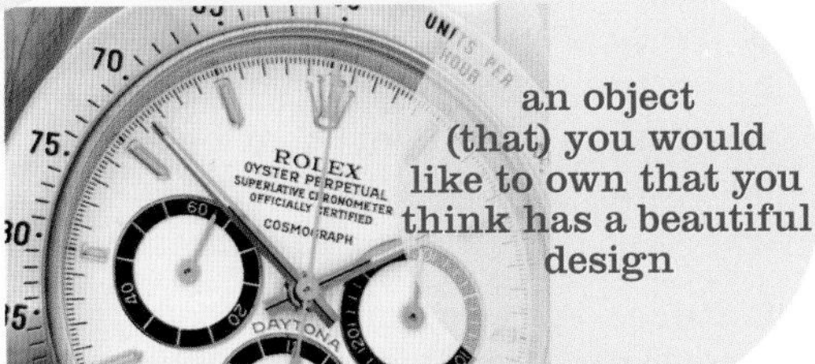

an object (that) you would like to own that you think has a beautiful design

a DVD cover, movie poster, or book cover (that) you think has a great design

6 VOCABULARY & PRONUNCIATION

compound nouns, word stress

> **Compound nouns**
> We often put two nouns together, where the first noun describes the second one, e.g., an *album cover* (= the cover of an album), the *subway map* (= the map of the subway). Compound nouns can be two words, e.g., *tourist attraction* or one word, e.g., *website*.

a Match a noun from column **A** with a noun from column **B** to make compound nouns.

A	B
soccer	picture
speed	case
sun	hall
town	field
book	mate
class	glasses
profile	camera

b 5 32 Listen and check. Which three are written as one word? Which noun is usually stressed more in compound nouns? Practice saying the compound nouns in **a** with the right stress.

c In pairs, try to answer all the questions in **three minutes** with compound nouns from Files 1–10.

COMPOUND NOUNS RACE

1 What kind of job do you have if you only work 20 hours a week?
2 What do you need to have before you can get on a plane?
3 What might you have to pay if you park in a bus lane?
4 What should you put on when you get into a car?
5 What do you call a long line of cars that can't move?
6 What do you need to book if you want to play tennis with someone?
7 Where do people go if they want to watch a basketball or handball game?
8 What do you call the noise a phone makes?
9 What kind of books or movies are about the future, and often outer space?
10 What do you call a school that is paid for by the government?
11 If you are in an elevator and you press 2, where do you want to go to?
12 What device do you use when you want to transfer files from one computer to another?

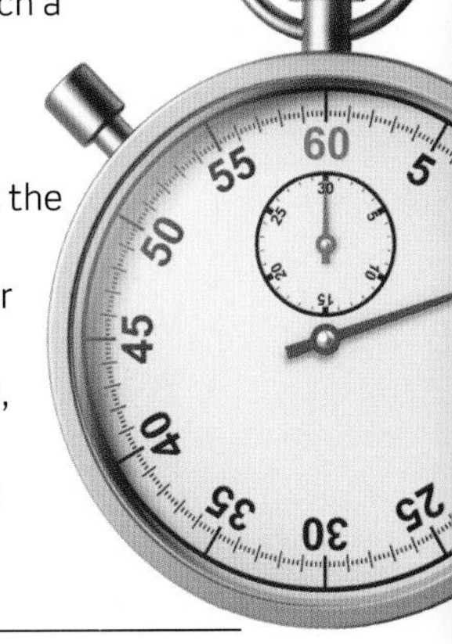

7 5 33 SONG *Greatest Love of All* ♫

G tag questions
V crime
P intonation in tag questions

You were a detective with the Los Angeles Police Department, weren't you?

Yes, I was.

10B Two crime stories

1 VOCABULARY crime

a Have you heard of Natalie Wood? What do you know about her?

b Match the words and definitions.

detectives evidence murder murderer
prove solve suspects victim witnesses

1 ________ *noun* police officers who investigate crimes
2 ________ *noun* people who see something that has happened, and then tell others (e.g., the police) about it
3 ________ *noun* a person who is hurt or killed by somebody in a crime
4 ________ *noun* a person who plans and kills another person
5 ________ *noun* the crime of killing a person illegally and deliberately
6 ________ *noun* the facts, signs, etc., that tell you who committed a crime
7 ________ *noun* people who are thought to be guilty of a crime
8 ________ (a mystery) *verb* to find the correct answer to why something happened
9 ________ (something) *verb* to use the facts and evidence to show something is true

c 5 34 Listen and check. Practice saying the words.

d Read *How did Hollywood actress Natalie Wood die?* and fill in the blanks with words from **b**.

e Read the article again and find the answer to these questions.

1 When did Natalie Wood die?
2 What was the weather like on the night she died?
3 Where was her body found?
4 Who was on the boat with her when she died?
5 Who did Natalie Wood have an argument with the night she died?
6 How many years later did the police reopen the investigation into her death?

HOW DID HOLLYWOOD ACTRESS NATALIE WOOD DIE?

WAS SHE THE [1]*victim* OF A CRIME OR DID SHE DIE AS A RESULT OF AN UNFORTUNATE ACCIDENT?

On the cold and rainy night of November 29, 1981, the beautiful and talented actress Natalie Wood mysteriously fell off her boat, *The Splendour*, and died. She was found the next morning, nearly a mile away, floating in the water with bruises and scratches on her body.

More than thirty years later, officials still haven't been able to [2]__________ the mystery of Natalie Wood's death. On the boat with Natalie that night were her husband—actor Robert Wagner, a friend—actor Christopher Walken, the captain—Dennis Davern, and a few others. Police know that Wagner and Walken had an argument early in the evening, but they made up and Walken went to bed. Police also know that Wood and Wagner had an argument. Wood then went to bed and when Wagner went to look in on her later, she wasn't in her room. No one heard or saw Natalie fall off the boat. Therefore there were no [3]__________ to say whether her death was a [4]__________ or an accident. In addition, [5]__________ who were working on the case at the time were not able to find any solid [6]__________ to [7]__________ whether Natalie Wood was pushed to her death from the boat. Therefore her death was officially ruled an accident—meaning there was no [8]__________ for police to arrest and put in jail.

In 2012, a TV news show investigating Natalie Wood's death brought new information to Los Angeles County officials. The TV news show claimed the bruises and scratches on her body were proof that she was indeed the victim of a murder. Officials have reopened the case and are currently conducting interviews; however none of the people who were on the boat that night have been officially named as [9]__________ in Natalie's death. Will LA police eventually discover the truth about her death? Only time will tell.

2 LISTENING

a 5 35 Now listen to the first part of an interview with a retired police officer who has done a lot of research about Natalie Wood's death. Complete the information about the people who were on *The Splendour* the night Natalie Wood died.

Robert Wagner,
Natalie Wood's ________

Christopher Walken,
Natalie Wood's ________ and movie actor

Dennis Davern,
________ captain

b 5 36 Listen to the second part of the interview and mark the sentences **T** (true) or **F** (false).

1 It's possible that Ms. Wood was hit before she fell into the water.
2 The LA County Coroner's Office recently changed Natalie Wood's cause of death because of new evidence found on the boat.
3 Ms. Wood was jealous of Mr. Wagner and Mr. Walken's friendship.
4 Mr. Wagner wrote about his wife's death in a book.
5 Ms. Wood and Mr. Walken acted in a movie together.
6 Mr. Walken has spoken to many people about the night of November 29, 1981.
7 The boat captain and Mr. Walken had an argument the night Ms. Wood died.
8 The boat captain says he didn't tell the truth in 1981.
9 The detective doesn't want to say how Ms. Wood died.
10 He doesn't think the mystery will ever be solved.

c Listen again. Say why the F sentences are false.

d Do you know of any famous unsolved crimes in your country?

3 GRAMMAR tag questions

a Look at four questions from the interview and complete them with the missing words.

1 "You were a detective with the Los Angeles Police Department, ________ ________?"
2 "That's incredible, ________ ________?"
3 "And you don't think they're suspects, ________ ________?"
4 "The boat captain changed his story about what happened that night, ________ ________?"

b 5 37 Listen and check. What's the difference between these questions and direct questions, e.g., between **1** and *Were you a detective with the Los Angeles Police Department?*

c ➤ **p.151 Grammar Bank 10B.** Learn more about tag questions and practice them.

4 PRONUNCIATION & SPEAKING
intonation in tag questions

a 5 39 Listen and complete the dialogue between a police officer and a suspect.

P Your last name's Jones, ______?
S Yes, it is.
P And you're 27, ______?
S Yes, that's right.
P You weren't at home last night at 8:00, ______?
S No, I wasn't. I was at the movie theater.
P But you don't have any witnesses, ______?
S Yes, I do. My wife was with me.
P Your wife wasn't with you, ______?
S How do you know?
P Because she was with me. At the police station. We arrested her yesterday.

b 5 40 Listen and repeat the tag questions. Copy the rhythm and intonation.

c ➤ **Communication** *Just checking* **A** *p.108* **B** *p.112.* Role-play a police interview.

d Which detective TV shows or movies are popular in your country right now? Do you enjoy watching these kinds of shows?

5 READING & LISTENING

a Do you enjoy reading crime novels? If so, which ones? If not, why not? Have you read a crime story recently? What was it about?

b 5 41 Read and listen to **Part 1** of a short story. Use the glossary to help you. Then answer the questions with a partner.

1 Where did the murder take place?
2 What did the prisoner look like?
3 How many witnesses saw him?
4 Why did Mrs. Salmon go to the window?
5 When did Mr. MacDougall see Adams?
6 Did Mr. Wheeler see Adams's face?

The Case for the Defense is a short story written by novelist Graham Greene. The story takes place in England around the time it was written, in the late 1930s, when the death penalty for murder still existed. It was abolished in 1965.

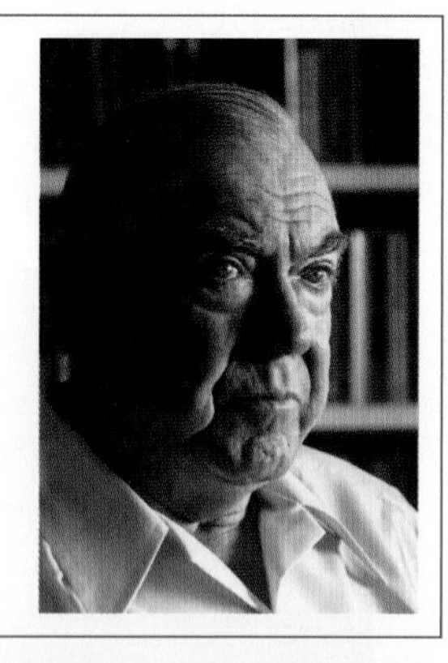

The Case for the Defense

BY GRAHAM GREENE

PART 1

It was the strangest murder trial I have ever attended. They named it the Peckham murder in the headlines, although Northwood Street, where Mrs. Parker was found murdered, was not actually in Peckham.

The prisoner was a well-built man with bloodshot eyes. An ugly man, one you wouldn't forget in a hurry – and that was an important point. The prosecution intended to call four witnesses who hadn't forgotten him and who had seen him hurrying away from the little red house in Northwood Street.

At two o'clock in the morning Mrs. Salmon, who lived at 15 Northwood Street, had been unable to sleep. She heard a door shut and so she went to the window and saw Adams (the accused) on the steps of the victim's house. He had just come out and he was wearing gloves. Before he moved away, he had looked up – at her window.

Henry MacDougall, who had been driving home late, nearly ran over Adams at the corner of Northwood Street because he was walking in the middle of the road, looking dazed. And old Mr. Wheeler, who lived next door to Mrs. Parker, at number 12, and was woken up by a noise and got up and looked out of the window, just as Mrs. Salmon had done, saw Adams's back and, as he turned, those bloodshot eyes. In Laurel Avenue he had been seen by yet another witness.

Glossary 1
trial /ˈtraɪəl/ the process where a judge, and sometimes a jury, listens to evidence and decides if somebody is guilty or innocent
Peckham /ˈpɛkəm/ an area in South London
the prosecution /prɑsəˈkyuʃn/ the lawyer(s) who try to show that somebody is guilty of a crime

PART 2

"I understand," the lawyer for the prosecution said, "that the defense intends to plead 'mistaken identity.' Adams's wife will tell you that he was with her at two in the morning on February 14. However, after you have heard the witnesses for the prosecution and examined carefully the features of the prisoner, I don't think you will be prepared to admit the possibility of a mistake."

Mrs. Salmon was called again. She was the ideal witness, with her slight Scottish accent and her expression of honesty and kindness. There was no malice in her, and no sense of importance. She told them what she had seen and how she had rung the police station.

"And do you see the man here in court?"

She looked straight at the big man in the dock, who stared hard at her with his bloodshot eyes, without emotion.

"Yes," she said, "there he is."

"You are quite certain?"

She said simply, "I couldn't be mistaken, sir."

"Thank you, Mrs. Salmon."

The lawyer for the defense began to cross-examine Mrs. Salmon.

"Now, Mrs. Salmon, you must remember that a man's life may depend on your evidence."

"I do remember it, sir."

"Is your eyesight good?"

"I have never had to wear spectacles, sir."

"You're fifty-five years old, aren't you?"

"Fifty-six, sir."

"And the man you saw was on the other side of the road, is that right?"

"Yes, sir, he was."

"And it was two o'clock in the morning. You must have remarkable eyes, Mrs. Salmon?"

"No, sir. There was moonlight, and when the man looked up, he had the lamplight on his face."

"And you have no doubt whatever that the man you saw is the prisoner?"

"None whatever, sir. It isn't a face you can easily forget."

Glossary 2
the defense /dɪˈfɛns/ the lawyer(s) who try to show that somebody is not guilty of a crime
plead (guilty) /plid/ to say in court that you are guilty (or not guilty) of a crime
court /kɔrt/ the place where crimes are judged
dock /dɑk/ the place in a court where a person who is accused sits or stands
cross-examine /krɔs ɪgˈzæmən/ to question a witness carefully about answers he or she have already given

c 5 42 Now read and listen to **Part 2**. Then answer the questions with a partner.

1 Adams's defense was "mistaken identity." What does this mean?
2 Where did Adams say that he was?
3 What did the prosecution lawyer ask Mrs. Salmon?
4 What three reasons did she give to explain how she had seen Adams's face so clearly?

d 5 43 Read the glossary for **Part 3** of the story, and check how the words are pronounced. Then listen to **Part 3** and answer the questions with a partner.

Glossary 3
swear /swɛr/ to make a public promise that something is true
case /keɪs/ something that is being officially investigated by the police, e.g., a murder case
alibi /ˈæləbaɪ/ evidence that proves somebody was in a different place at the time that a crime was committed
be acquitted /bi əˈkwɪtɪd/ to be declared not guilty of a crime

1 Who was the man at the back of the court?
2 How was he dressed?
3 What did the defense lawyer say to Mrs. Salmon?
4 What was the man's alibi?
5 Why was the man acquitted?
6 Why was there a big crowd outside the court?
7 Why did the brothers refuse to leave by the back entrance?
8 What happened to one of the brothers?
9 Why does the writer ask the question at the end, *If you were Mrs. Salmon, could you sleep at night?*

e Do you like the way the story ends? Why (not)?

9&10 Review and Check

GRAMMAR

Circle a, b, or c.

1 If you ______ here on time, we wouldn't have missed the beginning of the movie.
a were b had been c would have been

2 What ______ if that man hadn't helped you?
a you would do b you would have done
c would you have done

3 If she ______ me that she was arriving this morning, I would have gone to the airport to pick her up.
a told b would tell c had told

4 I would have finished the exam if I ______ about another ten minutes.
a would have had b had had
c would have

5 I'm afraid there's ______ time left.
a no b none c any

6 There are ______ good TV shows on tonight. I don't know what to watch.
a lots of b a lot c plenty

7 Is there ______ in the car for me, too?
a room enough b enough room
c too much room

8 Most people have ______ close friends.
a very little b very few c not much

9 Is he the man ______ you met at the party?
a – b whose c which

10 Is that the woman ______ husband is a famous writer?
a who b that c whose

11 The *Mona Lisa*, ______ was painted in about 1510, is in the Louvre in Paris.
a which b what c that

12 I'm very fond of Susan, ______ I used to share an apartment with in college.
a who b – c that

13 They're very rich, ______?
a are they b aren't they c isn't it

14 Your brother's been to New Zealand, ______?
a wasn't he b isn't he c hasn't he

15 You won't be late, ______?
a will you b won't you c are you

VOCABULARY

a Complete the sentences with a word formed from the **bold** word.

1 I got to the airport late, but ______ the flight was delayed. **luck**
2 He's ______ with his work. It's always full of mistakes. **care**
3 This sofa is really ______. It's too hard. **comfort**
4 I found a great jacket online, but ______ it was sold out. **fortunate**
5 Don't be so ______! The bus will be here soon. **patience**

b Complete with a verb.

1 It was too hot in the room, so I ______ the heat down a little.
2 I need to ______ my alarm for 5:30 because I have an early flight.
3 It's always a good idea to ______ your computer during a storm.
4 Could you ______ up the volume? I can't hear very well.
5 If you're not watching the TV, please ______ it off.

c Complete with the right words.

1 you use it to change the TV channel **r**______ **c**______
2 you use this on a computer to write **k**______
3 you use this to transfer files or photos **f**______ **dr**______
4 you use these to listen to music, e.g., on a plane **h**______**s**
5 you use this to move the cursor on a computer **m**______

d Complete the compound nouns.

1 soccer **f**______
2 **pr**______ picture
3 first **fl**______
4 gas **s**______
5 speed **c**______

e Complete the missing words.

1 The **d**______ was convinced that the man's alibi was false.
2 I'm sure he's guilty, but I can't **pr**______ it.
3 Natalie Wood was the **v**______ of an unlucky accident.
4 The police are not sure they will be able to **s**______ the mystery.
5 There is no **s**______ in the Natalie Wood's death.

PRONUNCIATION

a Circle the word with a different sound.

1	daughter	bought	caught	through
2	luck	tough	although	enough
3	charge	plug	gadget	program
4	keyboard	speaker	headphones	screen
5	murder	turn	perfect	careful

b Underline the stressed syllable.

1 comfor|ta|ble 2 a|dap|tor 3 ca|ble 4 wit|ness 5 e|vi|dence

CAN YOU UNDERSTAND THIS TEXT?

a Read the article once. Then read it again with the glossary and mark the sentences **T** (true), **F** (false), or **DS** (doesn't say).

1 The boy was on the Isle of Wight to attend the festival.
2 Bob Dylan and the boy had communication problems.
3 There was a beautiful view from the kitchen.
4 The boy liked the song that the American sang to him.
5 Some years later the boy committed a crime.
6 He was very moved when he heard *North Country Blues*.
7 Bob Dylan taught him to read and write.

b Choose five new words or phrases from the text. Check their meaning and pronunciation and try to learn them.

The ICON and the GYPSY

I was a young Gypsy boy trying to grow up in the 1960s in a country that was very hostile to our lifestyle, and with no access to education, and no chance to listen to music, or to attend festivals.

By chance, my family was on the Isle of Wight during the famous 1969 music festival. I was knocking on doors, trying to sell our homemade clothespins. One day I came to a very large house, somewhere in the middle of the island. A very charming American invited me in. He gave me orange juice and asked me a lot of questions about my life. He couldn't understand what I was saying very well because of my accent, and I couldn't understand him much either – he talked very quietly. I sat at his large wooden kitchen table and told him all about Gypsy life, how hard it could be, but also the fun we had.

I must have been there for most of the morning, and he got me to sing a couple of the Gypsy songs I knew. Before I left he played me a song on his guitar and gave me a record, which he said was his, and had the song on. But I didn't have a record player, and I soon lost the record.

I had no idea who he was, and I forgot about him until I was in my early twenties. Unfortunately I had gotten into some trouble and was in Brixton Prison for burglary. My sentence was for two years. We had a vicar who used to visit twice a week, and because we were bored, we would sometimes attend his sessions. At one of the sessions he played some music on an old record player, and as soon as I heard it, I recognized the singer. He told me it was a man named Bob Dylan and said that if I liked it, he would bring more of his records to the next meeting. The following week I spent hours transfixed as I listened to the records. One song stood out – *North Country Blues* – it was the song he had sung to me in the kitchen on the Isle of Wight all those years ago. When the song had finished, I cried – all the troubles and hardship I had lived with just poured out of me.

Those sessions with the vicar became my education. With his guidance and Dylan's poetry, a world opened up to me. He taught me to read and write, and by the time my prison sentence came to an end, I had started a journey that transformed my life. With the vicar's support I went to college and became a carpenter – I didn't look back.

Adapted from The Times

Gypsy a member of a race of people who spend their lives traveling around from place to place, living in caravans
Isle of Wight a small island off the south coast of England
vicar an Anglican priest

VIDEO CAN YOU UNDERSTAND THESE PEOPLE?

5 44))) On the street Watch or listen to five people and answer the questions.

Ryder

Elizabeth

Sean

Isobel

Giles

1 Ryder helped someone who ______.
 a had an electronic device taken from him
 b was run over by a car
 c couldn't make a phone call
2 Elizabeth thinks that technology ______.
 a is helpful in certain situations
 b helps people learn important skills
 c doesn't work as well as it should
3 Sean ______ guess who the murderer is.
 a can usually b likes to try to c doesn't try to
4 Isobel's favorite thing about Alexander McQueen's clothes is ______.
 a they are reasonably priced
 b the different designs and materials
 c that they are based on designs from the past
5 Giles thinks he's lucky because he ______.
 a caught a flight from Australia at the last minute
 b is generally happy
 c once won some money in the lottery

CAN YOU SAY THIS IN ENGLISH?

Do the tasks with a partner. Check (✓) the box if you can do them.

Can you...?

1 ☐ complete these three sentences:
 If you had told me about the party earlier,...
 I would have bought those shoes if...
 I wouldn't have been so angry if...
2 ☐ describe something that you do too much, and something that you don't do enough
3 ☐ talk about a gadget that you use and why it is useful
4 ☐ describe a person that you admire (who he or she is / what you know about him or her / why you admire him or her)
5 ☐ check five things you think you know about your partner using tag questions

VIDEO **Short movies** Brooklyn Bridge
Watch and enjoy the movie.

Communication

9A GUESS THE CONDITIONAL
Student A

a Look at sentences 1–6 and think of the missing verb or verb phrase ([+] = positive, [−] = negative). **Don't write anything yet!**

1 We ________ the hotel if we hadn't had GPS. [−]
2 If I ________ that it was your birthday, I would have bought you something. [+]
3 If I ________ about the concert earlier, I would have been able to get a ticket. [+]
4 The cat wouldn't have gotten in if you ________ the window open. [−]
5 If our best player hadn't been ejected, we ________ the game. [+]
6 I wouldn't have recognized her if you ________ me who she was. [−]

b Read your sentence 1 to **B**. If it isn't right, try again until **B** tells you "That's right." Then write it. Continue with 2–6.

c Listen to **B** say sentence 7. If it's the same as your sentence 7 below, say "That's right." If not, say "Try again" until **B** gets it right. Continue with 8–12.

7 I **wouldn't have been** so angry if you had told me the truth right from the start.
8 If I hadn't gone to that party that night, I **wouldn't have met** my wife.
9 If we hadn't taken a taxi, we **would have missed** the train.
10 If I'd known that show was on last night, I **would have watched** it.
11 I **would have gone out** with you last night if I hadn't had to work late.
12 If I **had listened** to my friends, I would never have married James.

PE5 ASKING POLITELY FOR INFORMATION
Student A

a You are a tourist in **B**'s town. You want to ask **B**, who you have stopped on the street, questions 1–5 and you want to be very polite. Rewrite 2–5 as indirect questions.

1 Do stores open on Sundays?
Could you tell me *if stores open on Sundays*?
2 Is there a post office near here?
Do you know ________________________________?
3 What time do banks close here?
Could you tell me ________________________________?
4 Where's the train station?
Do you know ________________________________?
5 Does the number 21 bus go to the city?
Could you tell me ________________________________?

b Ask **B** your indirect questions 1–5. Always begin with *Excuse me*.

c Now **B** is a tourist, and is going to stop you on the street and ask you some questions. Answer politely with the necessary information.

6B JUDGING BY APPEARANCES
Students A+B

Dominic McVey, born in 1985, is a British entrepreneur from London, who set up a business at the age of 13 importing micro-scooters from the United States. He was a millionaire by the age of 15. His business interests now include website publishing and fashion.

Mira Sorvino is an American actress of Italian descent. She won an Oscar as best supporting actress in 1995 for her role in Woody Allen's *Mighty Aphrodite*. Before becoming an actress she studied Chinese at Harvard University, where she graduated *magna cum laude* (with great honor).

Olga Rutterschmidt, an 80-year-old California woman, and her friend Helen Golay were convicted in 2008 of murdering two homeless men. They committed the murders to collect millions of dollars from the men's life insurance policies.

7A THREE IN A ROW
Students A+B

Play the game in small groups.

One team is **X** and one is **O**. Take turns choosing a square. Finish the sentence so that it is grammatically correct and makes sense. If you are right, put your **X** or **O** in the square. The first team to get "three in a row" is the winner.

Unless we hurry...	I'll leave home when...	I won't get married until...
I'll give you the money as soon as...	If I see him...	When I can speak English fluently...
He'll lose his job if...	As soon as he gets here...	You'll never be rich unless...

7B GUESS THE SENTENCE
Student A

a Look at sentences 1–6 and think of the missing verb phrase (+ = positive, − = negative). **Don't write anything yet!**

1 I'd cook dinner every day if I ____________ earlier from work. +

2 If we ____________ this summer, maybe we could afford to get a new car. −

3 I think you ____________ more if you saw the original version. +

4 I'd see my grandparents more often if they ____________. +

5 I ____________ the fish if I were you. It isn't usually very good here. −

6 I ____________ if the water was a little warmer. +

b Read your sentence 1 to **B**. If it isn't right, try again until **B** tells you "That's right." Then write it. Continue with 2–6.

c Listen to **B** say sentence 7. If it's the same as your sentence 7 below, say "That's right." If not, say "Try again" until **B** gets it right. Continue with 8–12.

7 The house would look better if you **painted it**.

8 If I met my ex on the street, I **wouldn't say hello** to him.

9 If it **weren't so late**, I'd stay a little longer.

10 The flight **would be more comfortable** if we were in business class.

11 I wouldn't mind the winter so much if it **didn't get dark** so early.

12 If I had more money, I'**d buy a house** with a beautiful yard.

8A I WANT TO SPEAK TO THE MANAGER
Student A

Look at the situations and role-play the conversations. Spend a few minutes preparing what you are going to say.

1 **You're a customer.** You bought something in a clothing store on sale yesterday (decide what) and there's a problem (decide what). Go back to the store. **B** is the salesperson. You'd like to exchange it for another identical one. If you can't, you'd like a refund.

You start. *Excuse me. I bought...*

2 **You're the manager of a restaurant.** Your regular chef is off this week, and you have a temporary chef who is not very good. One of the waiters has had a problem with a customer, who would like to speak to you. When customers complain, you usually offer them a free drink or a coffee. If it's absolutely necessary, you might give a 10% discount on their bill, but you would prefer not to. **B** is the customer.

B will start.

8B THE RIGHT JOB FOR YOU Students A+B

In which group(s) do you have the most check marks? Read the appropriate paragraph to find out which jobs would suit you. Would you like to do any of them?

If you have the most check marks in 1-4, the best job for you would be in the "caring professions." If you are good at science, you could consider a career in medicine, for example becoming a doctor or nurse. Alternatively, teaching or social work are areas that would suit your personality.

If you have the most check marks in 5-8, you should consider a job involving numbers, for example becoming an accountant or working in the stock market. The world of business would also probably appeal to you, especially sales or marketing.

If you have the most check marks in 9-12, you need a creative job. Depending on your specific talents you might enjoy a job in the world of music, art, or literature. Areas that would suit you include publishing, journalism, graphic design, fashion, or the music industry.

If you have the most check marks in 13-16, you have an analytical mind. You would be suitable for a job in computer science or engineering. You also have good spatial sense which would make architecture and related jobs another possibility.

9A GUESS THE CONDITIONAL Student B

a Look at sentences 7–12 and think of the missing verb or verb phrase (+ = positive, − = negative). **Don't write anything yet!**

7 I __________ so angry if you had told me the truth right from the start. −

8 If I hadn't gone to that party that night, I __________ my wife. −

9 If we hadn't taken a taxi, we __________ the train. +

10 If I'd known that show was on last night, I __________ it. +

11 I __________ with you last night if I hadn't had to work late. +

12 If I __________ to my friends, I would never have married James. +

b Listen to **A** say sentence 1. If it's the same as your sentence 1 below, say "That's right." If not, say "Try again" until **A** gets it right. Continue with 2–6.

1 We **wouldn't have found** the hotel if we hadn't had GPS.

2 If I **had remembered** that it was your birthday, I would have bought you something.

3 If **I'd known** about the concert earlier, I would have been able to get a ticket.

4 The cat wouldn't have gotten in if you **hadn't left** the window open.

5 If our best player hadn't been ejected, we **would have won** the game.

6 I wouldn't have recognized her if you **hadn't told me** who she was.

c Read your sentence 7 to **A**. If it isn't right, try again until **A** tells you "That's right." Then write it. Continue with 8–12.

10A RELATIVES QUIZ Student A

a Complete the questions with a relative clause to describe the **bold** words. Start the clause with *who, which, that, whose,* or *where*, or no relative pronoun when there is a new subject.

1 **a pedestrian** What do you call someone...?
2 **a loan** What do you call some money...?
3 **fans** What do you call people...?
4 **a private school** What do you call a place...?
5 **a coach** What do you call the person...?
6 **traffic light** What do you call the thing...?
7 **soccer field** What do you call the place...?
8 **selfish** What do you call somebody...?
9 **an ATM** What do you call a thing...?

b Ask **B** your questions.

c Answer **B**'s questions.

10B JUST CHECKING Student A

a You are a detective. **B** is a suspect in a crime. Ask **B** the questions below, but **don't write anything down**. Try to remember **B**'s answers.

- What's your name?
- Where do you live?
- How old are you?
- Where were you born?
- Are you married?
- What do you do?
- What car do you drive?
- How long have you lived in this town?
- What did you do last night?
- Where were you at 7:00 this morning?

b Now check the information with **B** using a tag question.

Your name is Tom Gibson, isn't it?

You live in New York City, don't you?

c Change roles. Now you are the suspect and **B** is the detective. Answer **B**'s questions. You can invent the information if you want to.

d **B** will now check the information he / she has. Just say, "Yes, that's right" or "No, that's wrong" and correct the wrong information.

7B GUESS THE SENTENCE Student B

a Look at sentences 7–12 and think of the missing verb phrase (+ = positive, − = negative). **Don't write anything yet!**

7 The house would look better if you ____________. +
8 If I met my ex on the street, I ____________ to him. −
9 If it ____________, I'd stay a little longer. −
10 The flight ____________ if we were in business class. +
11 I wouldn't mind the winter so much if it ____________ so early. −
12 If I had more money, I ____________ with a beautiful yard. +

b Now listen to **A** say sentence 1. If it's the same as your sentence 1 below, say "That's right." If not, say "Try again" until **A** gets it right. Continue with 2–6.

1 I'd cook dinner every day if I **got home** earlier from work.
2 If we **didn't go on vacation** this summer, maybe we could afford to get a new car.
3 I think you **would enjoy the movie** more if you saw the original version.
4 I'd see my grandparents more often if they **lived closer by**.
5 I **wouldn't have** the fish if I were you. It isn't usually very good here.
6 I'**d go swimming** if the water were a little warmer.

c Read your sentence 7 to **A**. If it's not right, try again until **A** tells you "That's right." Then write it. Continue with 8–12.

8A I WANT TO SPEAK TO THE MANAGER Student B

Look at the situations and role-play the conversations. Spend a few minutes preparing what you are going to say.

1 **You're a salesperson in a clothing store. A** is going to come to you with a problem with something he / she bought on sale yesterday. You can't exchange it for an identical one because there are no more in his / her size.

Try to persuade **A** to exchange it for something else because you don't usually give refunds during a sale.

A will start.

2 **You're a customer in a restaurant.** You have just finished your meal and you didn't enjoy it at all (decide what was wrong with it). You complained to the waiter, but the waiter didn't solve the problem. You have asked the waiter to call the manager. Try to get at least a 50% discount on your meal. **A** is the manager.

You start. *Good evening. Are you the manager?.*

PE5 ASKING POLITELY FOR INFORMATION Student B

a You are a tourist in A's town. You want to ask **A**, who you have stopped on the street, questions 1–5 and you want to be very polite. Rewrite 2–5 as indirect questions.

1 Do stores close at lunchtime?
Could you tell me *if stores close at lunchtime?*
2 Is there a cash machine near here?
Do you know ____________________?
3 Where's the closest drugstore?
Could you tell me ____________________?
4 What time do the buses stop running at night?
Do you know ____________________?
5 Do banks open on Saturday mornings?
Could you tell me ____________________?

b **A** is a tourist, and is going to stop you on the street and ask you some questions. Answer politely with the necessary information.

c Ask **A** your indirect questions 1–5. Always begin with *Excuse me*.

10A RELATIVES QUIZ Student B

a Complete the questions with a relative clause to describe the **bold** words. Start the clause with *who, which, that, whose*, or *where*, or no relative pronoun when there is a new subject.

1 **shy** What do you call somebody...?
2 **a flash drive** What do you call a thing...?
3 **a referee** What do you call the person...?
4 **a bicycle lane** What do you call the place...?
5 **a murderer** What do you call somebody...?
6 **a receipt** What do you call the piece of paper...?
7 **a taxi stand** What do you call the place...?
8 **a colleague** What do you call a person...?
9 **a motorcycle** What do you call a thing...?

b Answer **A**'s questions.

c Ask **A** your questions.

10B JUST CHECKING Student B

a You are a suspect in a crime. **A** is a detective. Answer **A**'s questions. You can invent the information if you want to.

b **A** will now check the information he / she has. Just say, "Yes, that's right" or "No, that's wrong" and correct the wrong information.

c Change roles. Now you are a detective and **A** is a suspect. Ask **A** the questions below, but **don't write anything down**. Try to remember **A**'s answers.

- What's your name?
- Where do you live?
- How old are you?
- Where were you born?
- Are you married?
- What do you do?
- What car do you drive?
- How long have you lived in this town?
- What did you do last night?
- Where were you at 7:00 this morning?

d Now check the information with **A** using a tag question.

Your name is Olivia Montoya, isn't it?

You live in New York City, don't you?

5 A MOVIE REVIEW

CLASSIC MOVIES YOU MUST SEE

PLEASE POST YOUR SUGGESTIONS

The Godfather (1972)

The movie *The Godfather* is [1]*based* on the book by Mario Puzo. The movie was [2]_________ by Martin Scorsese. It [3]_________ Marlon Brando as Vito Corleone and Al Pacino as his son, Michael. The movie won three Oscars in 1973 for Best Actor (Marlon Brando), Best Movie, and Best Screenplay.

The movie is [4]_________ in New York in the 1940s and 50s. It was filmed on [5]_________ in New York and in Sicily.

The movie is about the Corleone family. Vito, "The Godfather," is head of one of the most powerful criminal families in the US. Don Vito is a fair but ruthless man, who runs his business by doing favors and expecting favors in return. The Corleones get involved in a war with other criminal families because they don't want to sell drugs. Don Vito is shot and he is seriously injured. While Don Vito is in the hospital, control of the family passes to his eldest son, Sonny. Sonny is a hothead, and with him in charge, the war between the various families becomes more violent. Don Vito's youngest son, Michael, has always stayed outside the family business, but when Don Vito is shot, he returns home to do what he can to help the family. He also takes his revenge against the people who are trying to kill his father. In the end, Sonny is shot and Michael becomes the new Godfather.

I strongly [6]_________ *The Godfather.* It has [7]_________, drama, an unforgettable [8]_________, and an important message: that violence never really solves anything. The two [9]_________, *The Godfather II* and *The Godfather III* are also good, but the first movie is definitely my favorite.

a Read the movie review and complete it with the words in the list.

action ~~based~~ directed location recommend
sequels set soundtrack stars

b Read the review again and number the paragraphs in order 1–4.

Paragraph ☐	The plot
Paragraph ☐	The name of the movie, the director, the stars, and any prizes it won
Paragraph ☐	Why you recommend the movie
Paragraph ☐	Where and when it is set Where it was filmed

c Look at paragraph three again. What tense do we use to tell the story of a movie or book?

d Have you seen *The Godfather*? If yes, do you agree with the review? If no, does the review make you want to see it?

Useful language: describing a movie

It was directed / written by...
It is set in...
It is based on the book...
It's about...
It stars...
In the end...
My favorite scene is...
I strongly recommend (the movie) because...

e **Write** a movie review about a movie you would recommend people to buy on DVD or see at the movie theater. **Plan** what you are going to write in the four paragraphs. Use the **Useful language** and **Vocabulary Bank** *Movies p.159* to help you.

f **Check** your review for mistakes (grammar, vocabulary, punctuation, and spelling).

◄ p.57

Writing

6 DESCRIBING A HOUSE OR APARTMENT

a The website Homerent.net is for people who want to rent out their houses while they are away on vacation. Read two posts from the website. Which one would you prefer to stay in for a two-week vacation? Why?

b Read about the apartment in Mexico City again. Underline any adjectives that help to "sell" the apartment. What do they mean?

c Now read about the Thai villa again. Improve the description by replacing the word *nice* with one of the adjectives below. Often there is more than one possibility.

amazing beautiful breathtaking great ideal
luxurious magnificent perfect spacious superb

Useful language: describing location

It is perfectly situated in...
It is walking distance from...
It is a (fifteen-minute) walk from...
It is a short drive from...
The neighborhood is (safe, friendly, etc.)...
It's a (beautiful) area...

d **Write** a description of your house or apartment for the website. **Plan** what you're going to write. Use the **Useful language** and **Vocabulary Bank** *Houses p.162* to help you.

Paragraph 1	A brief introduction. What kind of house / apartment is it? Where is it exactly?
Paragraph 2	Describe the house / apartment. What rooms does it have? Does it have any special characteristics?
Paragraph 3	Describe the neighborhood. How far is it from places of interest, public transportation, etc.?
Paragraph 4	Say who the house / apartment is suitable for. Are there any restrictions?

e **Check** your description for mistakes (grammar, vocabulary, punctuation, and spelling).

p.71

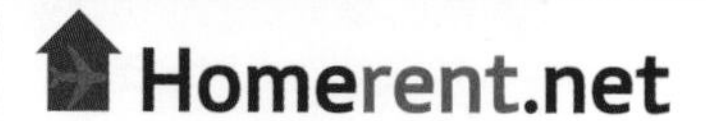

Homerent.net

Home | Search | Join our community | Help

Beautiful one-bedroom apartment in Mexico City

This apartment is perfectly situated on a quiet street in Mexico City's Reforma area.

It's a cozy, 750-square-foot apartment on the first floor of a three-story building. It has one bedroom with a queen-size bed, a spacious living / dining room, a modern, well-equipped kitchen, and a bathroom. There's a beautiful view of a flower-filled courtyard from the living room windows. The living room has a big table, which is ideal for having a meal with friends, and there is also a large flat-screen TV. The apartment has tile floors, air conditioning, satellite TV, and Wi-Fi Internet.

The Reforma area is a lively neighborhood near the center of Mexico City, with plenty of stores and cafes. The apartment is walking distance to Paseo de la Reforma, one of Mexico City's widest streets designed to look like a grand European boulevard. It's ten minutes away from a subway station and a bus stop, so you can visit the city very easily.

This apartment is ideal for a couple who would like to go sightseeing in this beautiful city. It's a non-smoking apartment, and pets are not allowed.

Beach villa in Hua Hin, Thailand

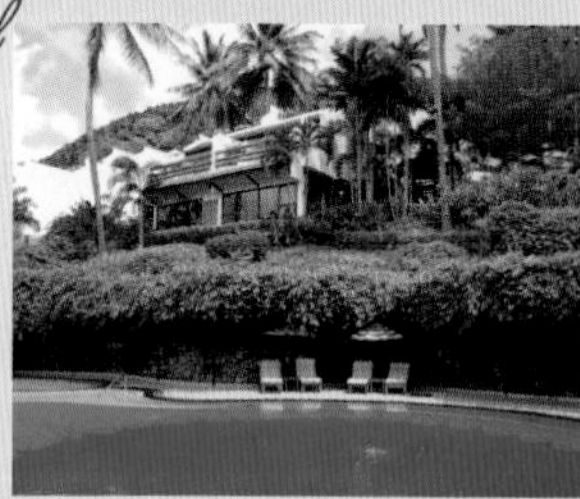

Hua Hin is a ~~nice~~ *beautiful* vacation resort town on the northern part of the Malay Peninsula, about 120 miles south of Bangkok.

Our house is *nice*. It has three double bedrooms, a living room, a *nice* kitchen, and four bathrooms. All the rooms have air conditioning, and the bedrooms all have an attached, private bathroom. There is a *nice* patio with a table and chairs, so you can eat outside. There is a *nice* view of the mountains in the distance. There is a *nice* yard with flower gardens and a swimming pool. There is also a hot tub, which is relaxing to use after a long day of sightseeing.

The house is near a *nice* beach, where you can play a lot of water sports. It's also a short drive to two floating markets where you can buy food, flowers, jewelry, and souvenirs.

This house is perfect for a family with children or for two or three couples. The house is not suitable for pets.

7 A LETTER OF COMPLAINT

a Read the letter of complaint. Then answer the questions.

1. Who is Chris Mason complaining to?
2. What item is he complaining about? Why?
3. Who did he contact first?
4. What problem did he have when he called to complain?
5. In which paragraph does Chris use flattery? How?

b Read it again and complete the blanks with a word from the list.

~~Dear~~ delivered forward However in stock number service unhelpful yours

 **Useful language: a formal letter (or email)**

You don't know the person's name
Start: *Dear Sir / Madam:*
Finish: *Kind regards,*

You know the person's name
Start: *Dear + Mr. / Ms. / Mrs. Garcia:*
Finish: *Sincerely yours,*

Style
- Don't use contractions
- Write *I look forward to hearing from you.* as the final sentence
- Write your full name under your signature

Note: a formal email is exactly the same as a formal letter, except in an email we don't write the address or date.

c **Write** a letter (or an email) of complaint about something you bought online. **Plan** what you're going to write. Use the **Useful language** to help you.

d **Check** your letter or email for mistakes (grammar, vocabulary, punctuation, and spelling).

◀ *p.77*

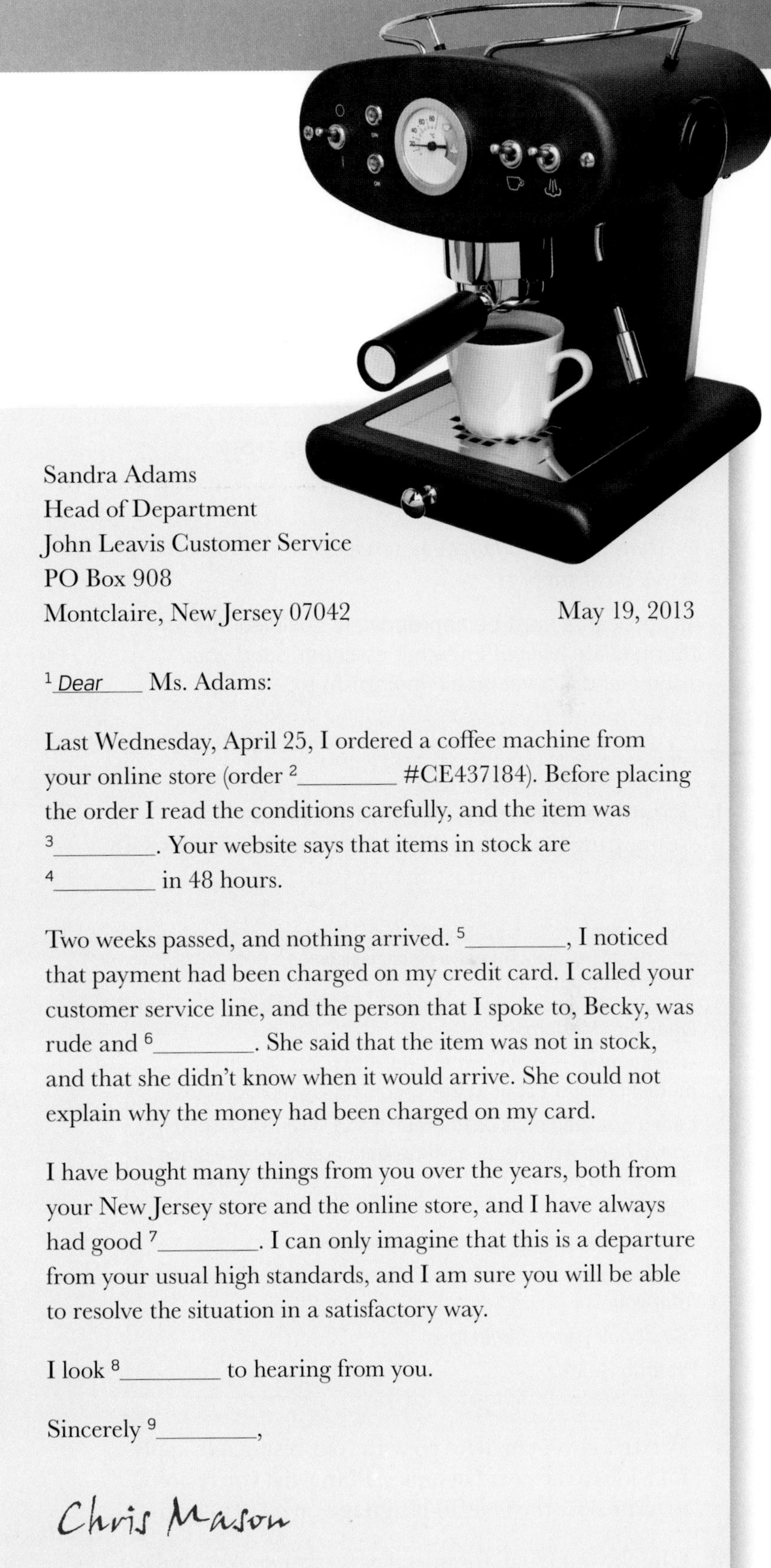

Sandra Adams
Head of Department
John Leavis Customer Service
PO Box 908
Montclaire, New Jersey 07042

May 19, 2013

[1] *Dear* Ms. Adams:

Last Wednesday, April 25, I ordered a coffee machine from your online store (order [2]________ #CE437184). Before placing the order I read the conditions carefully, and the item was [3]________. Your website says that items in stock are [4]________ in 48 hours.

Two weeks passed, and nothing arrived. [5]________, I noticed that payment had been charged on my credit card. I called your customer service line, and the person that I spoke to, Becky, was rude and [6]________. She said that the item was not in stock, and that she didn't know when it would arrive. She could not explain why the money had been charged on my card.

I have bought many things from you over the years, both from your New Jersey store and the online store, and I have always had good [7]________. I can only imagine that this is a departure from your usual high standards, and I am sure you will be able to resolve the situation in a satisfactory way.

I look [8]________ to hearing from you.

Sincerely [9]________,

Chris Mason

Chris Mason

8 A COVER EMAIL WITH YOUR RÉSUMÉ

a Look at the job advertisement. Which job could *you* apply for?

We are looking for dedicated, enthusiastic, and energetic people to work at the upcoming Olympic Games.

There are opportunities in the following areas:

- *Administration*
- *Hospitality and catering*
- *Translation and language services*
- *Medical support*

All applicants must be appropriately qualified and an intermediate level of English is essential. Send your résumé and a cover email (in English) to:
recruitment@theolympicgames.com

b Ricardo Suarez wants to apply for a job, and is submitting his résumé. Read the cover email to go with it. Circle the best phrase in each pair.

From: Ricardo Suarez [Suarezr@chatchat.com]
To: recruitment@theolympicgames.com
Subject: Job application

Dear Sir / Madam:

1 *I am writing / I'm writing* to apply for a job with the medical support staff at the upcoming Olympic Games.

I am a qualified physical therapist, and 2 *I've been working / I have been working* at a rehabilitation center here since January 2006. 3 *My English is great / I speak English fluently.*

4 I've enclosed / I've attached my résumé.

5 *Hope to hear from you soon! / I look forward to hearing from you.*

6 *Sincerely yours, / With love,*

Ricardo Suarez

c **Write** a cover email (to go with your résumé) to apply for a job in the next Olympics. **Plan** what you're going to write. Use the **Useful language** on *p.119* to help you.

d **Check** your email for mistakes (grammar, vocabulary, punctuation, and spelling).

◀ p.81

9 A MAGAZINE ARTICLE - ADVANTAGES AND DISADVANTAGES

a Read an article for a student magazine about the advantages and disadvantages of living without a TV. The computer has found ten mistakes (grammar, vocabulary, punctuation, and spelling). Can you correct them?

Living without a TV

Almost every family today 1 have a TV, in fact probably more than one, and people everywhere spend hours watching it. But a few families choose to live without a TV because they think there are advantages.

The first advantage is that families spend more time 2 talk to each other. Second, they spend more time doing more creative things like reading or painting. Third, they spend more time outdoors, and are usually 3 in gooder shape.

But on the other hand, there are also disadvantages. For example, children who don't have a TV may feel 4 differents from 5 there school friends, and often won't know what they are talking about. Also, it is not true that all TV 6 showes are bad. There are good ones, like 7 documentarys, and people who live without a TV may know less about 8 whats happening in the world.

In conclusion, 9 althought living without a TV has some advantages, I think today it's unrealistic and that we should just try to turn the TV 10 out when there's nothing good on.

b Read the article again. Then cover it, and in pairs, answer the questions from memory.

1. What are the three advantages?
2. What are the two disadvantages?
3. Is the writer for or against having a TV?

c You are going to write a similar article about smartphones. First with a partner, make a list of the advantages and disadvantages.

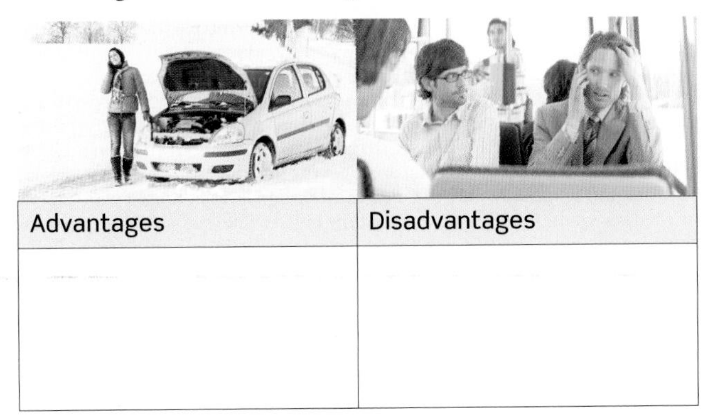

Advantages	Disadvantages

d Now decide which are the three biggest advantages and number them 1–3 (1 = the biggest). Do the same with the disadvantages.

Useful language: writing about advantages and disadvantages

Listing advantages
Firstly / First,... *Second,...* *Third,...*

Listing disadvantages
On the other hand, there are also (some) disadvantages...
For instance / For example...
Also,...

Conclusion
In conclusion / To sum up, I think...

e **Write** an article called "Smartphones – A great invention?" Start the article with this introduction.

> Many people today don't just have a cell phone, they have a smartphone like an iPhone or a Blackberry. But is it a great invention? I think there are both advantages and disadvantages.

Write three more paragraphs. **Plan** what you're going to write. Use the **Useful language** to help you.

Paragraph 2	Write two or three advantages.
Paragraph 3	Write two or three disadvantages.
Paragraph 4	Conclusion – decide if you think smartphones are a great invention or not.

f **Check** your article for mistakes (grammar, vocabulary, punctuation, and spelling).

◀ p.91

10 A BIOGRAPHY

a Read a text about Mark Zuckerberg. Then rewrite the text with the extra information (sentences A–F) as relative clauses.

Mark Zuckerberg, the American computer programmer, was one of the founders of Facebook.

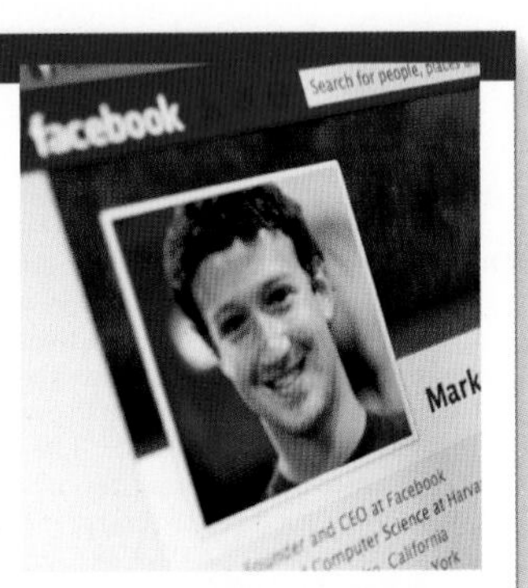

In his teens he began to write software programs as a hobby. After graduating from high school he went to Harvard. While he was there he created a website called Facemash. It was shut down by the university, but it inspired him to create Facebook.

He left Harvard and moved to California with Dustin Moskovitz, and together they made Facebook an international success.

In 2012 Zuckerberg married Priscilla Chan.

Paragraph 1	A Mark Zuckerberg was born in New York in 1984
Paragraph 2	B He studied computer science and sociology at Harvard C Facemash allowed students to share photos D He launched Facebook from his room in 2004
Paragraph 3	E Dustin Moskovitz had been his roommate
Paragraph 4	F He had dated Priscilla Chan for nine years

1 *Mark Zuckerberg, the American computer programmer,* ***who was born in New York in 1984****, was one of the founders of* Facebook.

b Cover **A–F**. Read the text again and try to remember the extra information.

c **Write** a short biography of an interesting or successful person you know about. **Plan** what you're going to write, and try to use some relative clauses.

d **Check** your biography for mistakes (grammar, vocabulary, punctuation, and spelling).

◀ p.95

3 36

Interviewer So tell me, how did you get involved in the movie, Dagmara?

Dagmara Well, as you probably know, *Schindler's List* was shot in Krakow, in Poland, which is where I live. I was a university student at the time studying English. And the film company set up their production office here three months before they started shooting the film, and I got a job there as a production assistant, preparing and translating documents and the script.

Interviewer But how did you get the job as Steven Spielberg's interpreter?

Dagmara Well, it was a complete coincidence. Just before the shooting started, there was a big party in one of the hotels in Krakow for all the actors and the film crew, and I was invited, too. When I arrived at the party, the Polish producer of the film came up to me and said, "The woman who was going to interpret for Steven Spielberg can't come, so we need you to interpret his opening speech."

Interviewer How did you feel about that?

Dagmara I couldn't believe it! I was just a student – I had no experience of interpreting – and now I was going to speak in front of hundreds of people. I was so nervous that I drank a couple of glasses of champagne to give myself courage. I must have done a pretty good job though, because soon afterwards Spielberg came up to me to say thank you and then he said, "I'd like you to be my interpreter for the whole film." I was so stunned I had to pinch myself to believe that this was happening to me.

3 37

Interviewer So what exactly did you have to do?

Dagmara I had to go to the film set every day and translate Spielberg's instructions to the Polish actors, and also to the extras. I had to make them understand what he wanted them to do. It was really exciting, and I often felt as if I was a director myself.

Interviewer So, was it a difficult job?

Dagmara Sometimes it was really hard. The worst thing was when we had to shoot a scene again and again because Spielberg thought it wasn't exactly right. Some scenes were repeated as many as 16 times – and then sometimes I would think that maybe it was my fault – that I hadn't translated properly what he wanted, so I'd get really nervous. I remember one scene with lots of actors in it which we just couldn't get right, and Spielberg started shouting at me because he was stressed. Eventually we got it right and then he apologized, and I cried a little, because I was also very stressed – and after that it was all right again.

Interviewer So, was Spielberg difficult to work with?

Dagmara Not at all. I mean he was very demanding, I had to do my best every day, but he was really nice to me. I felt he treated me like a daughter. For instance, he was always making sure that I wasn't cold – it was freezing on the set most of the time – and he would make sure that I had a warm coat and gloves and things.

Interviewer Did you ever get to be an extra?

Dagmara Yes, twice! I was going to be in two party scenes, and I got to wear beautiful long dresses and high heels. Unfortunately, one scene didn't make it to the final cut of the film, and before we started shooting the other one I tripped walking down some stairs and twisted my ankle really badly. I was in so much pain that I couldn't take part in the filming, and that was the end of my "acting career." I still have the photos of me looking like a girl from the 40s, though!

Interviewer Have you ever worked with Spielberg again?

Dagmara Yes. A year later he invited me to interpret for him again, this time during the premiere of *Schindler's List* in Poland, which was broadcast live on national television! Before that, he had also asked me come to work as a production assistant on his next movie in Hollywood. I was very tempted and thought really hard about it, but I hadn't finished my studies yet, and all my family and friends were in Poland – so in the end I decided not to go.

Interviewer Do you regret it?

Dagmara Not at all. I had my moment, and it was unforgettable, but that was it!

3 47

A few months ago I was with a Vietnamese friend of mine named Ny in California, and we were driving around the West Hollywood area, which is a pretty famous part of Los Angeles – you know – the Sunset Strip, Melrose Avenue, lots of cool shops and restaurants…and lots of movie stars!! Anyway, it was a hot, sunny day, and we were thirsty, so we stopped at a cafe for a cold drink and a snack. So, we sat down at an outside table waiting for the server when we saw a man walking toward us. He was wearing a crazy combination of clothing, and he kind of looked like a mess. He had a beard, long messy brown hair, and he was wearing a winter hat in the middle of summer! Ny said, "Oh, look at that poor man. He must be homeless. He looks like he hasn't taken a shower for some time. He's also really thin. He must be hungry – should I give him some money? She started to look in her bag for some money, but I looked at him again and just said, "Don't!" She couldn't understand why I didn't want her to give the man some money, and she thought I was being very mean and unfriendly.

3 48

When the man had gone past, I said, "Ny, that man isn't homeless. He's Russell Brand, the British comedian and actor." He's one of the funniest people in show business. And he definitely isn't homeless – he has a house in the Hollywood Hills and an apartment in New York City! And he definitely doesn't need any money! He just enjoys wearing comfortable, old, mismatched clothing. In fact, Russell Brand often talks to the homeless people he sees on the streets and gives them money or buys them food. Even though he looks a little messy and scary, he's actually a very kind person. Ny was really surprised. She said that she thought all US celebrities dressed in designer clothes, and had perfect hair and makeup all the time. I told her that in the US, you can't always judge people by their appearance. A lot of people, even famous celebrities, like to dress in old, mismatched clothing because it's comfortable, and it helps them blend in with the crowd better so they can go quietly about their business.

4 8

Part 1

Gareth had only eight weeks for the experiment, during which time he would be teaching three days a week. His aim was to try to improve the boys' reading age by six months. On the other two days the boys would have normal classes with the girls.

His plan was based on his own experience of being a learner and from talking to educational experts. He had three main principles:

First, that it was essential to make the work feel like play. "If I can do that, the boys will learn," said Gareth. The second principle was competition. Gareth says, "Boys absolutely love competition! It has gone out of fashion in many schools, but I think it's really important. Boys have to learn to lose and to fail and to come back from that. If you've never done that until you go for your first job interview and don't get the job, then you've got a problem."

The third thing Gareth thought was important was to allow boys to take risks. All kinds of risks. Not just physical risks like climbing trees, but doing things like acting in front of other people. Doing things that are a little scary, but that are very motivating if you manage to do them.

4 9

Part 2

When Gareth started, he made some changes to the way the children were learning. The boys spent a lot of time outside, and they had PE (physical education) every day before regular classes began. They even made their own outdoor classroom. Gareth also tried to involve the boy's parents as much as possible in their education, and he visited them at their homes on several occasions.

Gareth set up three major activities for the boys to help improve their language skills. The first activity was a school debating competition against the girls. The topic that the children had to debate was "Computer games should be banned."

When they started to prepare for the debate, the boys weren't very enthusiastic, but soon they started to get more involved. In the end the girls won the debate, but the boys had learned to argue and make points, to express themselves better. They were disappointed not to have won, but they wanted to do it again.

Next, Gareth organized a Reading World Cup, where the boys had to read in teams. Some of the boys couldn't read very well, but they all got very excited about the World Cup and became much more enthusiastic readers! There was a prize for the winners, and this really motivated the boys.

Finally, the boys, working with the girls, had to write their own play and perform it at the local theater. The play they wrote was about Romans and aliens. All the children, boys and girls, worked really hard and although some of them felt very nervous before they performed the play, it was a great success and the boys especially were thrilled. Gareth said afterwards, "It was a risk, and it was scary – but it was good scary."

4 10

Part 3

The boys had a great time with Gareth as their teacher. But at the end of the eight weeks, had their reading really improved? In the last week of the quarter, they had to take their national reading exams. The exams were independently marked, and when the results were announced, the boys had made great progress – all of them had improved by six months and some of them had advanced the equivalent of two years in just eight weeks!

4 23

1 My dream house would be in one of our national parks like Yellowstone or Redwood. It would be totally green – I'd have solar panels and wind turbines, and I'd collect rainwater. The house would be made of wood and would be heated

by wood fires. I would try to live off the land as much as possible, and I'd plant vegetables and fruit, and maybe have chickens. It would all be organic, with no pesticides or anything like that.

2 My dream house would be in Paris. It'd be on the top floor of an old apartment building, and I'd have a view of the Eiffel Tower or Notre Dame. It would be full of furniture that I'd found in antique shops, places like that, and amazing paintings, one of which would turn out to be an undiscovered Picasso or Matisse. There would be a beautiful old dining table and chairs for candlelit dinners... then all I'd need would be the right person to share it with.

3 My dream house would be an apartment in SoHo in New York City. It wouldn't be too big – it'd just have a couple of bedrooms, and a huge living room with a home theater. It would be very modern and incredibly practical, with things like automatic temperature control, a kitchen with all the latest gadgets – and if possible a stove that would produce amazing meals on its own – I'm a lazy kind of guy.

4 If I had to choose where to live, I'd choose Hawaii. So my dream house would be made of glass with the most amazing view of the beach from every room in the house, and it would have indoor and outdoor pools, and maybe a tennis court – I'm really into sports. It would also have a big indoor aquarium. There's something so peaceful about looking at fish. And fabulous bathrooms of course.

4 26

Paul Bad luck, mate.
Rob Nice shot.
Paul I've had years of practice.
Rob You used to play pool a lot at university.
Paul You did, too.
Rob Yeah. I don't really have the time anymore.
Paul Or anybody to play with.

Paul So what do you do in your free time?
Rob The magazine keeps me pretty busy. And when I'm free, I'm usually with Jenny.
Paul Ah. Your turn. Don't blow it.
Rob What is it?
Paul I was just thinking about you.
Rob What about me?
Paul Do you remember the great times we had at uni? You had such crazy hair – the last time I saw you it was blond!
Rob Don't remind me.
Paul Those were the days. But look at you now with your girlfriend and your 9 to 5 job. If you don't come back to London soon, you'll become an all-American boy!
Rob Come off it.
Paul It's true! I mean, just look at that shirt.
Rob What's wrong with my shirt?
Paul You look like a businessman! Did you buy it?
Rob Me? No. It was... it was a present from Jenny.
Paul I thought so.
Rob What does that mean?
Paul Well, it's Jenny's taste.
Rob Yes, and I really like it.
Paul Jenny seems to know what she wants – and she probably gets it.
Rob That's one of the things I like about her. Terrible.
Paul You said it.
Rob Sorry, Paul. We've got to go.
Paul Oh come on, Rob. We haven't even finished the game.
Rob Another time. Jenny's waiting for us.
Paul Jenny. Right.

4 27

Paul Oh, yeah. That was good. So! What shall we do now?
Rob What do you want to do?
Paul Well... I haven't been on a dance floor for weeks now. I've got to move my body. Let's go dancing!
Jenny I'm going running in the morning. Why don't you join me?
Paul No, thanks. I'm not very keen on running. But I've read about this place called Deep Space, where they play great music. We could go there.
Jenny A club?
Paul Don't you feel like dancing?
Jenny Not on a Wednesday night. How about going to the late show at MOMA?
Paul MOMA? What's that?
Jenny MOMA. It's the Museum of Modern Art. There's a Kandinsky exhibition.
Paul That isn't exactly my idea of a great night out.
Jenny What about staying in and watching a movie on TV?
Paul I'm in New York. I can watch TV anywhere.
Jenny Who's that?
Rob It's a text from Kerri. She's doing a gig at the Bowery Ballroom.
Paul Kerri who?
Rob Kerri Johnson. I interviewed her last week.
Paul Kerri Johnson? I've seen her play live. She's cool. Do you like her Jenny?
Jenny I have to admit I'm not crazy about her music ... or her for that matter.
Paul I didn't think so. So shall we go there?
Rob Why not? Actually Kerri's staying very near here and she doesn't know New York very well. We could meet her outside and go together.
Paul That's a great idea!
Rob I'll send her a text.
Jenny I think I might have an early night. You two can go on your own.
Rob Are you sure you don't mind?
Paul Of course she doesn't mind!
Jenny No, Rob, it's fine. I have another busy day tomorrow. You do too, actually.
Rob I know, we're meeting Don. I haven't forgotten.
Rob It's Kerri. She's on her way now.
Paul What are we waiting for? Let's go!

Monica Hello?
Jenny Hi Monica – it's not too late to call is it?
Monica Jenny! No, why? Are you OK?
Jenny I need to talk.
Monica Can you come over? Why don't you take a cab?
Jenny OK, thanks.

4 30

Jenny Rob?
Rob Hi, Jenny.
Jenny Are you OK? Where are you anyway?
Rob I'm at home. I'm feeling terrible. We got back really late last night.
Jenny Now why doesn't that surprise me? You know, you're not a student anymore.
Rob I know. There was a party after the gig – Kerri invited us – and of course Paul said yes.
Jenny And this morning's meeting? In... ten minutes?
Rob That's why I'm calling. I'm not going to make it. I'm really sorry.
Jenny Rob! It's a very important meeting! I'll cover for you this time, but I won't be able to do it again.
Rob It won't happen again. I promise. Anyway, Paul's leaving.
Jenny He's leaving?
Rob That's right. He's off to Boston this afternoon.
Jenny Maybe that's a good thing. I mean, it's not that I don't like Paul, but...
Rob I know, I know.
Jenny I have to go. Talk to you later.
Don Jenny, have you seen Rob? I wanted to have a word with him before the meeting and he isn't even here.
Jenny I know. He just called to say he can't make it.
Don He what?
Jenny I was with him last night. He wasn't feeling very well. But it's OK. He told me everything I need to know for the meeting.
Don Oh. OK then.
Jenny You know Rob. He's such a professional.

4 32

Host We're talking about great new shopping websites and I think we have time for one more. Janice, can you tell us about it?
Janice Well, it's called "neverlikeditanyway.com." It's a very creative name for a website, as you'll hear. This site was the idea of an American woman named Annabel Acton. She was living in New York City with her boyfriend, who was English. He had invited her to travel to London with him at Christmas to meet his family. But five days before Christmas, they broke up. Now, unlike some of us, Annabel didn't want to sit around crying and eating ice cream. She wanted to do something positive.
Host So what gave her the idea for the website?
Janice Well, after the breakup Annabel was left with a plane ticket to London that she didn't need. She also had jewelry that she didn't want anymore, and she had tickets to a concert that she didn't want to go to without her boyfriend. She also had paintings that they had bought together, that she didn't want on her wall anymore. She didn't want any of these things herself, but she thought someone somewhere would probably like to buy them, and that's what gave her the idea to set up the website.
Host What exactly is it?
Janice Well, it's a website where people who have just broken up with a partner can sell presents and other things that they don't want any more, maybe because they remind them of their ex, or maybe, as the name suggests because they never liked these things anyway! And the idea, which I think is genius, is that they also tell the personal story behind the thing they're selling. Annabel calls it "sell and tell"!
Host What kind of things do people sell on the website?
Janice Oh, everything – from something as small as a teddy bear to really expensive things like an engagement ring or a vacation. To give you an idea, today on the site one seller is offering a three-day honeymoon package at a luxury hotel in New York City, and a woman is selling her ex-boyfriend's car. And they're selling all these things at very good prices. So on "neverlikeditanyway" you can get a bargain, and also help someone who's going through a breakup.
Host Thanks Janice, and that's all we have time for today ...

4 40

1 I was at Sydney Airport, in Australia, and I got a taxi to take me to the hotel. A few minutes after he'd left the airport, the taxi driver said that his meter was broken, but that he would charge me $50, which was what he said the trip usually cost. It was my first time in Sydney and of course I didn't have a clue what the usual fare was, so I just said OK. But later when I was checking in to the hotel, I asked the receptionist what the usual taxi fare was from the airport, and she said about $35. I was really annoyed and I sent an email to the taxi company, but I never got a reply.

2 I was traveling in the UK. It was a work trip, and I knew that I was going to have to answer a lot of emails during that time, so I booked a hotel in Liverpool where they advertised Wi-Fi in all the rooms. When I arrived it turned out the hotel charged £16 for 24 hours Wi-Fi, which is about the same as I pay for a month of Internet at home! I complained to the man at reception, but all he said was that I could use the Wi-Fi in the lobby, which was free. I wasn't very happy about it. Hotels used to make a lot of money from customers by charging a ridiculous amount for phone calls. Now that everybody uses their cell to make phone calls, some hotels now charge a ridiculous amount for Wi-Fi.

3 I was in an Italian restaurant in New York City

recently, and I ordered manicotti, which is a kind of pasta, a little like cannelloni , and it's filled with cheese and served with tomato sauce. Well, when it arrived, the tomato sauce was really hot, but the pasta and the filling were cold – it was like they were still frozen. Anyway, I called the waitress and she said that it couldn't be cold. So I said "Sorry, it is cold. Do you want to try it?" So she took it back to the kitchen, and later the manager came out and apologized, and when I finally got the dish, it was good, hot all the way through. But I'd had to wait a long time for it. But later the manager came out again and offered me a free dessert. So I had a deleicious tiramisu for free.

4 49

Johnson Bailey presented Man Candles. He argued that most candles smell like perfume and are designed for women. One day he was having some friends over to watch a football game, and his house smelled like old Chinese food and dirty clothes. The only candle he had at the time was a vanilla-scented one, and he didn't want his house to smell like perfume. That's why Bailey invented manly candles that smell like things men enjoy: basketballs, golf courses, the beach, popcorn, and barbecue sauce. He even has a horrible-smelling candle you can burn to get people you don't like – perhaps your mother-in-law – out of your house. He tried to convince the Sharks to invest by passing out his candles and asking them to smell them. The Sharks most wanted to smell the bad candle, which is Bailey's best-selling candle.

Kim Nelson's idea was a cake business that sells homemade cakes across the US. These cakes are made from all natural ingredients like fresh oranges in the "Oh! Oh! Orange" cake or one pound of grated carrots in "Daisy's Carrot Cake." Kim came up with the idea because many people don't have the time or the talent to bake a delicious, homemade cake for special occassions like birthdays, graduations, or anniversaries. Kim says that she has a talent for baking cakes, and more importantly, she feels it's her passion. Kim's products are currently sold online in her local area, but she would like to increase production and sell more cakes across the US. The cake business is called Daisy Cakes.

4 50

The Sharks asked Johnson a lot of questions, for example they asked him how much the candles sell for (10–12 dollars a candle) and how much money they made in sales the year before ($53,000). Johnson explained that currently, he and his wife had put over $40,000 of their own money into this product. The Sharks also asked how the candles were made, to which he answered that he poured them all into their containers by himself – he didn't have any help in his entire candle-making process.

In the end, they decided that they weren't interested. Their main reason was they thought the business just wasn't big enough or interesting enough, so they couldn't believe that it would ever make any money.

The Sharks were impressed by Kim's presentation, and they immediately asked to try her cakes. They really loved her cakes and complimented her on their fresh and delicious taste. Even though the male Sharks liked Kim's product, they were concerned that her company had reached its potential – making a respectable $27,000 in the last three months. In the end, Barbara Corcoran, the only female Shark decided to invest $50,000 in Kim's business because she thought there was a market for Kim's product.

And since then?

Kim's Daisy Cakes are now being sold online across the US. She was able to pay Barbara Corcoran back in only three weeks! And she has expanded her business by offering new products like lemon curd.

Although the Sharks thought Johnson's candles were funny, it's a good thing they didn't invest in his company. Johnson's website has been shut down and his candles have disappeared from store shelves.

5 6

Apart from the hockey players, he also gives the examples of The Beatles, the most famous rock band of all time and Bill Gates, the founder of Microsoft. The Beatles were really lucky to be invited to play in Hamburg in 1960. The club owner who invited them usually only invited bands from London, but on one trip to the UK he met an entrepreneur from Liverpool who told him that there were some really good bands in that city. When The Beatles arrived in Hamburg, they had to work incredibly hard. They had to play for up to eight hours a night in the club seven nights a week. As John Lennon said later, "We got better and we got more confidence. We couldn't help it, with all the experience we got from playing all night long in the club." By 1964, when they became really successful, The Beatles had been to Hamburg four times, and had already performed live an estimated 1,200 times, far more than many bands today perform in their entire careers.

Bill Gates's huge stroke of good luck came in 1968, when the high school he was attending decided to spend some money they'd been given on a computer. This computer was kept in a little room that then became the computer club. In 1968, most *colleges* didn't have a computer club, let alone schools. From that time on Gates spent most of his time in the computer room because he and his friends taught themselves how to use it. "It was my obsession," Gates says of those early high school years. "I skipped sports. I went up there at night. We were programming on weekends. It would be a rare week that we wouldn't get 20 or 30 hours in." So Gates was unbelievably lucky to have access to a computer, but of course he also put in all those hours of practice, too.

Talent, Gladwell concludes, is obviously important, but there are many talented people out there. What makes just a few of them special is that they are lucky and that they put in far more hours of practice than the rest.

5 19

Part 1

Host And now it's time for our book of the week, which is *The Winter of our Disconnect* by Susan Maushart. Jeremy, to start with, it's a good title, isn't it?

Jeremy Yes, amazing. And it was a fascinating experiment and a good read.

Host Tell us about it.

Jeremy Well, Susan Maushart is a journalist who's raising three teenage children. She decided to do the experiment after reaching a point where she felt that the whole family, especially her children, were all living in their own little worlds, with headphones on, plugged into their laptops or their iPods or their smartphones and that they weren't relating to the other people in the family.

Andrew So it wasn't just her children who were permanently plugged into an electrical device?

Jeremy Well, she admits that she herself was addicted to her phone and to her iPod and her laptop and that she was constantly reading news sites and googling information, but it was really her children who were totally dependent on new technology. In the book she makes the interesting distinction between "digital immigrants" and "digital natives."

Chloe What does that mean?

Jeremy She describes herself as a digital immigrant, that's to say someone who didn't grow up with digital technology, which is really anyone who was born before1980. Her children are digital natives, which means that they were born *after* computers and the Internet were already part of life.

Chloe Well, that's me then.

Jeremy Yes, well, the main difference, she says, is that digital immigrants use the technology, to find information or to listen to music, but digital natives live and breathe the technology. So for them living without it is like living without water, without electricity…in the dark ages.

Chloe What were the rules of the experiment?

Jeremy The family had to live for six months without using any electrical gadgets in the house with a screen. So no smartphones, no TVs, no laptops or computers, no video consoles, and no iPods. They *were* allowed to use technology at school or at friends' houses, or in Internet cafés, and they were allowed to use landline phones. But everything else was switched off for the whole six months.

Sally Six months? How on earth did she get the children to agree?

Jeremy She bribed them. She told them she was going to write a book about the experiment, and that they would share in any profits that she made from the book!

Sally Wow, that was very smart of her…

5 20

Part 2

Host So what were the results? Was it a positive experience?

Jeremy At the end of the book Susan says that it was a positive experience in every way. At first, of course, the kids complained bitterly; they kept saying they were bored. But then they they started to talk to each other again, to go and sit in each other's rooms and talk. They got interested in cooking and reading; they went to the movies together. They played CDs on the CD player and they actually sat and listened to the music instead of just having music on their headphones all the time as background music. And Susan's 15-year-old son started playing the saxophone again. He had stopped playing a few years before, but then he started taking lessons again and even started giving concerts… Oh, and the children said that they slept better!

Sally Oh, well that's good, yeah. What about the childrens's' schoolwork? I mean, nowadays we sort of assume that everyone needs the Internet to do research for homework and so on.

Jeremy In fact, the children's school report cards showed that they all improved. When they needed the Internet, they used the computers at school or at college (the eldest daughter was in college), or they went to friends' houses. But when they did their homework they did it better than before because they weren't multitasking – they weren't doing homework and listening to music and sending messages all at the same time. So they concentrated better, and their schoolwork improved.

Andrew What about, Susan, the mother? Did she find it difficult to live without modern technology?

Jeremy What she found most difficult was writing her weekly article for the newspaper because she had to do it by hand, and not on her laptop. She says that at the beginning her hand used to really ache; she just wasn't used to writing by hand anymore. But that was just a small problem.

Chloe Any other negatives?

Jeremy Well, of course the phone bill for their landline was huge!

Chloe Has the experiment had a lasting effect?

Jeremy Susan says that it has. She thinks that they all get along much better as a family, her son is still playing the saxophone, and he sold his video console. They've all realized that we live in a digital world, but that we need to disconnect from time to time and to reconnect with the people around us. So they have new rules in the house – like no TVs in bedrooms and no TV in the kitchen where they eat. And no wasted hours on the Internet.

Sally Sounds great. That would be a good rule for

me, too!

5 21

Part 3

Host OK, so imagine you all did the experiment. What would you miss the most? Sally?

Sally Well, I already live without the Internet many weekends because we have a house in the country in the middle of nowhere where there's no Internet service. So I know that what I would miss most is being able to google information, like the phone number of a restaurant, or what time a movie starts. Or even, dare I say it, the sports scores. I don't have a TV, so I wouldn't miss that, but I would miss not having the Internet.

Host Andrew?

Andrew Well, I just couldn't live without a computer or a laptop because I work from home so I don't have an office to go to, and I absolutely need the Internet, too. I couldn't do the experiment – I just wouldn't be prepared to go to an Interent café all day to work. Susan, the journalist who did the experiment, only had to write one column a week, but I work from home eight hours a day.

Host Jeremy.

Jeremy I think I could do it. I think I could easily live without any of these electrical gadgets at home. I mean, I have my office, so I could use the Internet there. I don't use an iPod; I still prefer to listen to CDs…

Host You old dinosaur.

Jeremy Yes, yes I know… and I don't watch much TV. I am very attached to my Blackberry, but I wouldn't mind using a regular phone for six months. I don't think there's anything I'd miss too much…

Host And finally Chloe, our only digital native.

Chloe Well, I'm sorry, but I just wouldn't be prepared to even try the experiment, not even for a week let alone six months. I wouldn't be prepared to live without my phone. I use it for everything, calling, music, the Internet. So, no, I wouldn't do it.

Host Not even if you were offered money?

Chloe It would have to be a huge amount of money. No, I'm definitely not going to do it!

5 22

Paul Yeah?

Jenny Hi, there. It's me. Should I come up?

Jenny Paul!

Paul That's right.

Jenny Uh... hi.

Paul Hi. Are you OK?

Jenny Yes, fine. Thanks. It's just that I um...

Paul What?

Jenny I wasn't expecting to see you.

Paul Really? Well, as you can see, I'm still here. It seems Rob just can't live without me. Yeah, he's going to miss me when I'm gone. But not for long. We'll meet up again when he goes back to London.

Jenny Goes back...?

Paul Yeah, he told me last night that he was planning to leave New York pretty soon.

Jenny He what?

Rob Hi, Jenny. Do you want some breakfast? I've got bagels.

Jenny No thank you, Rob. Why don't you two enjoy them?!

Rob What's wrong?

Paul No idea. I just said you were planning to leave New York soon, and she ...

Rob You what? I didn't say that!

Paul You didn't have to. This New York life isn't you, Rob, and you know it.

Rob No, I don't! I like New York and Jenny's here.

Paul Oh, come on! What's the big deal? It's not like you want to marry her.

Rob Well ...

Paul What? You do?!

Rob Look Paul. I'm serious about New York, and I'm serious about Jenny. And I want you to leave. Today.

Paul You're joking, mate.

Rob No, I'm not. I'll even buy the ticket.

5 23

Rob Hi, Jenny

Jenny Rob.

Rob Paul told me what he said to you, and it's not true. I'm not planning to leave New York.

Jenny Oh, really? Could you tell me why Paul is still in your apartment?

Rob Well, he couldn't get a ticket to Boston.

Jenny But you told me he was going a few days ago. Or was that another lie?

Rob No, of course it wasn't! He couldn't get a ticket. The buses to Boston were all full.

Jenny So do you know if he's got one now?

Rob I bought it! He's leaving this evening. But that isn't really the issue here, is it? You have to believe me – I don't want to leave New York!

Jenny How can I believe you? I know you're missing London because you said the same thing to Kerri at the restaurant. Look Rob, I'd like to know what you really want.

Rob What do you mean?

Jenny When you and Paul were together, it was like you were a different person.

Rob You know what Paul's like. What was I meant to do? But that isn't the kind of life I want anymore. I'm not like that.

Jenny I know you're not, but I wonder if you really want to be here. I wonder if ...

Rob Jenny, what is it?

Jenny Forget it.

Rob Jenny... what are you worrying about?

Jenny I don't know if this is going to work out.

Rob You're not serious.

Jenny I'm just not sure if we want the same things anymore.

Rob That's crazy…

Don Jenny – oh, good morning, Rob.

Rob Don.

Don I need a word. Can you tell me what you decided at the last meeting?

Jenny Right away, Don. Rob was just leaving.

5 26

Rob But what can I do, Jenny? What can I say to convince you I'm serious?

Jenny I don't know, Rob.

Rob Wait! What Paul said just isn't true.

Jenny It isn't just what Paul said. It's obvious you want to go back.

Rob Of course I miss London, but I love my life here. What proof do you want of my commitment to New York, to you, to everything!

Jenny I don't know.

Rob There must be something I can do.

Jenny Look, we're going to see my parents later. I don't want us to be late.

Rob We won't be late. And I won't forget the chocolates this time either.

Jenny Well, that's a start, I guess.

Rob But Jenny – we need to talk about this.

Jenny We don't have time to discuss it now.

Rob Jenny!

Jenny What is it?

Rob What if I proposed to you?

Jenny "Proposed"?

Rob That's right. Proposed.

Jenny Like, "Will you marry me?"

Rob Exactly.

Jenny On one knee?

Rob I can do that. So what would you say?

Jenny Rob, stop it. It's embarrassing.

Rob Tell me.

Jenny Are you for real?

Rob Yes, I am actually. What about you?

Jenny Yes!

5 31

Barbie

Until the late 1950s, most American girls played with baby dolls, which often limited their imaginations to mother or caregiver roles. At around the same time, Ruth Handler noticed that her pre-teen daughter was playing with paper dolls, giving them adult roles such as actresses or secretaries. On a trip to Europe, Ruth saw an adult-figured doll in Germany and brought several of them back to the US. Handler had the idea that girls could expand their imagination and play-acting roles with a doll that looked like an adult. So she and engineer Jack Ryan redesigned the doll for the US market and called her Barbie after Ruth's daughter, Barbara. The first Barbie dolls were produced in 1959 and sold over 350,000 in the first year.

Barbie is still popular today, and billions have been sold around the world since 1959. Mattel, Inc. the company that produces Barbie, reports that 90 percent of American girls between the ages of three and ten have a Barbie doll.

The Chrysler Building

The Chrysler Building has been one of the most iconic New York City landmarks since it was completed in 1930. Architect William Van Alen designed the Art Deco building for Walter P. Chrysler, who owned the automobile company Chyrsler Corporation. In fact, Van Alen modeled many of the building's decorative features using Chrysler car parts as inspiration. For example, the decorations on the outside of the building for the thirty-first floor are fashioned after engine parts from a 1929 Chrysler car.

Today, the Chrysler Building is still considered one of the best examples of Art Deco architecture in the US. In fact, it was voted New York City's favorite building in 2005 by Skyscraper Museum. In addition, the building appears regularly in movies and TV shows that film in New York City.

The "LOVE" Sculpture

In 1965, artist Robert Indiana had an idea for a painting with the word "LOVE" as the main focus. He decided to break the word up into two lines, putting the "LO" on top of the "VE." He then tilted the "O" a little, and an iconic American design was born. In fact, it became so popular that the Museum of Modern Art and the United States Postal Service asked Indiana to create versions of his "LOVE" painting for cards and stamps. In the early 1970s, Indiana made a series of "LOVE" sculptures for display in public parks. The first of these "LOVE" sculptures was placed in New York City, on the corner of Sixth Avenue and Fifty-fifth Street. Additional "LOVE" sculptures were placed in New Orleans, Philadelphia, Vancouver, Tokyo, and Singapore, as well as many other cities.

Unfortunately, Indiana didn't make much money from his "LOVE" paintings and sculptures. He never signed his paintings or applied for copyright, so he didn't have legal protection against the many imitations of his work.

Air Jordan Sneakers

When Michael Jordan started playing basketball for the Chicago Bulls in 1984, he had special Nike sneakers designed for him by Peter Moore. These sneakers were called the Air Jordan 1, or more simply – Air Jordans. They were red and black – the Chicago Bulls's colors. Because the sneakers did not have any white on them, Jordan was fined $5,000 by the National Basketball Association each time he wore them for a game.

Every year since then, Nike has created a new pair of Air Jordans to sell. In 1987, Tinker Hatfield took over the design responsibilites for these sneakers, and he as been associated with them ever since. Hatfield introduced the Jumpman logo on the sneakers, which is a silhouette of Michael Jordan dunking a basketball with his legs spread wide. In 2010, Hatfield designed the Jordan 2010s to celebrate the sneakers' twenty-fifth anniversary.

5 35

Interviewer Good morning and thank you for coming, Mr. Ryan – or should it be Detective Ryan? You were a detective with the Los Angeles Police Department, weren't you?

Detective Ryan Yes, that's right. For twenty-five

years. I retired last year.

Interviewer People today are still fascinated by Natalie Wood's death even though it was more than 30 years ago. That's incredible, isn't it?

Detective Ryan Well, it's not really that surprising. People are always interested in unsolved mysteries – and Natalie Wood was a well-know and talented actress.

Interviewer Now, to be clear, none of the people on the boat the night Ms. Wood died were or are suspects. But – can you tell us *who* was on the boat that night?

Detective Ryan That is correct – none of them were or are suspects. But in order to get a better understanding about what happened that night, it *is* important to know who was on the boat. So, the people were her husband, movie and TV actor Robert Wagner; her friend and movie actor Christopher Walken; and the captain of the boat, Dennis Davern.

5 36

Interviewer Recently, the LA County Coroner's Office re-examined Ms. Wood's cause of death because of some new information about the bruises and scratches that were found on her body the night she died.

Detective Ryan Yes, that's correct. This new information suggests that Ms. Wood may have been hit or beaten right before she died. And the Coroner changed Ms. Wood's original cause of death from "accidental drowning" to "drowning and other undetermined factors."

Interviewer So what does this mean for the other people on the boat?

Detective Ryan Officially, it doesn't mean anything for them. They still aren't suspects.

Interviewer And you don't think they're suspects, do you?

Detective Ryan No, I don't. I don't think any of them can be considered suspects without some kind of convincing evidence.

Interviewer What about Robert Wagner? There are reports that he was jealous of his wife's friendship with Mr. Walken.

Detective Ryan Well, yes, Mr. Wagner wrote in his book *Pieces of My Heart* that he was jealous of the relationship, and that he and Mr. Walken argued that night on the boat. But that doesn't make him a suspect.

Interviewer And Christopher Walken, Ms. Wood's friend and co-star?

Detective Ryan Mr. Walken has remained mostly silent about what happened that night, but he has talked to the police.

Interviewer The boat captain changed his story about what happened that night, didn't he? That he originally lied to police the night Natalie died.

Detective Ryan Yes. Mr. Davern told a TV news program that he lied about the events of that night. He now says that Mr. Wagner and Ms. Wood had an argument, and that Ms. Wood went missing shortly after. Mr. Davern also claims that Mr. Wagner delayed contacting the police, implying that Mr. Wagner was responsible for Ms. Wood's death.

Interviewer Do you believe the captain's new story?

Detective Ryan Well, no. I think the timing of his new story is suspicious since he released it so close to the thirty-year anniversary of her death. I think he was looking to make some money by bringing this sad story back into the news.

Interviewer So, what do *you* think happened that night?

Detective Ryan I can't tell you because I don't know.

Interviewer So you don't think we'll ever solve the mystery?

Detective Ryan No, I wouldn't say that. I think one day the mystery *will* be solved. Some new evidence will appear and we'll be able to say that Natalie Wood's mysterious death is finally solved. But right now, it's still a mystery, and people like a good mystery.

the passive: *be* + past participle

1 A lot of movies **are shot** on location. 3 31
Our car **is being repaired** today.
Andy's bike **has been stolen**.
The director died when the movie **was being made**.
You'**ll be picked up** at the airport by one of our staff.
This bill **has to be paid** tomorrow.
2 *Batman Begins* **was directed by** Christopher Nolan.

A lot of movies are shot on location.

1 We often use the passive when it's not said, known, or important who does an action.
Andy's bike has been stolen. (= Somebody has stolen Andy's bike. We don't know who.)

2 If you want to say who did the action, use *by*.

- We can often say things in two ways, in the active or in the passive. Compare:
  Batman Begins *was directed by Christopher Nolan.* (= the focus is more on the movie)
  Christopher Nolan directed Batman Begins *in 2005.* (= the focus is more on Nolan)
- We form negatives and questions in the same way as in active sentences.
  Some movies ***aren't shot*** *on location.*
  Is *your car* ***being*** *repaired today?*
- We often use the passive to talk about processes, for example scientific processes, and in formal writing, such as newspaper reports.
  Then the water ***is heated*** *to 100 degrees...*
  Many buildings in the city ***have been damaged*** *by the earthquake.*

a Circle the correct form, active or passive.

The college *built* | *was built* in the 18th century.

1 The costumes for the show *are making* | *are being made* by hand.
2 The landscape *inspired* | *was inspired* him to write a poem.
3 This castle *hasn't inhabited* | *hasn't been inhabited* for almost a century.
4 The director's last movie *set* | *is set* in the present.
5 The movie *will shoot* | *will be shot* in the fall.
6 The actors *aren't recording* | *aren't being recorded* the dialogue until next week.
7 The house *wasn't using* | *wasn't being used* by the owners during the winter.
8 The makeup artist *has transformed* | *has been transformed* the actor into a monster.
9 They *hadn't owned* | *hadn't been owned* the company for very long before they went bankrupt.
10 The photo *took* | *was taken* by my husband on the balcony of our hotel.

b Rewrite the sentences with the passive. Only use *by* if necessary.

People don't use this room very often. *This room isn't used very often.*

1 They subtitle a lot of foreign movies.
A lot of foreign movies ________________.
2 García Márquez wrote *Love in the Time of Cholera.*
Love in the Time of Cholera ________________.
3 Someone is repairing my laptop.
My laptop ________________.
4 They haven't released the DVD of the movie yet.
The DVD of the movie ________________.
5 They won't finish the movie until the spring.
The movie ________________.
6 You have to pick up the tickets from the box office.
The tickets ________________.
7 They hadn't told the actor about the changes in the script.
The actor ________________.
8 James Cameron directed *Avatar.*
Avatar ________________.
9 They've already recorded the soundtrack.
The soundtrack ________________.
10 They were interviewing the director about the movie.
The director ________________.

p.55

6B

modals of deduction: *might, can't, must*

might / may (when you think something is possibly true)

Tony's phone is turned off. He **might** be on the plane now, or just boarding. 3 44
Laura **might not** like that skirt. It's not really her style.
I don't know where Kate is. She **may** be at work or at the gym.
I'm surprised that Ted isn't here. He **may not** know that the meeting is today.

can't (when you are sure something is impossible / not true)

Brandon **can't** earn much money at his job. He's still living with his parents. 3 45
That woman **can't** be Jack's wife. Jack's wife has dark hair.

must (when you are sure something is true)

The neighbors **must** be out. There aren't any lights on in the house. 3 46
Your sister **must** have a lot of money if she drives a Porsche.

- We often use *might* / *may*, *can't*, or *must* to say how sure or certain we are about something (based on the information we have).
- We don't use *can* instead of *might* / *may*, NOT ~~*He can be on the plane now*~~.
- In this context the opposite of *must* is *can't*.
  The neighbors must be out. There aren't any lights on in the house. / *The neighbors can't be out. All the lights are on in the house.* NOT ~~*The neighbors must not be out.*~~

The neighbors must be out. There aren't any lights on in the house.

The neighbors can't be out. All the lights are on in the house.

- We can use *could* instead of *might* in affirmative sentences.
  Jack could (or *might*) *be at the party – I'm not sure.*
- We often use *be* + gerund after *might* / *must* / *can't*.
  They must be having a party – the music is very loud.

a Match the sentences.

He might be American. *D*
1 He can't be a college student. ☐
2 He must be cold. ☐
3 He might be going to the gym. ☐
4 He could be lost. ☐
5 He must be married. ☐
6 He must be a tourist. ☐
7 He can't be enjoying the party. ☐
8 He may not have a job. ☐
9 He can't be a businessman. ☐

A He's carrying a sports bag.
B He's carrying a camera and a guide book.
C He's looking at a map.
D ~~He's wearing a baseball cap.~~
E He's looking at job ads in the newspaper.
F He isn't talking to anybody.
G He isn't wearing a suit.
H He's wearing a wedding ring.
I He's not old enough.
J He isn't wearing a jacket.

b Cover 1–9 and look at A–J. Remember 1–9.

c Complete with *must*, *might (not)*, or *can't*.

A What does Pete's new girlfriend do?
B I'm not sure, but she *might* be a model. She's very pretty.

1 **A** Do you know anyone who drives a Ferrari?
B Yes, my nephew. I don't know his salary, but he ______ earn a fortune!

2 **A** Why don't you buy this dress for your mom?
B I'm not sure. She ______ like it. It's a little short for her.

3 **A** My sister works as an interpreter for the United Nations.
B She ______ speak a lot of languages to work there.

4 **A** Did you know that Andy's parents have split up?
B Poor Andy. He ______ feel very happy about that.

5 **A** Are your neighbors away? All the windows are closed.
B I'm not sure. I suppose they ______ be on vacation.

6 **A** Where's your colleague today?
B She ______ be sick. She called to say that she's going to the doctor's.

7 **A** Jane is looking at you in a very strange way.
B Yes. I've grown a beard since I saw her last, so she ______ recognize me.

8 **A** My daughter has failed all her exams again.
B She ______ be working very hard if she gets such bad grades.

9 **A** Why is Tina so happy?
B I'm not sure, but she ______ have a new partner.

10 **A** Where's the manager's house?
B I don't know, but he ______ live near the office because he commutes every day by train.

◀ p.60

7A

first conditional and future time clauses + *when, until,* etc.

first conditional sentences: *if* + simple present, *will / won't* + base form

4 15

1. If you **work** hard, you**'ll pass** your exams.
   The boss **won't be** very happy if we**'re** late for the meeting.
2. **Come** and see us next week if you **have** time.
3. Alison **won't get** into college unless she **gets** good grades.
   I **won't go** unless you **go**, too.

- We use first conditional sentences to talk about a possible future situation and its consequence.
  1. We use the present tense (NOT the future) after *if* in first conditional sentences. NOT ~~*If you'll work hard you'll pass all your exams.*~~
  2. We can also use an imperative instead of the *will* clause.
  3. We can use *unless* instead of *if...not* in conditional sentences.
     She won't get into college ***unless*** *she gets good grades |* ***if*** *she* ***doesn't*** *get good grades.*

future time clauses

4 16

As soon as you **get** your test scores, **call** me.
We**'ll have** dinner when your father **gets** home.
I **won't go** to bed until you **come** home.
I**'ll have** a quick lunch before I **leave**.
After I **graduate** from college, I**'ll** probably **take** a year off and travel.

- Use the present tense (NOT the future) after *when, as soon as, until, before,* and *after* to talk about the future.

The boss won't be very happy if we're late for the meeting.

a Complete with the simple present or future with *will*.

If I fail my math class, I*'ll take* it again next semester. (take)

1. That girl ________ into trouble if she doesn't wear her uniform. (get)
2. If you hand in your homework late, the teacher ________ it. (not grade)
3. Don't write anything unless you ________ sure of the answer. (be)
4. Gary will be suspended if his behavior ________. (not improve)
5. They'll be late for school unless they ________. (hurry)
6. Ask me if you ________ what to do. (not know)
7. Johnny will be punished if he ________ at the teacher again. (shout)
8. My sister ________ from college this year if she passes all her exams. (graduate)
9. I ________ tonight unless I finish my homework quickly. (not go out)
10. Call me if you ________ some help with your project. (need)

b Circle the correct word or expression.

I won't go to college *if* | *unless* I don't get good grades.

1. Don't turn over the exam *after* | *until* the teacher tells you to.
2. Please check that the water's not too hot *before* | *after* the kids get in the bathtub.
3. Your parents will be really happy *when* | *unless* they hear your good news.
4. I'll look for a job in September *before* | *after* I come back from vacation.
5. The schools will close *unless* | *until* it stops snowing soon.
6. The job is very urgent, so please do it *after* | *as soon as* you can.
7. We'll stay in the library *as soon as* | *until* it closes. Then we'll go home.
8. Andrew will probably learn to drive *when* | *until* he's 18.
9. You won't be able to talk to the principal *unless* | *if* you make an appointment.
10. Give Mom a kiss *before* | *after* she goes to work.

◄ p.66

7B

second conditional

second conditional sentences: ***if*** **+ simple past,** ***would / wouldn't*** **+ base form**

1 If I **had** a job, **I'd get** my own apartment. 4 17
If David **spoke** good English, he **could get** a job in that new hotel.
I **would get along** better with my parents if I **didn't live** with them.
I **wouldn't do** that job unless they **paid me** a really good salary.
2 If your sister **were** here, she**'d know** what to do.
If it **was** warmer, we **could take** a swim.
3 If I **were** you, **I'd buy** a new computer.

- We use the second conditional to talk about a hypothetical / imaginary present or future situation and its consequence.
If I had a job... (= I don't have a job – I'm imagining it.)
1 We use the simple past after *if*, and *would / wouldn't* + base form in the other clause.
- We can also use *could* instead of *would* in the other clause.
2 After *if* we can use *was* or *were* with *I, he,* and *she*.
3 We often use second conditionals beginning *If I were you, I'd...* to give advice. Here we don't usually use *If I was you...*

First or second conditional?
If I have time, I'll help you. (= this is a real situation; it's possible that I'll have time – first conditional)
If I had time, I'd help you. (= this is a hypothetical / imaginary situation; I don't actually have time – second conditional)

would / wouldn't **+ base form**
We also often use *would / wouldn't* + base form (without an *if* clause) when we talk about imaginary situations.
My ideal vacation ***would be*** *a week in the Bahamas.*
I'd *never* ***buy*** *a car as big as yours.*

a Write second conditional sentences.

I (not live) with my parents if I (not have to)
I wouldn't live with my parents if I didn't have to.
1 Nick (not have to commute) every day if he (work) from home
2 If they (not have) such a noisy dog, they (get along) better with their neighbors
3 I (not buy) that bike if I (be) you – it's too expensive
4 We (sell) our house if somebody (offer) us enough money
5 If my mother-in-law (live) with us, we (get) divorced
6 you (share) an apartment with me if I (pay) half the rent?
7 If my sister (clean) her room more often, it (not be) such a mess
8 You (not treat) me like this if you really (love) me
9 If we (paint) the kitchen white, it (look) bigger
10 you (think) about camping if you (not can afford) to stay in a hotel?

b First or second conditional? Complete with the correct form of the verb.

I*'ll stay* with my sister if I have to go to Boston for my job interview. (stay)
I'd buy my own apartment if I *had* enough money. (have)
1 My kids ________ earlier if they didn't go to bed so late. (get up)
2 Where ________ you ________ if you go to college? (live)
3 If you make dinner, I ________ the dishes. (do)
4 If you ________ your job, what will you do? (lose)
5 We wouldn't have a dog if we ________ a yard. (not have)
6 How will you get to work if you ________ your car? (sell)
7 If we sit in the shade, we ________ sunburned. (not get)
8 If you could change one thing in your life, what ________ it ________? (be)
9 He won't be able to pay next month's rent if he ________ a job soon. (not find)
10 If she had a job, she ________ so late every night. (not stay up)

◀ p.68

reported speech: sentences and questions

reported sentences

direct statements	reported statements 4 33
"**I like** traveling."	She said (that) **she liked** traveling.
"**I'm** leaving **tomorrow**."	He told her (that) **he was** leaving **the next day**.
"**I'll** always love **you**."	He said (that) **he would** always love **me**.
"**I passed** the exam!"	She told me (that) **she had passed** the exam.
"**I've** forgotten **my** keys."	He said (that) **he had** forgotten **his** keys.
"**I can't** come."	She said (that) **she couldn't** come.
"**I may** be late."	He said (that) **he might** be late.
"**I must** go."	She said (that) **she had to** go.

- We use reported speech to report (i.e., to tell another person) what someone said.
- When the reporting verb (*said*, *told*, etc.) is in the past tense, the tenses in the sentence that is being reported usually change like this:
  present > past
  will > *would*
  simple past / present perfect > past perfect

When tenses don't change
When you report what someone said very soon after they said it, the tenses often stay the same as in the original sentence.
Adam *"I **can't come** tonight."*
*I've just spoken to Adam and he said that he **can't come** tonight.*
Jack *"I really **enjoyed** my trip."*
*Jack told me that he **really enjoyed** his trip.*

- Some modal verbs change, e.g., *can>could, may>might, must>had to*. Other modal verbs stay the same, e.g., *could, might, should*, etc.
- You usually have to change the pronouns, e.g., *"**I** like jazz." Jane said that **she** liked jazz.*
- Using ***that*** after *said* and *told* is optional.
- If you report what someone said on a different day or in a different place, some other time and place words can change, e.g., *tomorrow>the next day, here>there, this>that*, etc.
  *"I'll meet you **here tomorrow**." He said he'd meet me **there the next day**.*

say and tell
Be careful – after *said* don't use a person or an object pronoun:
He said he was tired. NOT ~~*He said me...*~~
After *told* you must use a person or pronoun:
Sarah told Cally that she would call her. NOT ~~*Sarah told that she...*~~
He told me he was tired. NOT ~~*He told he was...*~~

reported questions

direct questions	reported questions 4 34
"**Are you** married?"	She asked him if **he was** married.
"**Did** she **call**?"	He asked me whether she **had called**.
"What's your name?"	I asked him what his name **was**.
"Where **do you live**?"	He asked me where **I lived**.

- When you report a question, the tenses change as in reported statements.
- When a question doesn't begin with a question word, add *if* (or *whether*).
  *"Do you want a drink?" He asked me **if / whether** I wanted a drink.*
- You also have to change the word order to subject + verb, and not use *do / did*.

a Complete the sentences using reported speech.

"I'm in love with another woman."
My boyfriend told me he was in love with another woman.

1 "I'm selling all my books." My brother said ________.
2 "I've booked the flights." Emma told me ________.
3 "Your new dress doesn't suit you." My mother told me ________.
4 "I may not be able to go to the party." Matt said ________.
5 "I won't wear these shoes again." Jenny said ________.
6 "I didn't buy you a present." My girlfriend told me ________.
7 "I must get a dress for the party." Rachel said ________.
8 "I haven't been to the gym for a long time." Kevin said ________.
9 "I found a bargain at the sale." My sister told me ________.
10 "I can't find anywhere to park." Luke told me ________.

b Complete the sentences using reported speech.

"Why did you dump your girlfriend?" My friend asked me *why I had dumped my girlfriend*.

1 "When are you leaving?" My parents asked me ________.
2 "Have you ever been engaged?" She asked him ________.
3 "Will you be home early?" Anna asked Liam ________.
4 "Where do you usually buy your clothes?" My sister asked me ________.
5 "Did you wear a suit to the job interview?" We asked him ________.
6 "Do you ever go to the theater?" I asked Lisa ________.
7 "What time will you arrive?" He asked us ________.
8 "How much money did you spend at the sale?" I asked my girlfriend ________.
9 "Can you help me?" Sally asked the police officer ________.
10 "What size are you?" The salesperson asked me ________.

◀ p.74

8B

gerunds and infinitives

gerund (verb + *-ing*)

4 46

1 I'm not very **good at remembering** names.
Katie's **given up eating** junk food.
2 **Driving** at night is very tiring.
Shopping is my favorite thing to do on weekends.
3 I **hate not being** on time for things.
I **don't mind getting up** early.

- We use the gerund (verb + *-ing*)
  1 after prepositions and phrasal verbs.
  2 as the subject of a sentence.
  3 after some verbs, e.g., *hate, spend, don't mind.*
- Common verbs that take the gerund include: **admit**, **avoid**, **deny**, **dislike**, **enjoy**, **feel like**, **finish**, **hate**, **keep**, **like**, **love**, **mind**, **miss**, **practice**, **prefer**, **recommend**, **spend time**, **stop**, **suggest**, and phrasal verbs, e.g., **give up**, **go on**, etc.
- The negative gerund = *not* + verb + *-ing*

the infinitive

4 47

1 My apartment is very **easy to find**.
2 Simon is saving money **to buy** a new car.
3 My sister has never **learned to drive**.
4 **Try not to make** noise.

- We use the infinitive
  1 after adjectives.
  2 to express a reason or purpose.
  3 after some verbs, e.g., *want, need, learn.*
- Common verbs that take the infinitive include: **(can't) afford**, **agree**, **decide**, **expect**, **forget**, **help**, **hope**, **learn**, **need**, **offer**, **plan**, **pretend**, **promise**, **refuse**, **remember**, **seem**, **try**, **want**, **would like**.
- The negative infinitive = *not to* + verb.
- More verbs take the infinitive than the gerund.
- These common verbs can take either the infinitive or gerund with no difference in meaning: **start**, **begin**, **continue**, e.g., *It started to rain. It started raining.*

Verb + person + infinitive
We also use the infinitive after some verbs, e.g., *ask, tell, want, would like* + person.
Can you ask the manager to come?
She told him not to worry.
I want you to do this now.
We'd really like you to come.

the base form

4 48

1 I **can't drive**.
We **must hurry**.
2 She always **makes** me **laugh**.
My parents didn't **let** me **go** out last night.

- We use the base form
  1 after most modal and auxiliary verbs.
  2 after *make* and *let*.

Verbs that can take a gerund or an infinitive, but the meaning is different
Try *to be on time. (= make an effort to be on time)*
Try *doing yoga. (= do it to see if you like it)*
Remember *to call him. (= don't forget to do it)*
I ***remember*** *meeting him years ago. (= I have a memory of it)*

a Circle the correct form.

I'm in charge of *recruiting* | *to recruit* new staff.
1 It's important for me *spending* | *to spend* time with my family.
2 *Applying* | *Apply* for a job can be complicated.
3 The manager asked me *not saying* | *not to say* anything about the downsizing.
4 My boss wants me *start* | *to start* work earlier.
5 Be careful *not asking* | *not to ask* her about her boyfriend – they broke up.
6 We kept *working* | *to work* until we finished.
7 Dave is very good at *solving* | *to solve* logic problems.
8 The best thing about weekends is *not going* | *not to go* to work.
9 Layla gave up *modeling* | *to model* when she had a baby.
10 I took a training course *to learning* | *to learn* about the new software.

b Complete with a verb from the list in the correct form.

not buy commute leave lock not make
retire ~~set up~~ wear work not worry

I'd like <u>to set up</u> my own company.
1 My parents are planning ________ before they are 65.
2 Rob spends three hours ________ to work and back every day.
3 Mark's wife told him ________ about the problems he had at work.
4 Did you remember ________ the door?
5 In the end I decided ________ the shoes because they were very expensive.
6 The manager lets us ________ early on Fridays.
7 All employees must ________ a jacket and tie at work.
8 Please try ________ anymore mistakes in the report.
9 I don't mind ________ overtime during the week.

p.79

9A

third conditional

If **I'd known** about the meeting, I **would have gone.** 5 3
If James **hadn't gone** to the training course, he **wouldn't have met** his wife.
You **wouldn't have lost** your job if you **hadn't been** late every day.
Would you **have gone** to the party if you**'d known** Lisa was there?

- We usually use third conditional sentences to talk about how things could have been different in the past, i.e., for hypothetical / imaginary situations. Compare:
  Yesterday I got up late and missed my train. (= the real situation)
  If I hadn't got up late yesterday, I wouldn't have missed my train. (= the hypothetical or imaginary past situation)
- To make a third conditional, use *if* + past perfect and *would have* + past participle.
- The contraction of both *had* and *would* is *'d*.
- We can use *might* or *could* instead of *would* to make the result less certain.
  If she'd studied harder, she might have passed the exam.

a Match the phrases.

Billy wouldn't have injured his head [D]
1 If I'd driven any faster, [ ]
2 Jon might have gotten the job [ ]
3 She would have hurt herself badly [ ]
4 If Katy hadn't gone to the party, [ ]
5 What would you have studied [ ]
6 How would you have gotten to the airport [ ]
7 If you'd worn a warmer coat, [ ]
8 Your parents would have enjoyed the trip [ ]
9 Would you have helped me [ ]

A if you'd gone to college?
B you wouldn't have been so cold.
C if I'd asked you?
D ~~if he had worn his helmet.~~
E she wouldn't have met her new boyfriend.
F if he'd been on time for his interview.
G if they had come with us.
H if she'd fallen down the stairs.
I I could have gotten a speeding ticket.
J if the trains had been on strike?

b Cover A–J. Look at 1–9 and try to remember the end of the sentence.

c Complete the third conditional sentences with the correct form of the verbs.

If Tom *hadn't gone* to college, he *wouldn't have met* Sarah. (not go, not meet)
1 If you ________ me to the airport, I ________ my flight. (not take, miss)
2 We ________ the game if the referee ________ us a penalty. (not win, not give)
3 You ________ the weekend if you ________ with us. (enjoy, come)
4 If I ________ the theater tickets online, they ________ more expensive. (not buy, be)
5 Mike ________ his wife's birthday if she ________ him. (forget, not remind)
6 If the police ________ five minutes later, they ________ the thief. (arrive, not catch)
7 If you ________ me the money, I ________ to go away for the weekend. (not lend, not be able)
8 You ________ yourself if you ________ off the horse. (hurt, fall)
9 We ________ the hotel if we ________ the sign. (not find, not seen)
10 If I ________ about the job, I ________ for it. (know, apply)

◀ p.85

9B

quantifiers

large quantities

1 My uncle and aunt have **a lot of** money. 5 10
Nina has **lots of** clothes.
2 James eats **a lot**.
3 There aren't **many** cafes near here.
Do you have **many** close friends?
Do you watch **much** TV?
I don't eat **much** chocolate.
4 Don't run. We have **plenty of** time.

1 Use *a lot of* or *lots of* in [+] sentences.
2 Use *a lot* when there is no noun, e.g., *He talks a lot*. NOT ~~*He talks a lot of*~~.
3 *much* / *many* are usually used in [-] sentences and [?], but *a lot of* can also be used.
4 Use *plenty of* in [+] sentences. (= more than enough)

small quantities

1 **A** Do you want some more ice cream? 5 11
B Just **a little**.
The town only has **a few movie theaters**.
2 I'm so busy that I have **very little time** for myself.
Sarah isn't popular and she has **very few friends**.

1 Use *little* + uncountable nouns, *few* + plural countable nouns.
- *a little* and *a few* = some, but not a lot.

2 *very little* and *very few* = *not much* / *many*.

more or less than you need or want

1 I don't like this city. It's **too big** and it's **too noisy**. 5 12
2 There's **too much traffic** and **too much noise**.
There are **too many tourists** and **too many cars**.
3 There aren't **enough parks** and there aren't **enough trees**.
The buses aren't **frequent enough**.
The buses don't run **frequently enough**.

There's too much traffic and too much noise.

1 Use *too* + adjective.
2 Use *too much* + uncountable nouns and *too many* + plural countable nouns.
3 Use *enough* before a noun, e.g., *enough eggs*, and after an adjective, e.g., *It isn't big enough*, or an adverb, e.g., *You aren't walking fast enough*.

zero quantity

1 There **isn't any** room in the car. 5 13
We **don't have any** eggs.
2 There**'s no** room in the car. We **have no** eggs.
3 **A** How many eggs do we have?
B **None**. I've used them all.

1 Use *any* (+ noun) for zero quantity with a [-] verb.
2 Use *no* + noun with a [+] verb.
3 Use *none* (without a noun) in short answers.

a Circle the correct answer. Check ✓ if both are possible.

My husband has *too much* / *too many* electronic gadgets.
1 I just have to reply to *a few* / *a little* emails and then I'll be finished.
2 Do you spend *much* / *many* time on social networking sites?
3 My bedroom is a nice size. There's *enough room* / *plenty of room* for a desk.
4 I know *very few* / *very little* people who speak two foreign languages.
5 My brother has downloaded *a lot of* / *lots of* apps onto his new phone.
6 I have some cash on me, but not *a lot* / *a lot of*.
7 Their new TV is *too* / *too much* big. It hardly fits in the living room.
8 *There aren't any* / *There are no* potatoes. I forgot to buy some.
9 My niece isn't *old enough* / *enough old* to play with a game console.
10 I don't have *a lot of* / *many* friends on Facebook.

b Check ✓ the correct sentences. Correct the mistakes in the highlighted phrases.

My nephew got lots of video games for his birthday. ✓
I don't post much videos on Facebook. *many videos*
1 How many presents did you get? A lot of!
2 I buy very few paper books now because I have an e-reader.
3 I don't use no social networks because I don't like them.
4 Please turn that music down. It's too much loud!
5 There aren't many good shows on TV tonight.
6 My Internet connection isn't enough fast for me to download movies.
7 I make too much phone calls. My phone bill is enormous!
8 **A** How much fruit do we have?
B Any. Can you buy some?
9 There are only a little websites that I use regularly.
10 Karen has plenty of money, so she always has the latest gadgets.

◄ p.88

relative clauses

defining relative clauses (giving essential information)

1 Julia's the woman **who** / **that** works in the office with me. 5 29
It's a self-help book **that** / **which** teaches you how to relax.
That's the house **where** I was born.
2 Is Frank the man **whose** brother plays for the Lakers?
It's a plant **whose** leaves change color in spring.
3 I just got a text from the girl (**who** / **that**) I met on the flight to Paris.
This is the new phone (**that** / **which**) I bought yesterday.

To give important information about a person, place, or thing use a relative clause (= a relative pronoun + subject) + verb.

1 Use the relative pronoun *who* / *that* for people, *that* / *which* for things / animals, and *where* for places.
- *That* is more common than *which* in defining clauses.
  - You cannot omit *who* / *which* / *that* / *where* in this kind of clause. NOT ~~*Julia's the woman works in the office with me.*~~

2 Use *whose* to mean "of who" or "of which."

3 *who*, *which*, and *that* can be omitted when the verbs in the main clause and the relative clause **have a different subject**, e.g., *She's the girl I met on the plane.*
- *where* and *whose* can never be omitted, e.g., NOT ~~*Is that the woman dog barks?*~~

non-defining relative clauses (giving extra non-essential information)

This painting, **which** was painted in 1860, is worth millions of dollars. 5 30
Last week I visited my aunt, **who's** nearly 90 years old.
Burford, **where** my grandfather was born, is a beautiful little town.
My neighbor, **whose** son goes to my son's school, has just remarried.

- Non-defining relative clauses give extra (often non-essential information) in a sentence. If this clause is omitted, the sentence still makes sense.
  This painting, ~~which was painted in 1860~~, is worth millions of dollars.
- Non-defining relative clauses must go between commas (or a comma and a period).
- In these clauses, you can't leave out the relative pronoun (*who*, *which*, etc.)
- In these clauses, you can't use *that* instead of *who* / *which*. NOT ~~*This painting, that was painted in 1860, is worth millions of dollars.*~~

This painting, which was painted in 1860, is worth millions of dollars.

a Complete with *who*, *which*, *that*, *where*, or *whose*.

Mountain View is the area <u>*where*</u> Steve Jobs grew up.

1 Rob and Corinna, ________ have twins, often need a babysitter.
2 The White House, ________ the president of the United States lives, is in Washington, D.C.
3 The sandwich ________ you made me yesterday was delicious.
4 The woman ________ lived here before us was a writer.
5 Stieg Larsson, ________ books form the *Millennium Trilogy*, died in 2004.
6 My computer is a lot faster than the one ________ you bought.
7 The *Mona Lisa*, ________ has been damaged several times, is now displayed behind bulletproof glass.
8 Look! That's the woman ________ dog bit me last week.
9 On our last vacation we visited Stratford-Upon-Avon, ________ Shakespeare was born.
10 We all went to the game except Marianne, ________ doesn't like basketball.
11 That man ________ you saw at the party was my boyfriend!
12 That's the park ________ I learned to ride a bike.

b Look at the sentences in **a**. Check ✓ the sentences where you could leave out the relative pronoun.

c Add commas where necessary in the sentences.

Caroline, who lives next door to me, is beautiful.

1 This is the place where John crashed his car.
2 The museum that we visited yesterday was amazing.
3 Beijing which is one of the world's biggest cities hosted the 2008 Olympic Games.
4 Michael Jackson's *Thriller* which was released in 1982 was one of the best-selling albums of the 80s.
5 These are the shoes that I'm wearing to the party tonight.
6 Sally and Joe who got married last year are expecting their first baby.

◄ p.95

10B

tag questions

tag questions

affirmative verb, negative tag	negative verb, affirmative tag 5 38
It's cold today, **isn't it**?	**She isn't** here today, **is she**?
You're Peruvian, **aren't you**?	**You aren't** angry, **are you**?
They live in Ankara, **don't they**?	**They don't** like pizza, **do they**?
The game ends at 8:00, **doesn't it**?	**Lucy doesn't** eat meat, **does she**?
Your sister worked in the US, **didn't she**?	**You didn't** like the movie, **did you**?
We've met before, **haven't we**?	**Mike hasn't** been to Beijing before, **has he**?
You'll be OK, **won't you**?	**You won't** tell anyone, **will you**?
You'd go on vacation with me, **wouldn't you**?	**Sue wouldn't** quit her job, **would she**?

It's cold today, isn't it?

- Tag questions (*is he?, aren't they?, do you?, did we?*, etc.) are often used to check something you already think is true.
  Your name's Maria, isn't it?
- To form a tag question use:
  – the correct auxiliary verb, e.g., *do | does, be* for the present, *did* for the past, *will | won't* for the future, etc.
  – a pronoun, e.g., *he, it, they*, etc.
  – a negative auxiliary verb if the sentence is affirmative and an affirmative auxiliary verb if the sentence is negative.

a Match the phrases.

You know that man,	G	A	didn't you?
1 You're going out with him,		B	will you?
2 You haven't told your family about him,		C	did you?
3 You met him last month,		D	won't you?
4 You were at the same party,		E	have you?
5 You didn't know he was a criminal,		F	weren't you?
6 You aren't happy in the relationship,		G	~~don't you?~~
7 You don't want to see him again,		H	are you?
8 You'll tell us the truth,		I	aren't you?
9 You won't tell any lies,		J	don't you?
10 You understand what I'm saying,		K	do you?

b Complete with a tag question (*are you?, isn't it?*, etc.).

Your name's Jack, *isn't it*?
1 Your brother works at the gas station, ____________?
2 They don't have any proof, ____________?
3 That man isn't the murderer, ____________?
4 You were a witness to the crime, ____________?
5 The police have arrested someone, ____________?
6 The woman wasn't dead, ____________?
7 That girl took your bag, ____________?
8 He won't go to prison, ____________?
9 You haven't seen the suspect, ____________?
10 They didn't have enough evidence, ____________?

p.99

Movies

1 KINDS OF MOVIES

a Match the photos with the kinds of movies.

- [ ] an <u>ac</u>tion movie /'ækʃn 'muvi/
- [ ] an <u>an</u>imated movie /'ænəmeɪtəd 'muvi/
- [ ] a <u>co</u>medy /'kɑmədi/
- *1* a <u>dra</u>ma /'drɑmə/
- [ ] a his<u>tor</u>ical movie /hɪ'stɔrɪkl 'muvi/
- [ ] a <u>hor</u>ror movie /'hɔrər 'muvi/
- [ ] a <u>mu</u>sical /'myuzɪkl/
- [ ] a ro<u>man</u>tic <u>co</u>medy /roʊ'mæntɪk 'kɑmədi/
- [ ] a <u>sci</u>ence <u>fic</u>tion movie /'saɪəns 'fɪkʃn 'muvi/
- [ ] a <u>thril</u>ler /'θrɪlər/
- [ ] a war movie /wɔr 'muvi/
- [ ] a <u>wes</u>tern /'wɛstərn/

b 3 33 Listen and check.

c Think of a famous movie for each kind.

d What kind of movie is often...?

<u>fun</u>ny <u>vi</u>olent ex<u>ci</u>ting <u>sca</u>ry <u>mo</u>ving

e What kind of movies do you / don't you like? Why?

movie* and *film
Movie and *film* mean the same, but *film* is more common in British English.

2 PEOPLE AND THINGS

a Match the nouns and definitions.

<u>au</u>dience /'ɔdiəns/ ~~cast~~ /kæst/ <u>ex</u>tra /'ɛkstrə/ plot /plɑt/ <u>re</u>view /rɪ'vyu/ scene /sin/ script /skrɪpt/ <u>se</u>quel /'sikwəl/ <u>sound</u>track /'saʊndtræk/ <u>spe</u>cial ef<u>fects</u> /'spɛʃl ɪ'fɛkts/ star /stɑr/ <u>sub</u>titles /'sʌbtaɪtlz/

1 *cast* all the people who act in a movie
2 ________ (also *verb*) the most important actor or actress in a movie
3 ________ the music of a movie
4 ________ the story of a movie
5 ________ a part of a movie happening in one place
6 ________ the people who watch a movie in a movie theater
7 ________ a move that continues the story of an earlier movie
8 ________ images often created by a computer
9 ________ the words of the movie
10 ________ a person in a movie who has a small unimportant part, e.g., in a crowd scene
11 ________ the translation of the dialogue into another language
12 ________ an article that gives an opinion on a new movie, book, etc.

b 3 34 Listen and check. Cover the definitions and look at the words. Remember the definitions.

3 VERBS AND PHRASES

a Match sentences 1–6 with sentences A–F.

1 [ ] It **was directed** by Tate Taylor.
2 [ ] It **was dubbed** into other languages.
3 [ ] Viola Davis **played the part of** Aibileen Clark.
4 [ ] The movie **is set** in Mississippi in the US during the 1960s.
5 [ ] It **is based on** the novel of the same name by Kathryn Stockett.
6 [ ] It **was shot (filmed) on location** in Greenwood, Mississippi.

A It was situated in that place at that time.
B He was the director.
C This was her role in the movie.
D The voices of foreign actors were used.
E It was an adaptation of the book.
F It was filmed in the real place, not in a studio.

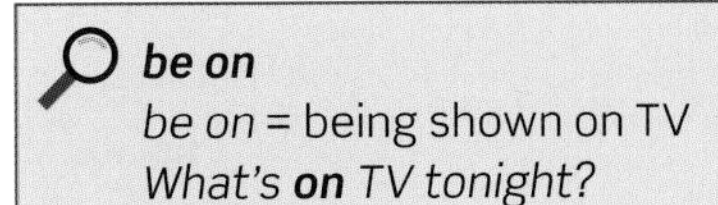

be on
be on = being shown on TV
What's ***on*** *TV tonight?*

b 3 35 Listen and check. Cover 1–6 and look at A–F. Remember 1–6.

◄ p.56

The body

1 PARTS OF THE BODY

a Match the words and pictures.

- arms /ɑrmz/
- back /bæk/
- ears /ɪrz/
- eyes /aɪz/
- face /feɪs/
- feet /fit/ (*singular* foot /fʊt/)
- fingers /ˈfɪŋɡərz/
- hands /hændz/
- head /hɛd/
- knees /niz/
- legs /lɛɡz/
- lips /lɪps/
- *1* mouth /maʊθ/
- neck /nɛk/
- nose /noʊz/
- shoulders /ˈʃoʊldərz/
- stomach /ˈstʌmək/
- teeth /tiθ/ (*singular* tooth /tuθ/)
- toes /toʊz/
- tongue /tʌŋ/

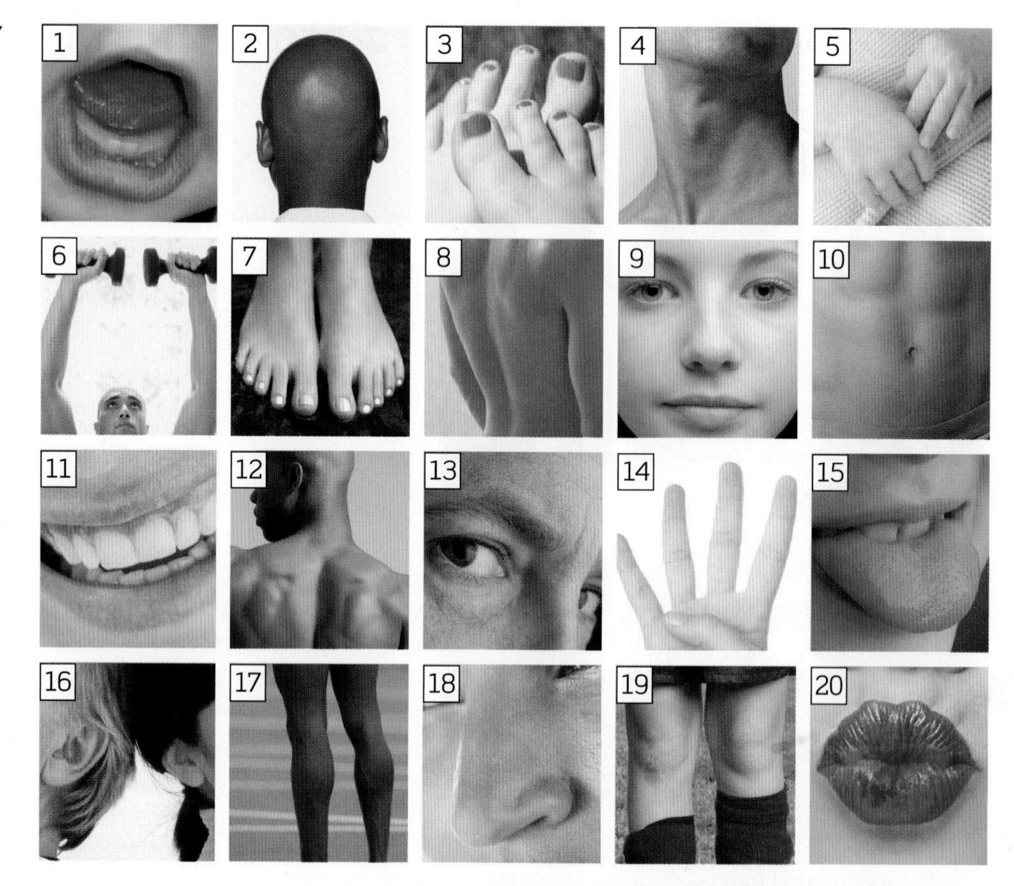

b 3 39 Listen and check.

c Cover the words and test yourself or a partner. Point to a part of the body for your partner to say the word.

> **Possessive pronouns with parts of the body**
> In English we use possessive pronouns (*my*, *your*, etc.) with parts of the body, not *the*.
> *Give me* ***your*** *hand.* NOT ~~*Give me the hand.*~~

2 VERBS RELATED TO THE BODY

a Complete the sentences with a verb from the list in the correct tense. Which two verbs are irregular in the past tense?

~~bite~~ /baɪt/ clap /klæp/ kick /kɪk/ nod /nɑd/ point /pɔɪnt/ smell /smɛl/ smile /smaɪl/ stare /stɛr/ taste /teɪst/ throw /θroʊ/ touch /tʌtʃ/ whistle /ˈwɪsl/

b 3 40 Listen and check. Which parts of the body do you use to do all these things?

◄ p.59

1. Don't be scared of the dog. He won't *bite*.
2. Jason ______ the ball too hard, and it went over the wall into the next yard.
3. Don't ______ stones – you might hit somebody.
4. Mmm! Something ______ delicious! Are you making a cake?
5. The stranger ______ at me for a long time, but he didn't say anything.
6. Can you ______ the rice? I'm not sure if it's cooked yet.
7. My dad ______ a tune as he raked the leaves.
8. Don't ______ the oven door! It's really hot.
9. The audience ______ when I finished singing.
10. The teacher suddenly ______ at me and said, "What's the answer?"
11. In Russia if you ______ at strangers, people think you're crazy!
12. Everybody ______ in agreement when I explained my idea.

Education

1 THE SCHOOL SYSTEM IN THE US AND THE UK

a Complete the text about the US with words from the list.

college elementary grades graduate high kindergarten ~~preschool~~ private public religious semesters twelfth

b 4 3))) Listen and check.

c Complete the text about the UK with the words from the list.

boarding head nursery ~~primary~~ pupils secondary terms university

d 4 4))) Listen and check.

e Cover both texts. With a partner, try to remember the different types of school (starting from the lowest level) in both countries.

In the US

Many children start their education between the ages of two and four in [1]*preschool*. Once a child turns five, he or she enters the US school system, which is divided into three levels, [2]________ school, middle school (sometimes called junior high school), and [3]________ school. In almost all schools at these levels, children are divided by age groups into [4]________. The youngest children begin in [5]________ (followed by first grade) and continue until [6]________ grade, the final year of high school. The school year is divided into two [7]________.

Most US schools (about 75%) are [8]________ schools, which means they are supported by US tax dollars and education is free. The other 25% are [9]________ schools, where parents have to pay. Many of these schools are [10]________ schools, where the teachers may be priests or nuns.

If you want to go to [11]________, you have to apply. Admission depends on high school grades, college aptitude test scores, and extracurricular activities. A person who has completed college and has earned a degree is called a college [12]________.

In the UK

Children start [1]________ school when they are five. Before that, many children go to [2]________ school. From 11–18, children go to [3]________ school. Some children go to [4]________ schools, where they study, eat, and sleep. School children are usually called [5]________ (not "students" which only refers to people who are at university), and the person who is in charge of a school is called the [6]________ teacher. The school year is divided into three [7]________. Higher education is often called [8]________.

2 VERBS

a Complete the texts with a verb from the list.

~~behave~~ /bɪˈheɪv/ be punished /bi ˈpʌnɪʃt/ be suspended /bi səˈspɛndəd/ cheat /tʃit/ fail /feɪl/ pass /pæs/ study /ˈstʌdi/ take /teɪk/ (*or* do)

1 Discipline is very strict in our school. If students *behave* badly, for example if they ______ on an exam, they will probably ______, and might even ______.

2 Marc has to ______ an important English exam next week. He hopes he'll ______, but he hasn't had much time to ______, so he's worried that he might ______.

b 4 5))) Listen and check. Cover the texts and look at the pictures. Remember the texts.

***educate* or *bring up*?**
educate = to teach somebody at a school
*Luke was **educated** at Cherry Creek High School and the University of Denver.*
bring up = to take care of a child and teach him / her how to behave. This is usually done by parents or a family member at home.
*Lily was **brought** up by her mother in a small city.*

***learn* or *study*?**
learn = to get knowledge or a skill (from somebody)
*I'm **learning** to drive right now. How long have you been **learning** Russian?*
study = to spend time learning about something
*Russell is **studying** economics in college.*

◀ p.64

Houses

1 WHERE PEOPLE LIVE

a Complete the **Preposition** column with *in* or *on*.

	Preposition
1 I live ___ **the country**, surrounded by fields.	*in*
2 I live ___ **the outskirts** of Boston, about 5 miles from the center of the city.	
3 I live ___ **a village** (**a town** / **a city**).	
4 I live in Del Mar, a small town ___ **the West Coast**.	
5 I live ___ **the second floor** of a large apartment building.	
6 I live ___ Littleton, **a suburb** of Denver about 11 miles from the center of the city.	

suburbs **or** ***outskirts?***
The *suburbs* is a residential area outside the center of a large city.
Littleton is ***a suburb of*** *Denver.*
The *outskirts* is the area around a city that is the farthest from the center of the city.
They live ***on the outskirts of*** *Vancouver.*

b 4 19 Listen and check.

c Cover the **Preposition** column. Say the sentences with the correct preposition.

d Describe where you live to your partner.

2 PARTS OF A HOUSE OR AN APARTMENT BUILDING

a Match the words and pictures.

An apartment building

- ☐ balcony /ˈbælkəni/
- ☐ basement /ˈbeɪsmənt/
- ☐ entrance /ˈɛntrəns/
- ☐ first floor /fərst flɔr/ (*BritE* ground floor)
- 1 top floor /tɑp flɔr/

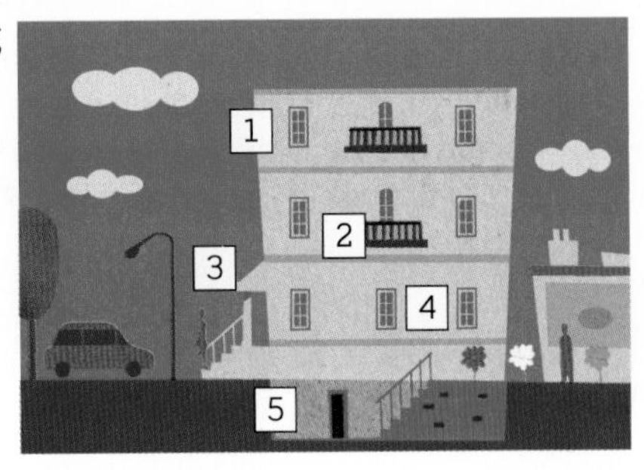

A house

- 1 chimney /ˈtʃɪmni/
- ☐ deck /dɛk/ / patio /ˈpætioʊ/
- ☐ gate /geɪt/
- ☐ roof /rʊf/
- ☐ steps /stɛps/
- ☐ walkway /ˈwɔkweɪ/
- ☐ wall /wɔl/

b 4 20 Listen and check. Cover the words and look at the pictures. Test yourself.

3 DESCRIBING A HOUSE OR AN APARTMENT

a Match the descriptions and photos.

☐ I live in a cabin in the woods. It's old and made of logs. The rooms have very low ceilings. There's a fireplace in the living room, and it's very cozy in the winter.

☐ I live in a modern apartment in the city. It's spacious and very light, with wood floors and big windows.

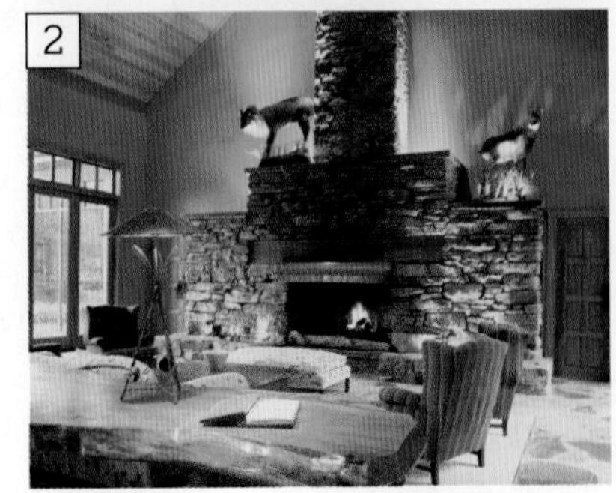

b 4 21 Listen and check. Focus on how the highlighted phrases are pronounced.

c Cover the descriptions and look at the photos. Describe the rooms.

chimney **or** ***fireplace?***
In English, *chimney* only refers to the structure on the roof of the house. *Fireplace* is the place where you burn wood or coal.

roof **or** ***ceiling?***
Roof is the top part of a house. *Ceiling* is the top part of a room.

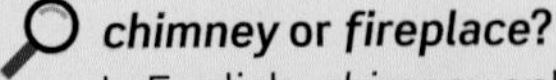

◀ p.69

Word building

1 MAKING NOUNS FROM VERBS

a Make nouns from the verbs in the list and write them in the correct column.

achieve /ə'tʃiv/ agree /ə'gri/ argue /'ɑrgyu/
attach /ə'tætʃ/ ~~choose~~ /tʃuz/ compensate /'kɑmpənseɪt/
complain /kəm'pleɪn/ deliver /dɪ'lɪvər/
demonstrate /'dɛmənstreɪt/ explain /ɪk'spleɪn/ lose /luz/
pay /peɪ/ respond /rɪ'spɑnd/ sell /sɛl/ succeed /sək'sid/

1 + *ation*	2 + *ment*	3 new word
		choice

b 4 38 Listen and check. Underline the stressed syllable in the nouns.

c Test a partner. Then switch roles.

A (book open) say the verb.
B (book closed) say the noun.

d Complete the questions with a noun from **a** in the singular or plural.

1 Have you ever opened an *attachment* on an email that contained a virus?
2 Do you often have ________ with your family? What about?
3 Do you prefer reading grammar ________ in your own language, or do you think it's better to read them in English?
4 Have you ever made a ________ to a company and gotten ________?
5 Do you think that there's too much ________ when you're shopping, e.g., for a new phone?
6 Have you ever been in a ________? What were you protesting about?

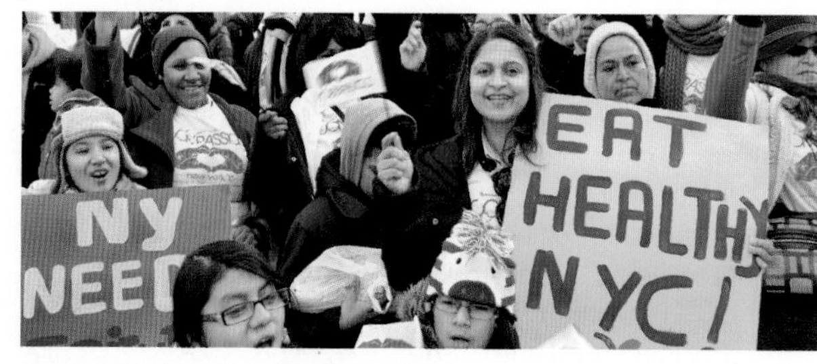

e 4 39 Listen and check. Then ask and answer the questions with a partner.

◀ p.77

2 MAKING ADJECTIVES AND ADVERBS

a Look at the adjectives and adverbs that can be made from the noun *luck* in the chart below. Then, in pairs, complete the chart.

noun	adjectives		adverbs	
	+	–	+	–
luck	lucky	unlucky	luckily	unluckily
fortune	fortunate	unfortunate		
comfort				
patience				
care				

b 5 7 Listen and check.

c Complete the sentences with the correct form of the **bold** noun.

1 The beach was beautiful, but *unfortunately* it rained almost every day. **fortune**
2 My new shoes are very ________. I wore them for the first time yesterday, and they didn't hurt at all. **comfort**
3 He took the exam quickly and ________, and so he made a lot of mistakes. **care**
4 We were really ________. We missed the flight by just five minutes. **luck**
5 Jack is a very ________ driver! He can't stand being behind someone who is driving slowly. **patience**
6 It was a bad accident, but ________ nobody was seriously hurt. **luck**
7 It was raining, but fans waited ________ in line to buy tickets for tomorrow's concert. **patience**
8 The roads will be very icy tonight, so drive ________. **care**
9 The temperature dropped to 20 degrees, but ________ we were all wearing warm coats and jackets. **fortune**
10 The bed in the hotel was incredibly ________. I hardly slept at all. **comfort**

d 5 8 Listen and check.

◀ p.87

Work

1 VERB PHRASES

a Complete the verb phrases with a word or phrase from the list.

applied for /ə'plaɪd fɔr/ was downsized /wəz 'daʊnsaɪzd/ was fired /wəz faɪərd/ got promoted /gɑt prə'moʊtɪd/ resign /rɪ'zaɪn/ retire /rɪ'taɪər/ set up /sɛt ʌp/ take /teɪk/ work (x2) /wərk/

1 Dan has to _work_ a lot of overtime. He has to work extra hours.
2 Matt ______ last week. He was given a more important job.
3 Most nurses have to ______ shifts. Sometimes they work during the day and sometimes at night.
4 A man in our department ______ yesterday. He lost his job because of poor performance.
5 Colin ______ last month. He lost his job because the company didn't need him anymore.
6 The politician is going to ______. He has decided to leave his job. (*also* quit)
7 Lilian is going to ______ next month. She's 65, and she's going to stop working.
8 Angela has ______ a business to sell clothes online. She had the idea and has started doing it.
9 Everyone in the office has to ______ a training course. They need to learn how to use the new software.
10 She ______ a job. She replied to an advertisement and sent in her résumé.

b 4 42 Listen and check. Cover the first sentence and look at the second. Can you remember the verb?

2 SAYING WHAT YOU DO

a Match the adjectives and definitions.

part-time /'pɑrt 'taɪm/ self-employed /sɛlf ɪm'plɔɪd/ temporary /'tɛmpərɛri/ unemployed /ʌnɪm'plɔɪd/ well qualified /wɛl 'kwɑləfaɪd/

for people

1 I'm ________. without a job
2 He's ________. working for himself
3 She's ________. with, e.g., a college degree or with a lot of experience

for a job or work

4 It's a ________ job. (opposite *permanent*) with only a short contract, e.g., for six months
5 It's a ________ job. (opposite *full-time*) only working a few hours a day

b Complete the sentences with the correct prepositions.

1 I **work** _for_ a multinational company.
2 I'm ______ **charge** ______ the marketing department.
3 I'm **responsible** ______ customer loans.
4 I'm ______ school (college).
5 I'm ______ my third year.

c 4 43 Listen and check **a** and **b**.

3 WORD BUILDING

a Make nouns from the following verbs by adding *-ment, -ion,* or *-ation*, and making any other necessary changes.

1 promote	*promotion*	4 employ	
2 apply		5 qualify	
3 retire		6 resign	

b Make nouns for the people who do the jobs by adding *-er, -or, -ian,* or *-ist*, and making any other necessary changes.

1 science		4 pharmacy	
2 law		5 farm	
3 music		6 translate	

c 4 44 Listen and check **a** and **b**. Underline the stressed syllable in the new words.

d Cover the nouns and look at 1–6 in **a** and **b**. Say the nouns. Think of two more jobs for each ending.

***job* or *work*?**
*I'm looking for **work**. I'm looking for a **job**.*
Work is an uncountable noun and has no plural.
NOT ~~*I'm looking for a work.*~~
Job is a countable noun.
There are several jobs available in this company.

◀ p.78

Irregular verbs

5 45

Infinitive	Simple past	Past participle
be /bi/	was /wəz/ were /wər/	been /bɪn/
beat /bit/	beat	beaten /ˈbitn/
become /bɪˈkʌm/	became /bɪˈkeɪm/	become
begin /bɪˈgɪn/	began /bɪˈgæn/	begun /bɪˈgʌn/
bite /baɪt/	bit /bɪt/	bitten /ˈbɪtn/
break /breɪk/	broke /broʊk/	broken /ˈbroʊkən/
bring /brɪŋ/	brought /brɔt/	brought
build /bɪld/	built /bɪlt/	built
buy /baɪ/	bought /bɔt/	bought
can /kæn/	could /kʊd/	–
catch /kætʃ/	caught /kɔt/	caught
choose /tʃuz/	chose /tʃoʊz/	chosen /ˈtʃoʊzn/
come /kʌm/	came /keɪm/	come
cost /kɔst/	cost	cost
cut /kʌt/	cut	cut
do /du/	did /dɪd/	done /dʌn/
draw /drɔ/	drew /dru/	drawn /drɔn/
dream /drim/	dreamed /drimd/ (dreamt /drɛmt/)	dreamed (dreamt)
drink /drɪŋk/	drank /dræŋk/	drunk /drʌŋk/
drive /draɪv/	drove /droʊv/	driven /ˈdrɪvn/
eat /it/	ate /eɪt/	eaten /ˈitn/
fall /fɔl/	fell /fɛl/	fallen /ˈfɔlən/
feel /fil/	felt /fɛlt/	felt
find /faɪnd/	found /faʊnd/	found
fly /flaɪ/	flew /flu/	flown /floʊn/
forget /fərˈgɛt/	forgot /fərˈgɑt/	forgotten /fərˈgɑtn/
get /gɛt/	got /gɑt/	gotten /ˈgɑtn/
give /gɪv/	gave /geɪv/	given /ˈgɪvn/
go /goʊ/	went /wɛnt/	gone /gɑn/
grow /groʊ/	grew /gru/	grown /groʊn/
hang /hæŋ/	hung /hʌŋ/	hung
have /hæv/	had /hæd/	had
hear /hɪr/	heard /hərd/	heard
hit /hɪt/	hit	hit
hurt /hərt/	hurt	hurt
keep /kip/	kept /kɛpt/	kept
know /noʊ/	knew /nu/	known /noʊn/

Infinitive	Simple past	Past participle
learn /lərn/	learned /lərnd/	learned
leave /liv/	left /lɛft/	left
lend /lɛnd/	lent /lɛnt/	lent
let /lɛt/	let	let
lie /laɪ/	lay /leɪ/	lain /leɪn/
lose /luz/	lost /lɔst/	lost
make /meɪk/	made /meɪd/	made
mean /min/	meant /mɛnt/	meant
meet /mit/	met /mɛt/	met
pay /peɪ/	paid /peɪd/	paid
put /pʊt/	put	put
read /rid/	read /rɛd/	read /rɛd/
ride /raɪd/	rode /roʊd/	ridden /ˈrɪdn/
ring /rɪŋ/	rang /ræŋ/	rung /rʌŋ/
run /rʌn/	ran /ræn/	run
say /seɪ/	said /sɛd/	said
see /si/	saw /sɔ/	seen /sin/
sell /sɛl/	sold /soʊld/	sold
send /sɛnd/	sent /sɛnt/	sent
set /sɛt/	set	set
shine /ʃaɪn/	shone /ʃoʊn/	shone
shut /ʃʌt/	shut	shut
sing /sɪŋ/	sang /sæŋ/	sung /sʌŋ/
sit /sɪt/	sat /sæt/	sat
sleep /slip/	slept /slɛpt/	slept
speak /spik/	spoke /spoʊk/	spoken /ˈspoʊkən/
spend /spɛnd/	spent /spɛnt/	spent
stand /stænd/	stood /stʊd/	stood
steal /stil/	stole /stoʊl/	stolen /ˈstoʊlən/
swim /swɪm/	swam /swæm/	swum /swʌm/
take /teɪk/	took /tʊk/	taken /ˈteɪkən/
teach /titʃ/	taught /tɔt/	taught
tell /tɛl/	told /toʊld/	told
think /θɪŋk/	thought /θɔt/	thought
throw /θroʊ/	threw /θru/	thrown /θrəʊn/
understand /ʌndəˈstaend/	understood /ʌndərˈstʊd/	understood
wake /weɪk/	woke /woʊk/	woken /ˈwoʊkən/
wear /wɛr/	wore /wɔr/	worn /wɔrn/
win /wɪn/	won /wʌn/	won
write /raɪt/	wrote /roʊt/	written /ˈrɪtn/

Vowel sounds

	usual spelling	! but also
 tree	**ee** beef speed **ea** peach team **e** refund medium	people magazine niece receipt
 fish	**i** dish bill pitch fit ticket since	pretty women busy decided village physics
 ear	**eer** cheers engineer **ere** here we're **ear** beard appearance	serious
 cat	**a** fan travel crash tax carry land	
 egg	**e** menu lend text spend plenty cent	friendly already healthy many said
 chair	**air** airport upstairs fair hair **are** rare careful	their there wear pear area
 clock	**o** shop comedy plot shot cottage on	watch want calm
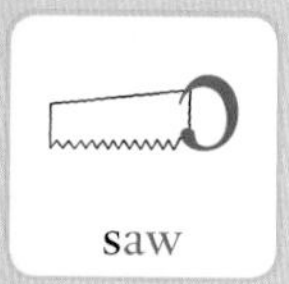 saw	**a** bald wall **aw** draw saw **al** walk talk	thought caught audience
 horse	**or** sports floor **ore** bore score	warm course board
 boot	**oo** pool moody **u*** true student	suitcase juice shoe move soup through

* especially before consonant + **e**

	usual spelling	! but also
 bull	**u** full **oo** cook book look good	could should would woman
 tourist	A very unusual sound. sure plural	
 up	**u** public subject ugly duck cup	money someone enough country tough
 computer	Many different spellings, /ə/ is always unstressed. about complain	
bird	**er** person prefer learn **ir** dirty third **ur** curly turn	work world worse picture
 owl	**ou** hour around proud ground **ow** town brown	
 phone	**o*** broke stone frozen stove **oa** roast coat	owe slow although shoulders
 car	**ar** garden charge starter	heart
 train	**a*** save gate **ai** railroad plain **ay** may say gray	break steak great weight they
 boy	**oi** boiled noisy spoil coin **oy** enjoy employer	
 bike	**i*** fine sign **y** shy motorcycle **igh** flight frightened	buy eyes height

vowels · vowels followed by /r/ · diphthongs

Consonant sounds

	usual spelling		! but also
parrot	**p** **pp**	plate transport trip shopping apply	
bag	**b** **bb**	beans bill probably crab stubborn dubbed	
key	**c** **k** **ck**	court script kind kick track lucky	chemisty school stomach squid account
girl	**g** **gg**	golf grilled colleague forget aggressive luggage	
flower	**f** **ph** **ff**	food roof pharmacy nephew traffic affectionate	enough laugh
vase	**v**	van vegetables travel invest private believe	of
tie	**t** **tt**	taste tennis stadium strict attractive cottage	worked passed
dog	**d** **dd**	director afford comedy confident address middle	failed bored
snake	**s** **ss** **c** (before *e, i, y*)	steps likes boss assistant twice city cycle	science scene
zebra	**z** **s**	lazy freezing nose loves cousins	
shower	**sh** **ti (+ vowel)** **ci (+ vowel)**	short dishwasher selfish cash ambitious explanation spacious sociable	sugar sure machine chef
television		decision confusion usually	

	usual spelling		! but also
thumb	**th**	throw thriller healthy path math teeth	
mother	**th**	the that with farther together	
chess	**ch** **tch** **t (+ ure)**	change cheat watch match picture future	
jazz	**j** **g** **dge**	jealous just generous manager bridge judge	
leg	**l** **ll**	limit salary until reliable sell rebellious	
right	**r** **rr**	result referee elementary fried borrow married	written wrong
witch	**w** **wh**	war waste western highway whistle which	one once
yacht	**y** before **u**	yet year yogurt yourself university argue	
monkey	**m** **mm**	mean arm romantic charming summer swimming	lamb
nose	**n** **nn**	neck honest none chimney tennis thinner	knee knew
singer	**ng** before **g/k**	cooking going spring bring think tongue	
house	**h**	handsome helmet behave inherit unhappy perhaps	who whose whole

voiced unvoiced

3B

American ENGLISH FILE

Workbook

Christina Latham-Koenig
Clive Oxenden
Jane Hudson

Paul Seligson and Clive Oxenden are the original co-authors of
English File 1 and *English File 2*

Contents

STUDY LINK iChecker SELF-ASSESSMENT CD-ROM

Powerful listening and interactive assessment CD-ROM

Your iChecker disc on the inside back cover of this Workbook includes:

- **AUDIO** – Download ALL of the audio files for the Listening and Pronunciation activities in this Workbook for on-the-go listening practice.
- **FILE TESTS** – Check your progress by taking a self-assessment test after you complete each File.

Audio: When you see this symbol iChecker, go to the iChecker disc in the back of this Workbook. Load the disc in your computer.

1

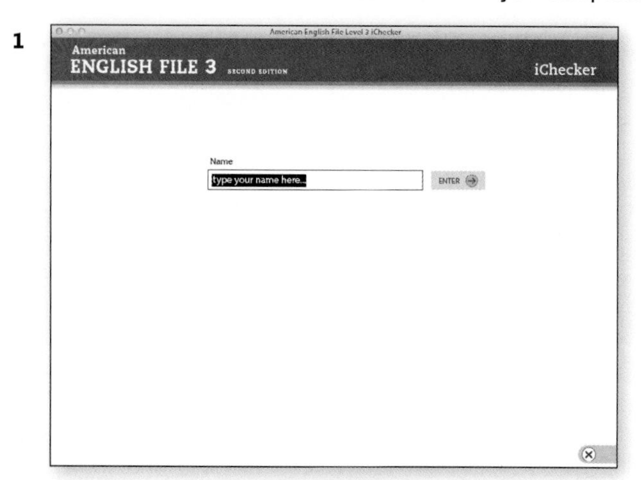

Type your name and press "ENTER."

2

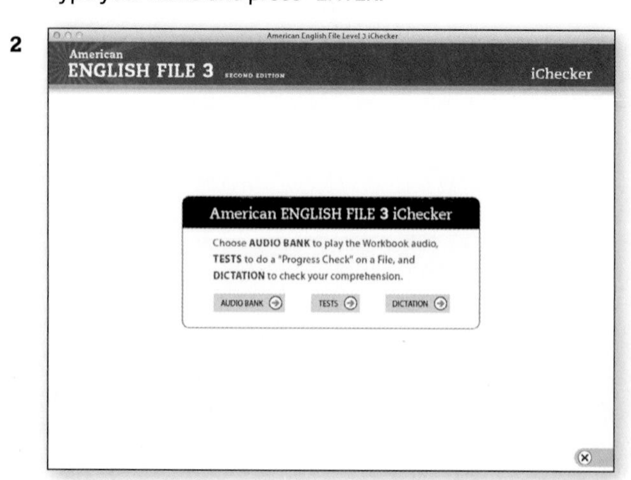

Choose "AUDIO BANK."

3

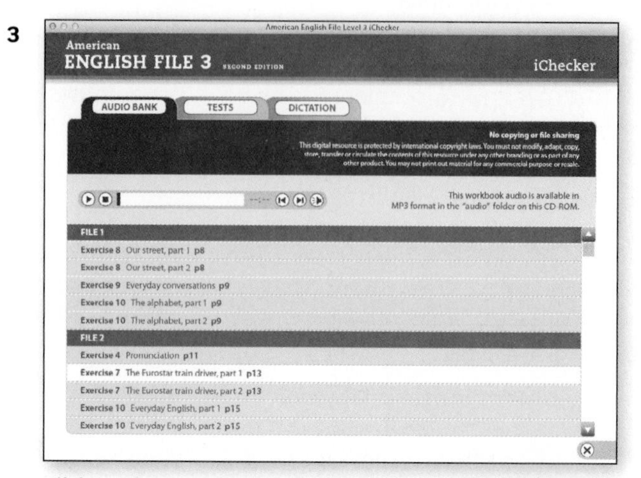

Click on the exercise for the File. Then use the media player to listen.

You can transfer the audio to a mobile device from the "audio" folder on the disc.

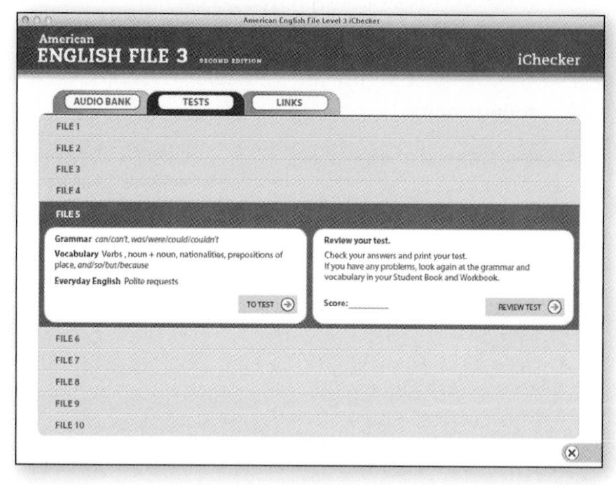

File test: At the end of every File, there is a test. To do the test, load the iChecker and select "Tests." Select the test for the File you have just finished.

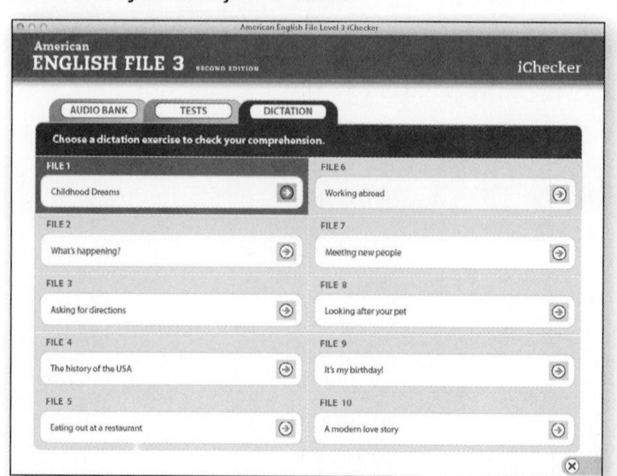

Dictation: At the end of every File, there is a dictation exercise. To do the dictation, select "Dictations" from the "File" menu.

Film is one of three universal languages, the other two: mathematics and music.

Frank Capra, US movie director

6A Shot on location

1 VOCABULARY movies

a Read the clues. Complete the puzzle on the right to find the hidden kind of movie.

1 A movie where images are drawn is an an*imated* movie.
2 A funny movie is a c________________.
3 A movie based on real events in the past is a h________________ movie.
4 A movie with an exciting plot is a th________________.
5 A scary movie is a h________________ movie.
6 A movie about cowboys is a w________________.
7 A movie with a serious story is a dr________________.
8 A funny movie about people falling in love is a r________________ comedy.
9 A movie about wars and battles is a w________________ m________________.
10 A movie where the cast sings and dances is a m________________.
11 A movie about imaginary events in the future is a sc________________-f________________ movie.

Hidden kind of movie: ________________

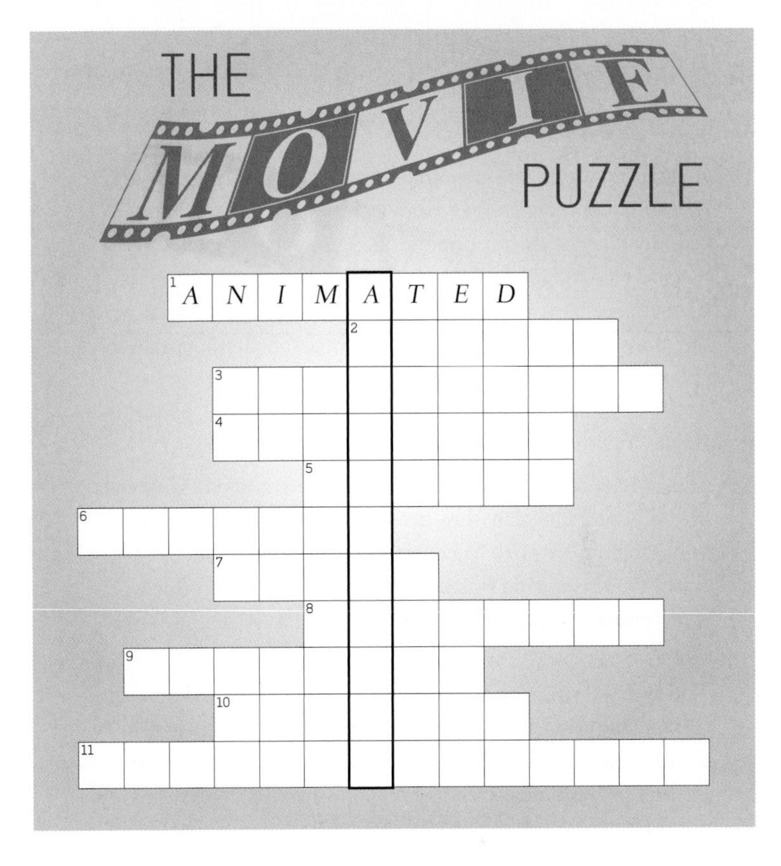

b Complete the sentences.

1 The st*ar* of the movie was a famous British actress.
2 I didn't understand the movie because the pl____________ was very complicated.
3 The actor accepted the part as soon as he read the sc____________.
4 Some members of the au____________ were crying at the end of the movie.
5 Most critics gave the movie an excellent r____________.
6 They only had to shoot the sc____________ once.
7 We don't speak French, so we saw the French movie with English s____________.
8 You'll have to wait for the s____________ to find out what happens next.
9 My favorite s____________ is the music from *The Artist*.
10 The best thing about the movie was the sp____________ ef____________. They looked very realistic.
11 The director is looking for ex____________ to appear in the crowd scenes.
12 The c____________ was a mixture of American and British actors.

2 GRAMMAR passive (all tenses)

a Complete the sentences with the correct passive form of the verbs in the box. Use the tense in parentheses.

~~direct~~ dub invite play release shoot show write

1 The movie *is directed* by Kathryn Bigelow. (simple present)
2 The part of Spider-Man ________________ by Andrew Garfield. (simple past)
3 It was very windy while the scene ________________. (past continuous)
4 The sequel ________________ next year. (future, *will*)
5 Some of the extras ________________ to the movie premiere. (future, *going to*)
6 The musical ________________ in movie theaters all over the country. (present continuous)
7 The drama ________________ into five other languages. (present perfect)
8 The script ________________ by the author of the book. (simple past)

b Circle the correct form, active or passive.

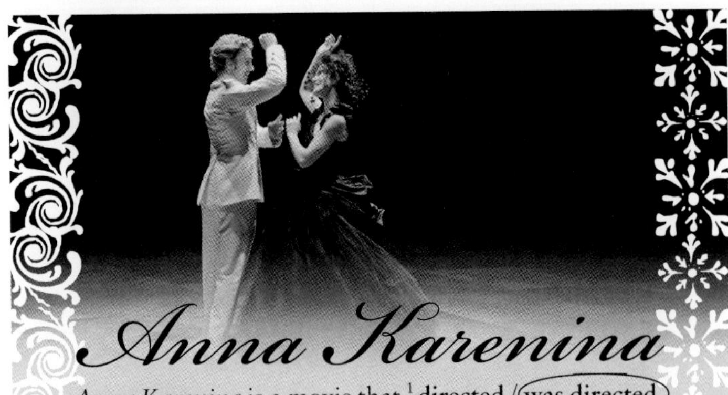

Anna Karenina

Anna Karenina is a movie that [1] **directed / was directed** by Joe Wright. Most of the movie [2] **shot / was shot** in an old theater outside of London, but some scenes [3] **filmed / were filmed** in Russia. It [4] **tells / is told** the story of a young Russian woman who is married to a government official, but [5] **falls / is fallen** in love with an aristocrat. Keira Knightley [6] **plays / is played** the part of Anna Karenina, and the part of her romantic interest, Count Vronsky, [7] **plays / is played** by Aaron Taylor-Johnson.

The movie [8] **starts / is started** when Anna arrives in Moscow. Her brother [9] **has seen / has been seen** with another woman, and Anna must speak to her sister-in-law about the situation. It is during this meeting that Anna [10] **introduces / is introduced** to the Count. The movie [11] **has based / is based** on the novel by Leo Tolstoy.

The superb soundtrack [12] **composed / was composed** by Italian composer Dario Marianelli, who also [13] **wrote / was written** the music for *Pride and Prejudice* and *Atonement*. Both of his previous soundtracks [14] **nominated / were nominated** for Oscars, and *Atonement* won an Oscar.

3 PRONUNCIATION sentence stress

a ONLINE Listen and repeat the sentences. Copy the rhythm.

1. The **movie** is **based** on a **true story**.
2. These **scenes** will be **shot** on **location**.
3. The **actor** has been **nominated** for an **Oscar**.
4. The **script** was **written** by the **author** of the **novel**.
5. The **sequel** is **going** to be **released next week**.
6. The **costumes** are **being made** by **hand**.

b Underline the stressed syllable in these words.

1. au|di|ence
2. hi|stor|i|cal mo|vie
3. co|me|dy
4. di|rec|tor
5. dra|ma
6. horr|or mo|vie
7. re|view
8. se|quel
9. sound|track
10. sub|ti|tles

c ONLINE Listen and check. Then listen again and repeat the words.

4 READING

a Read the text once. Check (✓) where you think it comes from.

1. an online newspaper ☐
2. a travel blog ☐
3. a website for tourists ☐
4. a movie program ☐

On location at Knebworth House

Knebworth House is famous worldwide for the major open-air rock concerts that have been held on its grounds since 1979. Knebworth is in the southeast England, and the Lytton family have lived there for over 500 years. The house itself is one of the oldest stately homes in the UK. It is also one of the most popular locations for the world's filmmakers.

Not surprisingly, the Gothic architecture of the house appealed to American movie director Tim Burton when he saw it. He was in the UK shooting a new version of the movie *Batman* at the time. He thought that the façade of the building would be perfect as the exterior of Wayne Manor, the home of Batman. But the inside of Wayne Manor was actually shot at another big house in the same area – Hatfield House.

The inside of Knebworth House has also been used in many movies. An important scene from the 2010 Oscar-winning movie *The King's Speech* was shot in the ballroom. This movie was made by the British director Tom Hooper. It starred Colin Firth as the young King George VI of England, who had a speech impediment. The ballroom was the venue for a party that was held by his older brother Edward. In a corner of the room, Edward tells George that he is planning to marry divorced American woman, Wallis Simpson, something that makes it impossible for him to be King of England. It is George who becomes King instead.

And, of course, like many other historic buildings in the UK, Knebworth has made an appearance in the Harry Potter movies. In the fourth movie of the series, *Harry Potter and the Goblet of Fire*, a holiday dance is held in Hogwarts School. Before the dancing starts, there is a scene where one of Harry's friends appears in a beautiful long dress. The staircase that she descends while her friends look on in amazement is, in fact, the one in Knebworth House.

These are just a few of the famous scenes filmed at Knebworth House. To discover more, why not visit Knebworth yourself? The house is only 27 miles from London, and is easy to get to by car or by train. Knebworth House is a must for all movie lovers visiting the UK.

b Read the text again. Mark the sentences T (true) or F (false).

1 Knebworth is a favorite destination for music lovers. *T*
2 The house isn't occupied anymore. ___
3 Many movies have been made at Knebworth. ___
4 Tim Burton used the outside of the house in one of his movies. ___
5 You can see the outside of the house in *The King's Speech*. ___
6 George VI makes an important announcement to all his guests at Knebworth. ___
7 Harry Potter walks down the staircase in Knebworth in one of the movies. ___
8 Knebworth House is not far from London. ___

c Look at the highlighted words and phrases. What do you think they mean? Use your dictionary to look up their meaning and pronunciation.

d Complete the sentences with one of the highlighted words or phrases.

1 My sister didn't really like the *new version* of *Pride and Prejudice*. She prefers the old one.
2 Palaces often have a ___________ where people come for a formal dance or party.
3 Nowadays, you can visit ___________ ___________ in the UK to see how very rich families lived in the past.
4 In the summer, I love going to ___________-___________ concerts. It's more fun than going to an indoor concert.
5 A hotel near a beach is a popular ___________ for weddings.
6 A person with a ___________ ___________ can find it very hard to speak in public.

5 LISTENING

a ONLINE Listen to a tour guide talking to a group before she takes them on the TV and Movie Walking Tour of Central Park in New York City. Number the places in the order she mentions them.

a a carousel ☐
b a bridge *1*
c a memorial ☐
d a skating rink ☐
e a hotel ☐
f a lake ☐
g a fountain ☐

b Listen again and correct any mistakes in the sentences. Check (✓) the sentences that are correct.

1 The tour will last for three hours.
two hours.
2 The Gapstow Bridge is made of wood.
___________.
3 The Plaza Hotel was featured in *The Great Gatsby*.
___________.
4 There is one skating rink in Central Park.
___________.
5 The Carousel has 47 wooden horses to ride on.
___________.
6 The Boathouse Restaurant is next to the smallest lake in Central Park.
___________.
7 The Bow Bridge was used as a location in the TV show *Glee*.
___________.
8 The last time sheep were in the Sheep Meadow was 1943.
___________.

c Listen again with the audioscript on p. 73.

Wollman Skating Rink

the Carousel

Bow Bridge

USEFUL WORDS AND PHRASES

Learn these words and phrases.

alley /'æli/
aristocratic /ə'rɪstəkrætɪk/
gangsters /'gæŋstərz/
servants /'sərvənts/
tomb /tum/
fictional /'fɪkʃənl/
spectacular /spɛk'tækyələr/
currently /'kərəntli/
on the edge of /ɑn ði 'ɛdʒ əv/

What lies behind appearance is usually another appearance.
Mason Cooley, US writer

6B Judging by appearances

1 VOCABULARY the body

a Label the picture.

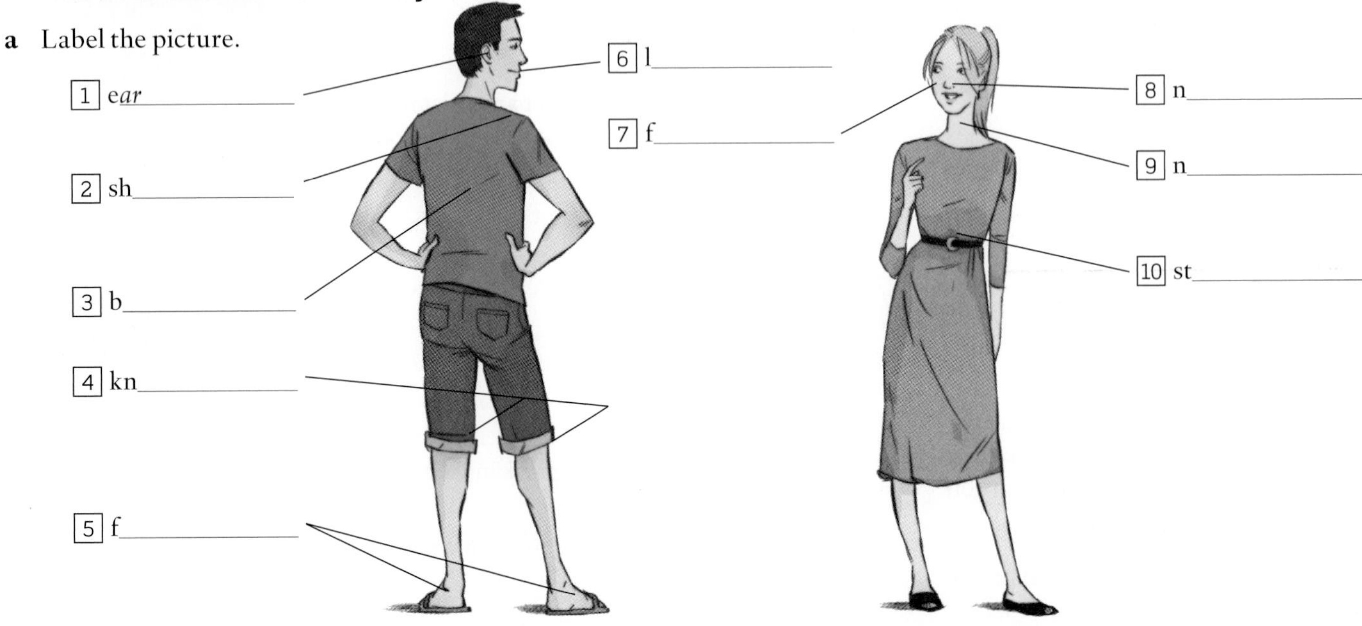

b Complete the sentences with the verbs in the box.

bite clap kick nod point smell smile ~~stare~~ taste touch throw whistle

1 It's rude to *stare* at people. It can make them feel uncomfortable.
2 You'll have to ________ the ball harder to score a goal.
3 Don't ________ the door – I just painted it.
4 Can you ________ the soup? I think it might need more salt.
5 I can ________ something burning. Did you turn off the oven?
6 When you're introduced to someone, you should ________, say hello, and shake hands.
7 We often ________ our heads when we agree with someone or understand what they said.
8 Did the audience ________ much at the end of the concert?
9 Lisa doesn't like dogs because she thinks they'll ________ her.
10 I often ________ a tune when I'm in the shower.
11 Don't drop your potato chip bag on the floor. ________ it in the trash.
12 When I'm abroad, it's sometimes easier to ________ at something I want in a store.

2 PRONUNCIATION diphthongs

a (Circle) the word with the different sound.

1 aɪ bike	bite smile height (weight)
2 eɪ train	face great eyes taste
3 oʊ phone	nose tongue throw toes
4 aʊ owl	sound crowd mouth shoulders
5 ɔɪ boy	point enjoy noise outgoing

b ONLINE Listen and check. Then listen again and repeat the words.

3 **GRAMMAR** modals of deduction: *might, can't, must*

a Circle the correct answers.

1 That woman *can't* / *must* be the new manager. Our new manager is a man.

2 You *must* / *can't* be tired. You had a long trip.

3 They *must* / *can't* have much money. They never go out.

4 Don't buy Oliver a book. He *might not* / *must not* like the same kind of things as you.

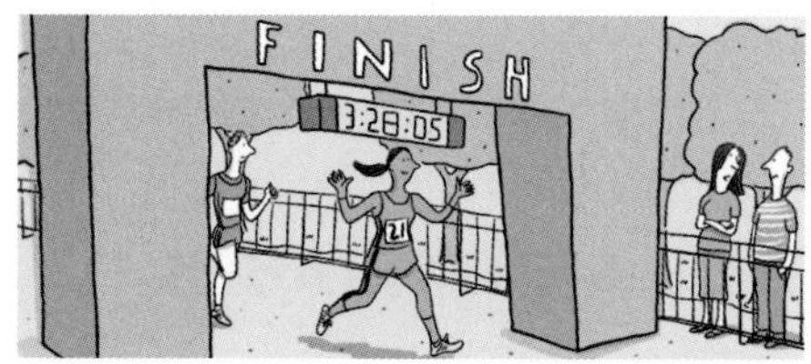

5 Paula *can't* / *might* be injured. That's her best time ever for a marathon.

6 Your neighbor *must* / *might not* have a good job. Those cars are really expensive!

b Complete the sentences with *must, might, might not,* or *can't*.

1 He lived in Argentina for five years so he _*must*_ speak Spanish well!
2 You ________ be very busy at work. You're always on Facebook!
3 I'm not sure, but Jenna ________ be on vacation. She didn't come to work today.
4 Mark passed all his final exams. His parents ________ be very proud.
5 Do you really think the US will win tonight? You ________ be serious! They have no chance!
6 Lucy wasn't feeling well this afternoon, so she ________ come to the party tonight. She said she would let us know later today.
7 I thought our neighbor was away for the weekend, but she ________ be – I just saw her in her yard.
8 It's very cold this evening and there are a lot of clouds. I think it ________ snow.

4 **LISTENING**

a ONLINE Listen to a radio program about the history of beauty. Check (✓) the three periods in history that the guest talks about.

1 ancient Greece ☐
2 the Egyptians ☐
3 the seventeenth century ☐
4 the Middle Ages ☐
5 the Romans ☐
6 the nineteenth century ☐

Glossary
lead = a soft, heavy, gray metal
powder = a dry substance in the form of very small grains

b Listen again and mark the sentences T (true) or F (false).

1 Women and men wore makeup in ancient Egypt. _*T*_
2 The Egyptians only wore black and white makeup. __
3 Egyptian men wore makeup to protect their skin from the sun. __
4 The Greeks thought that brown hair was the most beautiful. __
5 Greek women used a substance that was dangerous in their makeup. __
6 Beauty was very important to Roman people. __
7 Roman women put their makeup on themselves. __

c Listen again with the audioscript on p. 73.

5 READING

a Read the article once. What is the writer's opinion of Photoshopping?

1 Publishers should be able to use it as much as they want to. ☐
2 Publishers should be able to use it a little. ☐
3 Publishers shouldn't be able to use it at all. ☐

b Read the article again and choose the correct answers.

1 According to the article, publishers use Photoshopping to make people look...
(a) as good as possible.
b as interesting as possible.
c as thin as possible.

2 The article says that Photoshopped images have a bad effect on...
a girls of all ages.
b young teenagers.
c all kinds of people.

3 The new program gives a rating of 1 to an image with...
a no Photoshopping.
b a little Photoshopping.
c a lot of Photoshopping.

4 People complained about the Rachel Weisz ad because...
a it made her look a lot younger than she is.
b it showed the actress as she really is.
c it used an image of a different actress.

5 The people who will benefit most from the new tool are...
a advertisers.
b consumers.
c publishers.

c Look at the highlighted words and phrases. What do you think they mean? Use your dictionary to look up their meaning and pronunciation.

d Complete the sentences with one of the highlighted words or phrases.

1 Our neighbors are *relying* on us to water their plants while they're away.
2 Animal rights groups want experiments on animals to be ________.
3 We're ________ our vacation plans so that we arrive on Thursday instead of Saturday.
4 I can't ________ ________ how to download this program.
5 In general, the older you get, the more ________ you have in your skin.
6 In most countries, movies are given a ________ to show which age group they are suitable for.

Photoshopping: how much is too much?

Today, it is normal for magazines to show pictures of models and celebrities that have been "Photoshopped." This means that the original photos have been changed on a computer using Photoshop® software to make them look better. The beautiful people in the photographs have perfect skin, no fat on their stomachs, and no wrinkles on their faces. They look so perfect and beautiful that what we see can't be real. But some publishers and advertisers insist that Photoshopping is necessary so that celebrities and models always look their best.

On the other hand, health organizations have warned that digitally altering photographs may be dangerous. They say Photoshopped images are not realistic, and may have a negative effect on people. Psychologists agree with the health organizations. They say some people try so hard to look like the pictures in magazines that they get sick. In some cases, they want to be as thin as the models and so they stop eating enough. When they realize that it is impossible to look so good, they get depressed. This doesn't only happen to young girls, but it can happen to people of all ages. So what can be done to keep everybody happy? Two researchers at Dartmouth University in New Hampshire, think they have found the answer.

Professor Hany Farid and Doctor Eric Klee have developed a computer program that can detect how much Photoshopping has been used on an image. Their software gives a rating from 1 to 5 to the image – 1 for a few changes, and 5 for a lot of changes. Farid and Klee's idea is that publishers include the rating next to the image. That way, consumers will be able to figure out how realistic the image is.

News of Farid and Klee's system has come out at the same time as people have started criticizing the use of Photoshopping. They say that some advertisers are going too far with it. Recently, the actress Rachel Weisz appeared in an ad for an anti-aging beauty cream. In the ad, Ms. Weisz looked like a teenager – in fact, she's in her early forties. There were a lot of complaints about the image and the ad was eventually banned. Farid and Klee's system could solve two problems at the same time. First, it would serve as a kind of health warning for consumers, and second, it may stop advertisers from relying on Photoshopping so much.

USEFUL WORDS AND PHRASES

Learn these words and phrases.

stage /steɪdʒ/	go viral /goʊ 'vaɪrəl/
achieve /ə'tʃiv/	grow up /groʊ 'ʌp/
dye (hair) /daɪ/	take seriously /teɪk 'sɪriəsli/
judge (vb) /dʒʌdʒ/	vitally important /'vaɪtli ɪm'pɔrtnt/
carefree /'kɛrfri/	set an example /sɛt ən ɪg'zæmpl/

ONLINE FILE 6

Education is what survives when
what has been learned has been forgotten.

B. F. Skinner, US psychologist

7A Extraordinary school for boys

1 VOCABULARY education

a Complete the sentences with the correct word.

In the US

1 A school for children aged from about two to five is a p*reschool.*
2 A school for children aged from five to 10 is an el___________ school.
3 A school for children aged from 11 to 13 is a m___________ school.
4 A school for children aged from 13 to 18 is a h___________ school.
5 The class children are in is called a gr___________.
6 The school year is divided into two s___________.
7 Students have to apply to a c___________ before they can study there.

In the UK

8 A school for children aged from about two to five is a n___________ school.
9 A school for children aged from five to 11 is a pr___________ school.
10 A school for children aged from 11 to 18 is a s___________ school.
11 The person in charge of the school is the h___________ teacher.
12 The school year is divided into three t___________.
13 A school where children study, eat, and sleep is a b___________ school.
14 A person who goes on to study higher education usually studies at a u___________.

b Complete the sentences.

1 My friend was sick so she didn't t*ake* the exam.
2 Some of the students in that class b___________ very badly.
3 If you ch___________ on the exam, the teacher won't grade it.
4 A boy was s___________ for stealing money from other students.
5 You'll f___________ your classes if you don't work harder.
6 I'm taking my driver's test tomorrow. I hope I p___________!
7 I have exams next week, so I'm going to s___________ this weekend.
8 The students were p___________ by the teacher for being noisy in class.

2 PRONUNCIATION the letter *u*

a Circle the word with a different sound.

1 boot	2 up	3 bull	4 /yu/
(lunch)	couple	cut	cute
fruit	mussels	full	musical
scooter	pull	push	subtitles
true	tongue	put	uniform

b ONLINE Listen and check. Then listen again and repeat the words.

3 GRAMMAR first conditional and future time clauses + *when, until*, etc.

a Match the sentence halves.

1 Joe's parents will be furious [c]
2 As soon as I get my driver's license, [ ]
3 I'm sure we'll feel more relaxed [ ]
4 You'll have to go to a new school [ ]
5 He won't pass his test [ ]
6 Nina won't look for a job [ ]
7 I'll buy the book [ ]
8 If I don't feel well, [ ]

a unless he studies more.
b after we go on vacation.
~~c if he fails his exam again.~~
d before classes start.
e I'm going to buy a car.
f when your family moves to a new house.
g I'll stay in bed.
h until her daughter starts school.

b Complete the sentences with a word from the box.

if	until	~~when~~	after	unless	before

1 They won't have to wear a uniform *when* they go to high school.
2 I won't leave early ________ the teacher gives me permission.
3 Ella will be disappointed ________ she doesn't get good test scores.
4 I'll take a long vacation ________ classes end.
5 The teacher won't start the class ________ all the students are quiet.
6 I'll talk to my teachers ________ I choose which colleges to apply to.

c Complete the sentences with the correct form of the verbs in parentheses. Use the simple present or future (*will* / *won't*).

1 I*'ll do* do my homework as soon as I *get* home. (do, get)
2 We ________ late unless we ________. (be, hurry up)
3 My friends ________ a going-away party before they ________ to Korea. (have, go)
4 The bus ________ for you if you ________ on time. (not wait, not be)
5 If the teacher ________, we ________ the exam. (not come, not take)
6 James ________ home until he ________ a job. (not leave, find)
7 Alice ________ buy a car unless her parents ________ her the money. (not be able to, lend)
8 As soon as my boyfriend ________ his test scores, he ________ me. (get, call)
9 She ________ kindergarten until she ________ five years old. (not start, be)
10 You ________ better if you ________ every day. (play, practice)

4 READING

a Read the article once. What do South Korean students do in a *hagwon*?

1 sleep ☐
2 meet friends ☐
3 study ☐
4 have lunch ☐

When is it time to stop studying?

It's 10 p.m. and six government employees are out checking the streets of Seoul, South Korea. But these are not police officers looking for teenagers who are behaving badly. Their mission is to find children who are still studying. And stop them.

Education in South Korea is very competitive. The aim of almost every schoolchild is to get into one of the country's top universities. Only the students with the best grades get a place. The school day starts at 8 a.m. and students finish studying somewhere between 10 p.m. and 1 a.m. at night. This is because many go to private academies called *hagwon* after school. Around 74 percent of all students attend a hagwon after their regular classes finish. A year's course costs, on average, $2,600 per student. In Seoul, there are more private tutors than schoolteachers, and the most popular ones make millions of dollars a year from online and in-person classes. Most parents rely on private tutoring to get their children into a university.

With so much time spent in the classroom, all that students in South Korean high schools do is study and sleep. Some of them are so exhausted that they cannot stay awake the next day at school. It is a common sight to see a teacher explaining the lesson while a third of the students are asleep on their desks. The teachers don't seem to mind. There are even special pillows for sale that fit over the arms of the chairs to make sleeping in class more comfortable. Ironically, the students spend class time sleeping so that they can stay up late studying that night.

The South Korean government has been aware of the faults in the system for some time, but now they have passed some reforms. Today, schoolteachers have to meet certain standards or take additional training courses.

However, the biggest challenge for the government is the hagwons. Hagwons have been banned from having classes after 10 p.m., which is why there are street patrols looking for children who are studying after that time. If they find any in class, the owner of the hagwon is punished and the students are sent home. It's a strange world, where some children have to be told to stop studying while others are reluctant to start.

b Read the article again. Mark the sentences T (true) or F (false).

1 The street patrol in Seoul is looking for criminals. *F*
2 Most students in South Korea want to go to a university. ___
3 All private tutors in South Korea are paid well. ___
4 Schoolteachers are used to students who sleep in class. ___
5 The government is doing nothing to improve the education system. ___
6 Every academy must close before 9 p.m. ___
7 Students are punished if they are found in a *hagwon*. ___

c Look at the highlighted words and phrases. What do you think they mean? Use your dictionary to look up their meaning and pronunciation.

d Complete the sentences with one of the highlighted words or phrases from the text.

1 It's a real *challenge* for teachers to get all their students to pass their exams.
2 Jon hurt his neck, so he shouldn't use two ___________ in bed.
3 It's very ___________ to get into some universities. You need excellent grades.
4 My children are ___________ to go outside when it's cold.
5 People using laptops on the bus is a ___________ ___________ these days.
6 Mary needed extra help with math and history, so she has private ___________ to help her with these subjects.

5 LISTENING

a ONLINE Listen to a radio program about a new TV series. Which word describes the methods used by the teacher in the series?

1 unusual ☐
2 traditional ☐
3 old-fashioned ☐

b Listen again and correct the mistakes.

1 The series is a **drama**.
reality show
2 The students are **sixteen**.
____
3 A boy says he'll burn a **car**.
____
4 The teacher used to be a **soldier**.
____
5 He teaches **math** at a high school.
____
6 The students have to say **a number** in the game.
____
7 The students read Shakespeare to some **dogs**.
____
8 The punctuation lesson is in a **classroom**.
____
9 Some of the students think the teacher is **crazy**.
____
10 The next episode is the following **Friday**.
____

c Listen again with the audioscript on p.74.

USEFUL WORDS AND PHRASES

Learn these words and phrases.

a prodigy /ə 'prɑdədʒi/
determined (to do something) /dɪ'tərmənd/
resent (somebody) /rɪ'zɛnt/
take up (tennis) /'teɪk ʌp/
required /rɪ'kwaɪərd/
forbidden /fər'bɪdn/
outstanding /aʊt'stændɪŋ/
prestigious /prɛ'stɪdʒəs/
cause controversy /kɔz 'kɑntrəˌvəsi/
push (somebody) too hard /pʊʃ tu 'hɑrd/

Home is a place you grow up wanting to leave and grow old wanting to get back to.
John Ed Pearce, US journalist

7B Ideal home

1 GRAMMAR second conditional

a Match the sentence halves.

1 If we had the time, *d*
2 I would like my apartment more
3 Luke would be able to get a job in Tokyo
4 If my sister didn't work so hard,
5 If we bought a bigger house in the suburbs,
6 If they could live anywhere they wanted to,
7 We'd have more privacy
8 I wouldn't want to live in New York City,

a she could spend more time with her children.
b they'd move to California.
c if he could speak better Japanese.
~~d we'd do the housework ourselves.~~
e if we didn't have to share an apartment.
f unless I earned a lot of money.
g if it were on the top floor.
h we'd be able to have a dog.

b Complete the sentences with the correct form of the verbs in parentheses. Use the second conditional.

1 If I *had* more time, *I'd paint* my room myself. (have, paint)
2 Lucy's room ______ better organized if she ______ it more often. (be, clean)
3 I ______ my car to work if I ______ a parking space. (not take, not have)
4 ______ you ______ your job if you ______ a lot of money? (keep, win)
5 Jack ______ his mother every day if he ______ a girlfriend. (not call, have)
6 We ______ so often if our stove ______ broken. (not eat out, not be)
7 If I ______ a big argument with my neighbors because of a problem, I ______ away. (have, not move)
8 If our house ______ so small, you ______ all stay the night. (not be, can)
9 ______ you ______ if you ______ your alarm? (wake up, not set)
10 If we ______ another bathroom, there ______ a line for the shower. (have, not be)

2 PRONUNCIATION sentence stress

a ONLINE Listen and complete the sentences.

1 If I *exercised* more, I'd be a lot healthier.
2 I'd ______ my own ______ if I had a garden.
3 Would you ______ a ______ if you had enough money?
4 If it were my house, I ______ ______ the kitchen bigger.
5 I ______ ______ so hard if I didn't have pay so much rent.

b Listen again and repeat the sentences. Copy the rhythm.

c Match the words with the same sounds.

1 **co**sy — b
2 **c**eiling
3 t**ow**n
4 c**ou**ntry
5 spa**ci**ous
6 bal**c**ony

a s**u**burb
b **k**itchen
c wal**k**way
d **sh**ower
e gr**ou**nd
f ba**se**ment

d ONLINE Listen and check. Then listen again and repeat the words.

3 VOCABULARY houses

a Complete the sentences with *in* or *on* and a phrase from the box.

the fourth floor the outskirts ~~a suburb~~
the West Coast the woods

1 We're looking at apartments outside of the city. We want to live *in a suburb*.
2 Sara bought a small cabin ______ because she loves looking at the birds and trees.
3 Here's your key. Your room is ______.
4 I'd love to live by the ocean, maybe ______.
5 Chris lives ______ of the city, so he has to commute downtown every day.

b Complete the ads.

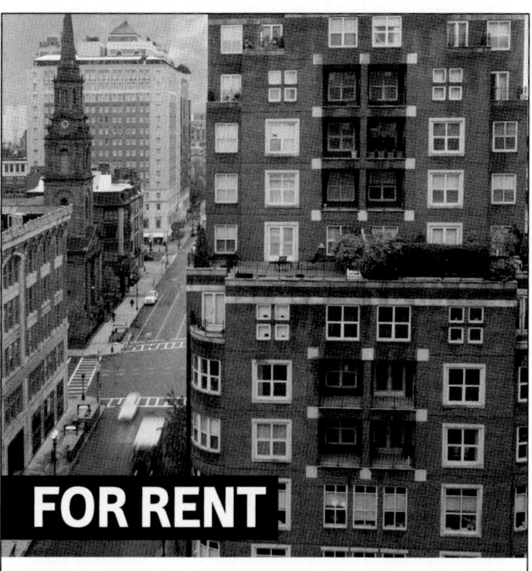

This [1] m*odern* apartment is on the [2] t__________ fl__________ of a building with magnificent views of the Charles River. It has three bedrooms, a bathroom, and a large [3] sp__________ kitchen. The living room has a [4] w__________ fl__________ and there is carpet in all the bedrooms. There is a large [5] b__________ outside the living room with space for a table, chairs, and plants. There is a garage in the [6] b__________ with room for two cars.

This old-fashioned [7] c__________ is situated on a quiet mountain road. It has a kitchen, living room, and two small, but [8] c__________ bedrooms. All the rooms have low [9] c__________, and the walls are made of [10] l__________. There is a [11] f__________ in the living room, but the house also has central heat. There is a small [12] d__________ on the side of the house with a pretty view of the mountains. Several beautiful stone [13] s__________ lead to the front [14] e__________ of the house.

4 LISTENING

a ONLINE Listen to a guide giving a tour of Elvis Presley's home, Graceland. Number the places and parts of the house in the order you hear about them.

a TV room ☐
b music room ☐
c living room ☐
d the front door *1*
e dining room ☐
f basement ☐
g the walls ☐

b Listen again and answer the questions.

1 When was the house built?
In the early twentieth century.

2 How long did Elvis Presley live in Graceland?

3 When did he get married?

4 How many children did he have?

5 How many TVs did Elvis Presley have in the TV room?

6 At what time did Elvis Presley usually wake up?

7 Other than eating meals, what did Elvis Presley like to do in the dining room?

8 On what floor did Elvis Presley's parents have a room?

c Listen again with the audioscript on p. 74.

5 READING

a Read the article once and choose the best title for it.

1 Top tips on buying a new house ☐
2 Finding out where you really live ☐
3 The most interesting houses to visit in London ☐

1 _D_

Are you interested in the history of your house? If you are, then you might want to get in touch with a house historian. A house historian's job is to find out what has happened to a particular house in the past. They try to discover who built the house, who has lived in the building since it was built, and what was on the site of the building before. Their research can uncover all kinds of interesting information.

2 __

We spoke to house historian Tracy Collins, who told us some of her stories. One of the houses she had to research was an apartment at 200 Oxford Street in London. She discovered that the author George Orwell had once stayed with the owners of the apartment. He had slept in the smallest bedroom in the apartment, which was very dark. Later, when he wrote his novel *1984*, he used the room as the inspiration for the famous Room 101. On another occasion, she was looking into the story of an apartment building in Orchard Court, also in London. She found out that the apartment had been used by spies during the World War II. First of all, the spies were invited to the building for a job interview. If they were successful, they took a training course. After the course, they returned to the apartment for their instructions. Then, they were sent on a mission. But Tracy's third story is even more dramatic. When she was investigating a house in another part of London, she discovered that a murder had happened there!

3 __

However, house historians do not only focus on one particular house. They also find out about the area where the house was built. Some areas are completely different now than they were in the past. One example is an area in Central London called Belgravia. Today, it is one of the richest neighborhoods in the world, but in the early nineteenth century, it was a poorer area. People used to go there during the day to hang their laundry or to collect plants for food. At night, many people would avoid the area because it was full of criminals.

4 __

If you can't afford to pay a professional to research the history of your house, you can try to research the past yourself. The best place to start is to find all the official documents belonging to your house. These should give you some idea of who the previous owners were. After that, you should go to the office that has the official documents of your area. Some of these go back hundreds of years! You may not find out anything particularly interesting about your house, but you'll definitely to enjoy the search.

b Match the headings with the paragraphs in the article. There are two extra headings that you do not need to use.

A What was there before?
B How much do house historians charge?
C How can you do it yourself?
~~D What does a house historian do?~~
E What do you need to become a house historian?
F What has one house historian discovered?

c Look at the highlighted words and phrases. What do you think they mean? Use your dictionary to look up their meaning and pronunciation.

d Complete the sentences with one of the highlighted words or phrases.

1 The police are _looking_ _into_ a robbery at the school.
2 I'm going to ________ my family history.
3 Some of the houses in this town ________ ________ to the seventeenth century.
4 I didn't paint my living room. It was done by the ________ owner of the house.
5 When the washing machine finishes, can you ________ the clothes to dry, please?
6 You should always read the ________ before you try to build a bookcase.

USEFUL WORDS AND PHRASES

Learn these words and phrases.

bookcase /ˈbʊkkeɪs/
property /ˈprɑpərti/
tower /ˈtaʊər/
hang (a picture) /hæŋ/
overlook (sth) /oʊvərˈlʊk/
remain /rɪˈmeɪn/
settle (in a village) /ˈsetl/
plain /pleɪn/
peace and quiet /pis ən ˈkwaɪət/
turn into /tərn ˈɪntə/

ONLINE FILE 7

Practical English Boys' night out

1 MAKING SUGGESTIONS

Complete the dialogue with the words in the box.

could Let's great going about ~~go~~
don't feel

Jess I'm hungry. Where should we [1] *go* for lunch?
Phil I think there's a burger place near here.
[2] ______________ go there.
Jess Phil, you know I don't eat meat.
Phil Oops! Sorry, I forgot. How about [3] ______________ to that Italian place you like?
Jess Aren't you on a diet?
Phil Well, yes. But we [4] ______________ order a salad.
Jess No, thanks . I don't [5] ______________ like a salad today. Why [6] ______________ we try that new sushi restaurant?
Phil I'd rather not. I'm not crazy about raw fish.
Jess Well, what [7] ______________ having some Chinese? I know a really good place.
Phil That's a [8] ______________ idea. Where is it?

2 SOCIAL ENGLISH

Complete the dialogue.

Ellie Joe?
Joe Hi, Ellie.
Ellie It's Mom's birthday, and you're late. Where are you, [1] *anyway*?
Joe That's [2] w______________ I'm calling. I'm not going to [3] m______________ it for dinner.
Ellie Why not?
Joe I'm at my sister's house. She's [4] o______________ to Miami tomorrow to start her new job and I wanted to say goodbye.
Ellie But why tonight? It's [5] n______________ that I don't think you should say goodbye, but couldn't you do it tomorrow?
Joe Not really. I wanted to have a [6] w______________ with her about something before she left.
Ellie Mom's going to be upset.
Joe Sorry, Ellie. It won't [7] h______________ again. I'll call you tomorrow.

3 READING

a Read the text and answer the questions.

1 Where can you get a map of New York?
From the Visitor Information Center.
2 How much is a seven-day MetroCard? ______________
3 What is the best time to visit the Empire State Building? ______________
4 How many islands do you visit on the Statue of Liberty tour? ______________
5 What time does the bike tour around Central Park leave? ______________
6 What day can you visit MoMA in the evening? ______________

What to do in New York

To explore New York, you'll need a map and a MetroCard. Maps are available at the Visitor Information Center and you can buy a MetroCard at any of the subway stations. A seven-day pass costs $30, and you can use it on the subways and city buses. Below are some places you might like to visit.

Empire State Building
Take an elevator to the 86th floor to get the best views of the city. Come at 8:30 a.m. to avoid the crowds, or try visiting during lunch and dinner hours from Monday to Wednesday when it's quieter. An adult ticket is $25, or you can get an express pass for $50. Buy your ticket online to reduce your time standing in line.

Statue of Liberty
This famous New York landmark is only accessible by ferry. You should get your tickets in advance either online, by phone, or in person at the ferry departure points. An adult ticket costs $24 and includes a tour of Liberty Island and a visit to the Immigration Museum on Ellis Island.

Central Park
Central Park is very big, so the best way to see it is by bike. It costs $20 to rent one for two hours and ride around the park on your own, or you can book a tour, which costs about $47 per person. The tour leaves daily at 9 a.m.

MoMA
MoMA is the most influential museum of modern art in the world, so it's definitely worth a visit. There are famous works by Picasso, Kandinsky, Andy Warhol, and many, many more. It is open from 10 a.m. to 5:30 p.m. (8 p.m. on Fridays) and tickets are $25 for adults.

b Underline five words or phrases you don't know. Use your dictionary to look up their meaning and pronunciation.

I always say shopping is cheaper than a psychiatrist.
Tammy Faye Bakker, US TV host

8A Sell and tell

1 VOCABULARY shopping

a Complete the sentences.

1 We always book our flights on*line*.
2 We spent all day checking out the different stores at the m__________.
3 Are you sure that jacket f__________ you?
4 My sister buys all her clothes at an ou__________ st__________ because it's cheaper.
5 There was a line at the b__________ st__________ because all the novels were half price.
6 That's a beautiful shirt. Why don't you t__________ it o__________?
7 They went to the ph__________ to buy some aspirin.
8 That store is having a s__________. All winter coats are 20% off.
9 I wouldn't buy that dress, if I were you. It doesn't s__________ you.
10 The sports section is on the top floor of the d__________ st__________.

making nouns from verbs

b Complete the text with the noun form of the verbs in parentheses.

A month ago, I bought a video game online for my son's birthday. They sent me an order confirmation saying that [1] *delivery* (deliver) would take about ten days. Two weeks later I began to worry. The seller had received my [2] __________ (pay), but the video game had not arrived. So I decided to make a [3] __________ (complain). I sent an email to the seller with a copy of the order confirmation as an [4] __________ (attach). I received a [5] __________ (respond) immediately saying that the seller would look into the incident. After that, I heard nothing for three days, so I sent another email demanding an [6] __________ (explain). This time I had more [7] __________ (succeed) and the seller said he would send another copy of the game. If I don't receive it before my son's birthday, I'm going to ask for [8] __________ (compensate).

2 GRAMMAR reported speech: sentences and questions

a Circle the correct answer. Check (✓) if both are correct.

1 Matt said yesterday that he *will* | *would* come shopping.
2 We asked the salesperson how much *it was* | *was it*.
3 My sister *said me* | *told me* that she had spent all her money at the sale.
4 I asked Lucy where *she bought* | *did she buy* her clothes.
5 You told me that you *may* | *might* go shopping on Saturday.
6 My brother asked me *if I can* | *if I could* lend him some money to buy a new video game.
7 Kate said that she *had to* | *must* go to the supermarket.
8 I asked my sister *whether* | *that* the dress suited me, and she said I looked great!
9 Carolina asked me what *I wanted* | *did I want* from the mall.
10 Nick said that he couldn't pay me back, because he *has forgotten* | *had forgotten* his wallet.

b Change the direct speech into reported sentences and questions.

1 I haven't been to the sale yet.
2 I hate buying clothes.
3 How much did you pay for your jacket?
4 I'll check the price online.
5 Where's the shoe department?
6 Does the shirt fit you?

1 Jackie said *(that) she hadn't been to the sale yet*.
2 My boyfriend told me __________.
3 They asked me __________.
4 You said __________.
5 I asked her __________.
6 The salesperson asked me __________.

3 READING

a Read the article once and match the headings with the paragraphs.

A Check out the company you are buying from
B Keep copies of all documents
C Check the terms and conditions of the seller
D Check your computer before and after buying online
~~E Always use a credit card~~
F Be security-conscious

b Look at the highlighted words and phrases. What do you think they mean? Use your dictionary to look up their meaning and pronunciation.

c Complete the sentences with one of the highlighted words or phrases.

1 I don't understand people who stand in line all night just to buy the most *up-to-date* smartphones.
2 You should change your passwords frequently so that ____________ can't get into your computer.
3 I put a ____________ on the garage door to protect my car.
4 My friend said she would meet me outside the movie theater, but she didn't ____________ ____________.
5 I forgot to ____________ ____________ of Facebook, and my boss read my messages.
6 Some people don't bother with a ____________ these days – they only have a smartphone.

Top tips for safe online shopping

US shoppers spent $202 billion buying items online in 2011. Experts predict that our spending will increase to $327 billion by 2016. Read on to find out how you can protect yourself when you are shopping online.

1 *E*

When you buy things on the Internet, there is always a chance that something may go wrong. The product could be broken when you get it, or it might not turn up at all. If this happens, your credit card will offer you the best protection. Some credit cards allow you to dispute a purchase, meaning the credit card company will stop payment on a purchase until the matter is resolved. This is why a credit card is the best way to pay.

2 __

Make sure that your device, for example your laptop or tablet, is safe to use at all times. It should be protected by up-to-date antivirus software, and you should also install a personal firewall, which will stop hackers from attacking your system. Make sure that your firewall is turned on before you start shopping, and when you finish be sure to log out of the system, especially if you share your computer with other people.

3 __

Take a minute to look at the website before you buy anything. Check that the company has a geographical address as well as a landline telephone number, and write down these details. It is generally better to use sellers that you know about or ones that have been recommended to you.

4 __

Somewhere on the seller's website, there should be a list of all your rights (for example, what to do if you have a problem with the item you bought, or if it hasn't arrived). Make sure you read this before you decide to shop there. If you can't find the list, you should probably choose a different website.

5 __

A special icon on your screen will tell you if the website you are using is safe. The icon is in the shape of a padlock, and you can find it on the browser bar at the top or bottom of the screen. Another indication of a safe website is its address. The address should begin with "https" and not "http" – the **s** stands for secure.

6 __

The final stage of online shopping is the order confirmation. This is proof that you have bought a product from this company, and it contains the special reference number for your order. You should always print this information and keep it somewhere safe – you might need it if there is a problem.

4 PRONUNCIATION the letters *ai*

a Circle the word where ***ai*** is pronounced differently.

1 barg**ai**n	vill**ai**n	(p**ai**d)
2 cert**ai**n	compl**ai**n	r**ai**n
3 p**ai**nting	s**ai**d	w**ai**t
4 **ai**rline	f**ai**r	r**ai**se
5 capt**ai**n	pl**ai**n	em**ai**l
6 br**ai**n	h**ai**r	st**ai**rs

b ONLINE Listen and check. Then listen again and repeat the words.

5 LISTENING

a ONLINE Listen to a conversation about a complaint. Answer the questions.

1 Where was Sam flying to when he had a problem?

____

2 How many emails did Sam send to the Airline?

____

b Listen again and choose the correct answers.

1 Sam usually pays for Preferred Access because…
  a he's always late for flights.
  (b) he hates waiting in line.
  c he's really scared of flying.
  d he likes sitting by the window.

2 Sam's problem at the airport was…
  a there wasn't any space left for baggage.
  b he'd forgotten to take his passport.
  c he didn't get the service he'd paid for.
  d there was a long line at the check-in desk.

3 In Sam's first email…
  a he complained about the airline staff.
  b he said the airline should stop Preferred Access.
  c he asked the airline for a small amount of money.
  d he told the airline he would never fly with them again.

4 The man who replied to the first email…
  a didn't offer to give Sam any money.
  b took a long time to write back.
  c said he would send Sam a check for $20.
  d didn't believe Sam's story.

5 The result of Sam's complaint was that…
  a the airline gave him two free flights.
  b he got exactly what he asked for.
  c he will never use the airline again.
  d the airline gave him more than he asked for.

c Listen again with the audioscript on p. 74.

USEFUL WORDS AND PHRASES

Learn these words and phrases.

hesitate /ˈhɛzəteɪt/
refund (vb) /riˈfʌnd/
slip (vb) /slɪp/
spoil /spɔɪl/
swear /swɛr/
faulty /ˈfɔlti/
a satisfied customer /ə sætəsfaɪd ˈkʌstəmər/
make (sth) clear /meɪk klɪr/
get into an argument /gɛt ˈɪntu ən ˈɑrgyəmənt/
waste your time /weɪst yər taɪm/

People who work sitting down get paid more than people who work standing up.
Ogden Nash, US poet

8B What's the right job for you?

1 VOCABULARY work

a Complete the text with a word from the box.

applied downsized self-employed ~~overtime~~ promoted resign retire set shifts training

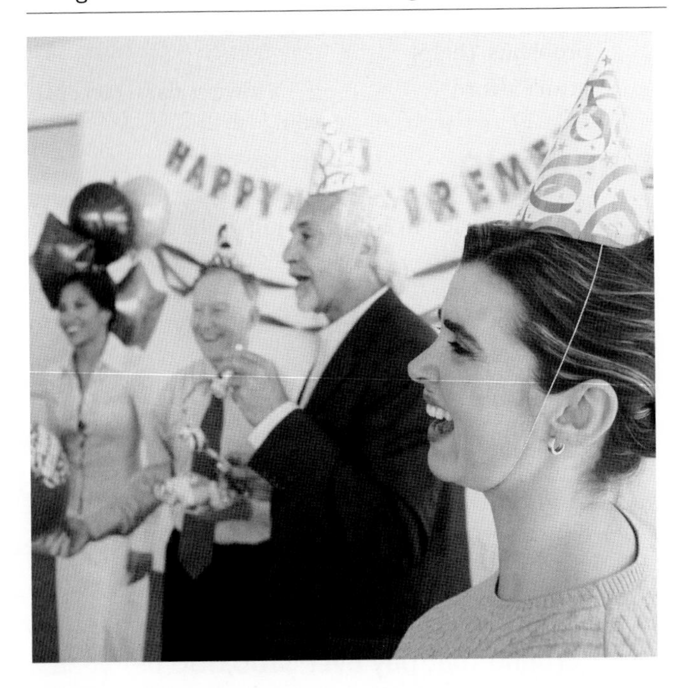

My father's first job was in a small local company. He had to work a lot of [1] *overtime*, which he really hated. One day, he decided to [2] ______ from the job. He [3] ______ for a new job with a multinational company. At first, he worked [4] ______ in a factory. Then, he was [5] ______ to supervisor. Later, he was [6] ______ because business was bad. After that, my dad took a [7] ______ course in business management, and he [8] ______ up his own business. He really enjoyed being [9] ______—he was his own boss so he could make all the rules! He didn't [10] ______ until he was 65 years old. This photo shows the party they gave him on his last day.

b Complete the sentences with a noun form of the word in **bold**.

1 A *musician* plays **music** for a living.
2 They're looking for a ______ to **translate** some documents into Chinese.
3 The company **employs** over 200 people – 150 of whom have full-time ______.
4 Hanna studied **pharmacy** because she wanted to be a ______.
5 When we **retire**, we'd like to spend our ______ with our grandchildren.
6 They're going to **promote** someone, but we don't know who's going to get the ______.
7 Ken got a **law** degree because he wanted to be a ______.
8 My son is studying **science** because he wants to be a ______.
9 My colleague tried to **resign**, but our boss wouldn't accept his ______.
10 I **applied** for the job, but I sent in the ______ too late.
11 A ______ has to get up early to take care of his **farm**.
12 He wasn't **qualified** for the job, because he didn't have the right ______.

c Complete the sentences with the correct words.

1 My niece is still *in* school, but she has a *part-time* job on Friday nights and Saturdays.
2 Oliver is ______ his third year of college, but he hopes to get a ______ job for the summer. He'll work until the end of August.
3 My boyfriend works ______ a multinational company. He's ______ charge ______ human resources.
4 Dan got a Ph.D when he was ______ college. Now, he's very ______ ______.
5 Teresa has a ______ job. She works from 8 a.m. to 6 p.m. every day. Her job is ______, so she hopes to stay there until she retires.
6 My cousin didn't use to have a job, so he was ______. Now he's ______-______ and he really enjoys working for himself.

2 PRONUNCIATION word stress

a Underline the stressed syllable.

1 a|pply
2 down|size
3 em|ploy|ment
4 far|mer
5 law|yer
6 o|ver|time
7 mu|si|cian
8 per|ma|nent
9 pro|mo|tion
10 qua|li|fy
11 re|sign
12 re|tire
13 sa|la|ry
14 tem|po|ra|ry
15 un|em|ployed

b ONLINE Listen and check. Then listen again and repeat.

3 GRAMMAR gerunds and infinitives

a Circle the correct answer.

1 She's going to practice *giving* | *to give* her presentation.
2 My colleague isn't very good at *making* | *to make* decisions.
3 Did they promise *paying* | *to pay* you on time?
4 The government is trying to make it easier for companies *firing* | *to fire* employees.
5 My brother regrets *not going* | *not to go* to college.
6 Can you remember *having* | *to have* your first job interview?
7 He really enjoys *working* | *to work* on a team.
8 Don't forget *signing* | *to sign* the application form.

b Correct any mistakes in the highlighted verbs. Check (✓) if the sentence is correct.

1 It isn't easy finding a good job these days.
to find
2 My brother has decided to resign from his job.
____
3 I'd like getting a job abroad, preferably in Canada.
____
4 She spent three months to take a training course.
____
5 They'll have to increase the salary to attract the right applicants.
____
6 He gave up to play basketball when he went to college.
____
7 The interviewer asked me to wait in the reception area.
____
8 Fill out an application form can take a long time.
____

c Complete the sentences with the gerund or the infinitive form of the verbs in parentheses.

1 I forgot *to tell* my boss I was going to the doctor's. (tell)
2 My girlfriend told me ___________ her outside the movie theater. (meet)
3 ___________ heavy weights can give you back problems. (lift)
4 It's always difficult ___________ good seats if we don't get to the theater early. (find)
5 They're afraid of ___________ fired. (get)
6 Why don't you try ___________ to a smaller company? (apply)
7 My colleague doesn't mind ___________ me with my problems. (help)
8 I can't afford ___________ a lower salary. (accept)

4 READING

a Read the article once. Which job / jobs require a special qualification?

Do something different and get a super salary!

Would you like your friends to be impressed by your job? Do you want to earn a better salary? Here are some of the strangest jobs around that pay over $100,000 per year.

A Ethical hacker

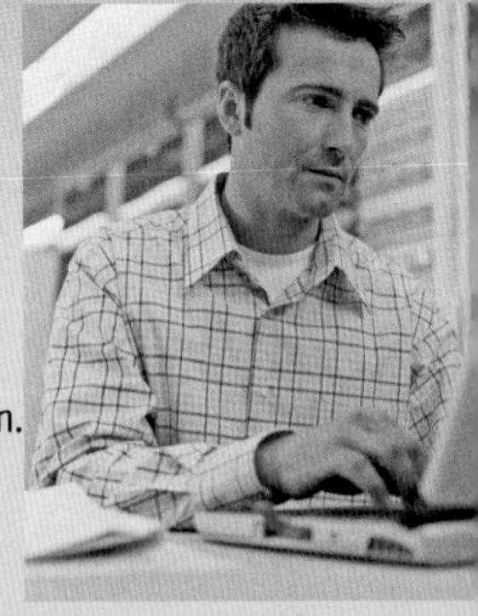

What they do

A hacker doesn't usually have permission to enter a company's computer system. But an ethical hacker is actually employed by a company to take care of the system. Ethical hackers have to protect a company's IT network from real hackers. Their job is to stop professional criminals from entering the company's system to steal confidential information.

How to get a job

After getting a degree in IT, you have to work in computers for a few years until you have enough experience in programming. After that, you need to get a special qualification called the Certified Ethical Hacker (CEH) certificate, which lets you work as an ethical hacker. Salaries start between $50,000 and $100,000, depending on your experience and where you work.

B Golf-ball diver

What they do

Not all of the golf balls on a golf course end up in the hole on the green. In fact, golfers hit a surprisingly high number of them into the lake. Golf-ball divers do exactly what the job title suggests: they dive into the lake to collect the balls. Professional divers only work during the day. They have to wear special diving equipment, as well as a pair of thick waterproof gloves to keep their hands from getting cold.

How to get a job

To be a golf-ball diver, you need an advanced certificate in scuba diving. Once you have the right qualifications, you can choose to work for a company or to work for yourself. If you work for a company, the company will organize your schedule for you, whereas if you're self-employed, you have to contact the golf courses yourself. Golf-ball divers are paid between seven and 12 cents per ball, and on an average day, they can collect about 4,000 balls. If you work from 7 a.m. to noon four days a week, you can earn up to $100,000 per year.

C Forensic dentist

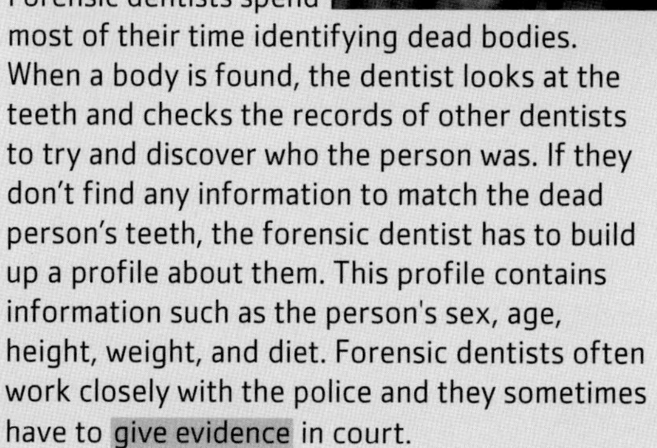

What they do

Forensic dentists spend most of their time identifying dead bodies. When a body is found, the dentist looks at the teeth and checks the records of other dentists to try and discover who the person was. If they don't find any information to match the dead person's teeth, the forensic dentist has to build up a profile about them. This profile contains information such as the person's sex, age, height, weight, and diet. Forensic dentists often work closely with the police and they sometimes have to give evidence in court.

How to get a job

First, you need to get a degree in dentistry and after that, you can take a postgraduate course to become a forensic dentist. You have to work in a laboratory for many years until you are promoted to department head. The starting salary is between $69,000 to $146,000 per year, but forensic dentists who go to court can earn up to $180,000.

b Read the article again. Answer the questions with the letters A, B, or C.

In which profession does the employee…?

1 work outside *B*
2 try to stop a crime ___
3 take part in criminal investigations ___
4 need two degrees ___
5 get paid depending on the results of a day's work ___
6 do something that could be illegal ___

c Look at the highlighted words and phrases. What do you think they mean? Use your dictionary to look up their meaning and pronunciation.

5 LISTENING

a ONLINE Listen to five speakers talking about their first job. Check (✓) the speakers who enjoyed their jobs and put an ✗ if they didn't enjoy them.

Speaker 1 ☑ Speaker 4 ☐
Speaker 2 ☐ Speaker 5 ☐
Speaker 3 ☐

b Listen again and mark the sentences T (true) or F (false).

1 Speaker 1 was downsized after three years. *F*
2 Speaker 2 went abroad when he was a student. ___
3 Speaker 3 didn't earn any money doing the job. ___
4 Speaker 4 got along well with his colleagues. ___
5 Speaker 5 wasn't wearing the right clothes for the job. ___

c Listen again with the audioscript on p. 75.

USEFUL WORDS AND PHRASES

Learn these words and phrases.

entrepreneurs /ɑntrəprə'nərz/
a product /ə 'prɑdʌkt/
be successful /bi sək'sɛsfl/
impressive /ɪm'prɛsɪv/
profitable /'prɑfətəbl/
to make it /tə 'meɪk ɪt/
make a presentation /meɪk ə prɛzn'teɪʃn/
reject somebody's idea /rɪ'dʒɛkt aɪdɪə/
share the profits /ʃɛr ðə 'prɑfəts/

ONLINE **FILE 8**

We must believe in luck. For how else can we explain the success of those we don't like?

Jean Cocteau, French writer and artist

9A Lucky encounters

1 GRAMMAR third conditional

a Complete the sentences with the correct form of the verbs in parentheses.

1 If you'd told me you weren't hungry, I *wouldn't have made* any dinner. (make)
2 They ______ on time if the train hadn't broken down. (arrive)
3 If he ______ his keys, he wouldn't have gone back home. (not forget)
4 You would have seen my message if you ______ ______ your cell phone. (check)
5 I ______ the flight if the plane hadn't been delayed. (miss)
6 If you'd concentrated on what you were doing, you ______ so many mistakes. (not make)
7 If I'd known it was going to snow, I ______ ______ a coat. (wear)
8 We ______ Joe if we'd known you didn't like him. (not invite)

b Complete the second sentence so that it means the same as the first.

1 I got to the restaurant late because I went to the wrong place first.
If I hadn't gone to the wrong place first, *I wouldn't have gotten to the restaurant late*.
2 They called us because they had a problem.
They wouldn't have called us ______ ______.
3 Helen didn't have the right qualifications so she didn't get the job.
If Helen had had the right qualifications, ______ ______.
4 Alex wasn't very careful with his glasses, so he broke them.
If Alex had been more careful with his glasses, ______ ______.
5 You got lost because you didn't follow my directions.
You wouldn't have gotten lost ______ ______.
6 We didn't play tennis this afternoon because it was windy.
If it hadn't been so windy this afternoon, ______ ______.

2 PRONUNCIATION sentence stress

a ONLINE Listen and complete the sentences.

1 We'd have gotten to the movie theater on time if we'd *taken* a *taxi*.
2 If you'd ______ me about the ______, I'd have gone.
3 She would have bought the coat if it ______ been so ______.
4 If I'd ______ you were ______, I wouldn't have called.
5 If they ______ ______ so badly in the second half, they would have won the game.
6 The flight would have been cheaper if we'd ______ last ______.

b Listen again and repeat the sentences. Copy the rhythm.

3 VOCABULARY making adjectives and adverbs

a Complete the chart with the two adjective forms of each noun in the box.

care ~~comfort~~ fortune luck patience

	+	–
adjective ending in *-able*	1 *comfortable*	2 *uncomfortable*
adjective ending in *-ate*	3 ______	4 ______
adjective ending in *-ful* / *-less*	5 ______	6 ______
adjective ending in *-ient*	7 ______	8 ______
adjective ending in *-y*	9 ______	10 ______

b Complete the text with the correct adjective or adverb of the nouns in parentheses.

An American teenager made a [1] *careless* (care) mistake yesterday when he forgot to check a river for alligators before going swimming. Kaleb Langdale found himself in the [2] ____________ (comfort) position of sharing the water with an alligator, which started to attack him. He was [3] ____________ (luck) enough to escape the first attack and he began to swim to the bank, where his friends were [4] ____________ (desperation) waiting for him. [5] ____________ (fortune), the ten-foot animal attacked again, and this time it held on to Kaleb's arm. [6] ____________ (luck), Kaleb managed to get away, but he lost his right arm in the process. Kaleb is now resting [7] ____________ (comfort) in the hospital, despite his horrific injuries. He recommends that anybody who goes swimming in the Caloosahatchee River in Florida check the water [8] ____________ (care) before jumping in.

4 LISTENING

a ONLINE Listen to five speakers talking about superstitions. Match the speakers with the pictures.

b Listen again and match the speakers with the sentences below.

Speaker 1 *b*

Speaker 2 ____

Speaker 3 ____

Speaker 4 ____

Speaker 5 ____

a He / She was frustrated by this superstition.

~~b He / She does something dangerous because of a superstition.~~

c He / She says that this superstition used to be a kind of self-defense.

d He / She does something to make something good happen.

e He / She says this superstition is associated with death.

c Listen again with the audioscript on p. 75.

5 READING

a Read the article once and number the paragraphs in the correct order.

A lucky escape

A __ After he had seen the pictures of the crash, Mr. Hamilton called emergency services. The police came immediately and an ambulance arrived on the scene soon after. A spokesperson from the ambulance service said that the couple both had minor injuries, but only one of them had been taken to the hospital. A neighbor said that she had seen the young couple having an argument in the car when the accident happened.

B __ Instead of going downstairs to talk to the couple in his yard, Mr. Hamilton went to look at the pictures on his security cameras. He had installed the cameras a few years earlier to deter people from stealing the potted plants outside his front door. The Hamiltons live on the corner of a road that leads to the main road, and passersby can easily step over the low wall that surrounds his yard. When he played back the pictures of the accident, he could not believe his eyes.

C _1_ An elderly couple from Central England, had a shock last night after they had gone to bed. Seventy-five-year old Howard Hamilton and his wife were just falling asleep when they heard a big bang in their front yard. They both jumped straight out of bed to look out the window and see what had happened. What they saw was a badly damaged car lying in their front yard. Next to the car there was a young couple hugging each other. Once Mr. Hamilton realized that nobody had been hurt, he decided to go and find out what had caused the accident.

D __ Apparently, this is the fourth time that a car has driven through the wall of Mr. Hamilton's yard. This is because drivers often go around the corner too fast, and lose control of their vehicles. Mr. Hamilton's sister Joyce, who lives next door, said that it had been lucky that nobody had been walking on the sidewalk. She said that she didn't know what would have happened if there had been somebody there. Regarding the number of accidents that have happened on the corner, she said, "We're getting used to it."

E __ On the recording, he saw that the girlfriend had been driving the car. He watched her turn the corner and lose control of the car. The car crashed right through the wall of his yard and came to a stop in the middle of the lawn. But the most dramatic thing is what had happened to her boyfriend. Before the crash, the sunroof of the car had been open. When the car hit the wall, Mr. Hamilton saw the boyfriend fly out of the sunroof and land heavily on the lawn. Miraculously, he was not hurt. Instead, he got up, and went to find his girlfriend. She didn't seem to be badly injured either – she appeared to be wearing her seat belt when the accident happened.

b Read the article in the correct order and answer the questions.

1 When did Mr. and Mrs. Hamilton hear the accident happen?
They heard it after they had gone to bed.
2 What did they see when they looked out their bedroom window?
______
3 Why had Mr. Hamilton installed security cameras in his yard?
______
4 Why did the car crash through the wall of Mr. Hamilton's yard?
______
5 What happened to the boyfriend?
______
6 What happened to the couple when emergency services arrived?
______
7 What did a neighbor say about the couple in the accident?
______
8 Why are there so many accidents on that corner?
______

c Look at the highlighted words and phrases. What do you think they mean? Use your dictionary to look up their meaning and pronunciation.

d Complete the sentences with one of the highlighted words or phrases.

1 I *had a shock* last night when the phone rang at midnight.
2 You should always call ______ ______ if there is a fire in your house.
3 The library is just ______ ______ ______ from my house.
4 Rachel fell off her bike yesterday, but luckily she only had ______ ______.
5 If you drive fast, it's easy to ______ ______ of the car and crash.
6 ______ described what happened to the police.

USEFUL WORDS AND PHRASES

Learn these words and phrases.

countryside /'kʌntrisaɪd/
stranger (noun) /'streɪndʒər/
hitchhike /'hɪtʃhaɪk/
miss (the connection) /mɪs/
pour (gas into a car) /pɔr/
shiver /'ʃɪvər/
upset (adj) /ʌp'sɛt/
feel lonely /fil 'loʊnli/
get to the (top) /'gɛt tə ðə/
in order to (do something) /ɪn 'ɔrdər tər/

Computers are useless. They only give you answers.

Pablo Picasso, Spanish artist

9B Too much information!

1 GRAMMAR quantifiers

a Circle the correct form.

1 *A lot of* | *A lot* people send text messages on the train.
2 There wasn't *no* | *any* bread left in the store by the time I got there.
3 Most of my friends spend *too many* | *too much* time on social networking sites.
4 This bag isn't *enough big* | *big enough* to put all my books in.
5 I like my coffee with just *a little* | *a few* hot milk.
6 I think people eat *too quickly* | *too much quickly* these days.
7 There were *lot* | *lots of* people waiting at the bus stop.
8 There's *no* | *any* time to stop for lunch. We'll just have to have a sandwich.
9 There were *very little* | *very few* tickets left for the concert.
10 There aren't *enough hours* | *hours enough* in the day to do everything.

b Complete each pair of sentences so that they have the same meaning. Sometimes more than one expression is possible.

1 There *aren't enough* chairs.
There are *too few* chairs.

4 He has __________ video games.
There aren't __________ shelves.

2 He can't afford it. He doesn't have __________ money.
He can't afford it. It's __________ for him.

5 There's __________ gas in the tank.
There isn't __________ gas in the tank.

3 We only had __________ sleep last night.
We didn't have __________ sleep last night.

6 She buys very __________ books these days.
She doesn't buy __________ books these days.

2 PRONUNCIATION *-ough* and *-augh*

a Circle the word with a different sound.

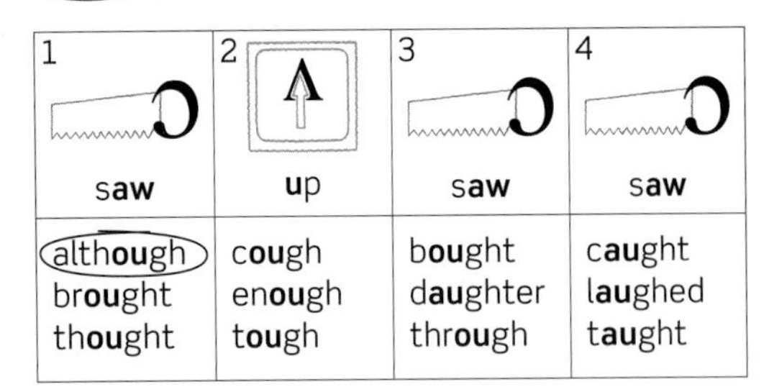

1 saw	2 up	3 saw	4 saw
(although)	cough	bought	caught
brought	enough	daughter	laughed
thought	tough	through	taught

b ONLINE Listen and check. Then listen again and repeat the words.

3 VOCABULARY phrasal verbs

a Complete the sentences with the simple past form of the phrasal verbs in the box. Replace the words in **bold** with a pronoun.

plug in ~~switch on~~ turn up turn down switch off

1 I wanted to listen **to the radio** so I *switched it on*.
2 **The music** was too loud so I ________________.
3 When I found **my adaptor**, I ________________.
4 I couldn't hear **my MP3 player** so I ________________.
5 There wasn't anything on **TV** so I ________________.

electronic devices

b Complete the crossword.

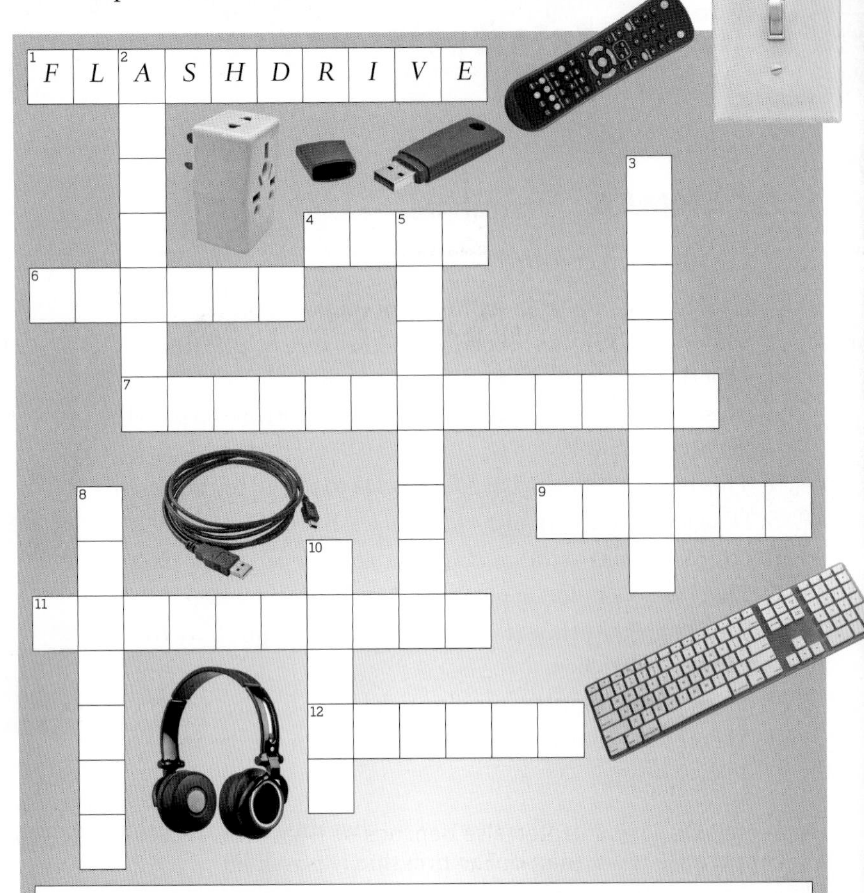

Clues across →

1 A small device that can be used to store data and to move it from one computer to another.
4 A plastic object with two or three metal pins that connects electrical equipment to the electricity supply.
6 The place on a wall where electrical equipment can be connected to the electricity supply.
7 A piece of equipment for controlling something from a distance.
9 The lighted surface of a computer where the information appears.
11 A piece of equipment worn over the ears that makes it possible to listen to music without other people hearing it.
12 A small button that you press up and down in order to turn on electricity.

Clues down ↓

2 A device for connecting pieces of electrical equipment that were not designed to be fitted together.
3 The set of keys on a computer.
5 The piece of equipment for connecting other pieces of equipment to a computer.
8 A part of an electrical device that the sound comes out of.
10 A piece of equipment connected to a computer for moving around the screen and entering commands without touching the keys.

4 READING

a Read the article once and choose the best heading.

1 Laptops and modern lifestyles ☐
2 Eat and drink while you work ☐
3 Liquid and laptops don't mix ☐

Have you ever dropped a drink on your laptop? If you have, you'll remember the panic when you thought that your machine would never work again. If you haven't, it may well happen to you in the future. Spilling drinks on a laptop is a common occurrence. Just in case it does happen, here are some basic tips that tell you what you should do.

The effect of the drink on your laptop depends on what it is. Water and green tea generally cause the least damage. The worst drinks to spill are those that contain milk and sugar, such as hot drinks like coffee and tea, and soft drinks like soda or lemonade.

What happens to your laptop also depends on what you do immediately after the spill. The first thing you should do is unplug the machine and take the battery out. This will hopefully stop any electrical damage. Then, you should turn it upside down and stop the liquid from getting to the motherboard. This is where some of the most important parts of the computer are, and if it gets wet, your laptop may be damaged permanently.

The next step is to clean up as much of the liquid as quickly as possible. If you don't have a cloth to do this, use some tissues instead. Try to touch the keyboard lightly instead of wiping it with the tissue.

If you spilled a lot of liquid, you'll have to work harder to save your machine. Put it near a window or somewhere with cold air, and shake it gently to get the liquid out. It might help if you take off the bottom of the case so that you can take out the hard drive. If you do this, remember not to touch any of the electronics. When you have done as much as you can, leave the laptop somewhere warm to dry. This will take at least a day. Do not use a hair dryer because this will make the machine dirty.

When you think the laptop is dry, turn it back on to see if it works. If you only spilled a little clean water, you might be lucky and the machine may turn on right away. However, you'll probably have problems if the drink was a large, milky coffee with lots of sugar in it. If your laptop still doesn't work, look at the keyboard and try taking it apart to clean it better. However, if you've gone this far, it's probably time to think about getting some help. You can either take the laptop to be repaired, or buy a new one. And in the future, remember to drink your coffee at someone else's desk!

b Read the article again. Mark the sentences T (true) or F (false).

1 Not many people spill drinks on their laptops. *F*
2 Green tea causes less damage than coffee with milk. ___
3 You shouldn't move your laptop after a spill. ___
4 You should only use a cloth. ___
5 You can try taking out the hard drive of the machine. ___
6 You should use a hair dryer to dry the electronics. ___
7 A little water doesn't usually cause much damage. ___
8 The advice in the article only works for laptops that haven't had a lot of liquid spilled on them. ___

c Look at the highlighted words and phrases. What do you think they mean? Use your dictionary to look up their meaning and pronunciation.

5 LISTENING

a ONLINE Listen to a conversation at the reception desk of a hotel. What does the guest want to know?

____

b Listen again and complete the notes.

Name	1 *Barry Gray*		**Type of Wi-Fi chosen** 6 ______
Room Number	2 ______		**Start time** 7 ______
Standard	3 ______	per day	
Advanced	4 ______	per minute	**End time** 8 ______
Maximum	5 ______	per day	

c Listen again with the audioscript on p. 76.

USEFUL WORDS AND PHRASES

Learn these words and phrases.

hits (on a website) /hɪts/
willpower /'wɪlpaʊər/
multitask /'mʌltitæsk/
relevant /'rɛləvənt/
be productive /bi prə'dʌktɪv/
feel anxious /fil 'æŋkʃəs/
common sense /kɑmən 'sɛns/
electronic device /ɪlɛk'trɑnɪk dɪ'vaɪs/
from time to time /frəm taɪm tə 'taɪm/
information overload /ɪnfər'meɪʃn oʊvər'loʊd/

ONLINE **FILE 9**

Practical English Unexpected events

1 INDIRECT QUESTIONS

Correct any mistakes in the highlighted phrases. Check (✓) the correct sentences.

Ticket agent Can I help you?
Max Yes. I'd like to know what time is the next bus to Boston.
[1] *what time the next bus to Boston is*
Ticket agent Well, the next bus leaves at 10 a.m.
Max Great. Could you tell me how much costs a one-way ticket?
[2] ______
Ticket agent Sure. A one-way ticket to Boston costs $35.95. Can you tell me do you have a Student Advantage Card?
[3] ______
Max Yes, here it is.
Ticket agent Then you get a 20% discount on your ticket. That means it'll cost you $28.75.
Max Great! Here's my credit card.
Ticket agent OK. And here's your ticket and your cards.
Max Thanks. Can you tell me if I need to change buses?
[4] ______
Ticket agent No, you don't. The bus goes straight through.
Max And do you know what time does it arrive?
[5] ______
Ticket agent Yes, it gets in at 2:20 p.m.
Max Thanks a lot.

2 SOCIAL ENGLISH

Complete the dialogue with the words and phrases in the box.

either | I guess | It's obvious | Of course | ~~Stop it!~~ | What if

A [1] *Stop it!* You keep yawning. Everyone will think you're bored.
B Oh, sorry. [2] ______ I'm a little tired.
A [3] ______ you're tired. You had a long day.
B Well, I did get up at six o'clock this morning.
A Oh, come on. Let's go. [4] ______ you aren't enjoying the party.
B I'm sorry. I think I need to go to bed.
A I know. [5] ______ we go home and do something fun tomorrow?
B That sounds like a great idea. And I promise I won't yawn all day, [6] ______.
A Perfect!

3 READING

a Read the text. Mark the sentences T (true) or F (false).

1. People made bread in the shape of bagels in many different cultures. *T*
2. Bagels were first made in Austria. ___
3. They were made by Jewish bakers. ___
4. Bagels first came to the US in 1900. ___
5. They became popular all over America in the 1960s. ___
6. New inventions were used to sell bagels across America. ___
7. One of the reasons bagels are popular is because they stay fresh longer than bread. ___

A Short History of the Bagel

The bagel is known around the world as a typically New York type of food. But it has a surprising and unusual history that goes back many years.

The basic idea of a bread roll with a hole is centuries old. In Roman times, soldiers ate hard bread called *buccellatum*, and in China there is similar-shaped traditional bread called *girde*. The ancient Egyptians ate a bagel-like snack, too, and there are even more examples from around the Mediterranean area.

But it was in Poland that today's bagel really began. According to legend, it was the product of the 1683 Battle of Vienna. The Polish king, Jan Sobieski, had saved Austria from the Turkish invaders. To celebrate, the Jewish bakers of Kraków made a roll in the shape of the king's stirrup – the metal objects you put your feet in when you ride a horse – and called it a "buegel" (from the German word for stirrup). There is, however, no evidence to show whether this was true or not, but the story still remains today.

It is unclear when the first bagels made their way to the United States, but by 1900, there were 70 bakeries that sold bagels on the Lower East Side of New York. What is also certain is that immigrants from Eastern Europe, with their cravings for the foods of the old country, sparked the New York bagel craze.

It was the 1950s that were the real turning point. As Jewish people began to move to other parts of New York, they started to share their traditional food with the rest of the city. Bagels were mentioned in a popular cookbook of the time, and demand started to grow across America. To meet this demand, a baker named Murray Lender began to use recent inventions like the freezer and plastic packaging to distribute freshly made bagels across America. Soon, Lender's bagels were available in almost every supermarket, and today they are part of a typical American diet and available all over the world.

But why has the bagel endured through all this time? Possibly because of its heroic legend, but also because it has the advantage of lasting longer than freshly baked bread. If it gets slightly stale, it can be dunked in hot liquid to soften it. So it lasts long, can be eaten in many ways, and of course tastes delicious.

b Underline five words or phrases you don't know. Use your dictionary to look up their meaning and pronunciation.

I don't think that I want to meet any of the icons. I don't think that anybody can quite live up to your expectations.

Jane Horrocks, English actress

10A Modern icons

1 GRAMMAR relative clauses: defining and non-defining

a Complete the sentences with a relative pronoun. Where two answers are possible, write both pronouns. There is one sentence where you can leave out the relative pronoun.

1 Espoo is the city in Finland *where* Nokia is based.
2 Apple is the company *which / that* makes the iPad.
3 Melinda Gates is the woman ______ husband founded Microsoft.
4 The thing ______ my son wants most for his birthday is a tablet computer.
5 Lee Byung-chull was the man ______ founded Samsung.
6 Minato, is the district in Tokyo ______ Sony has its headquarters.
7 Alexander Graham Bell is the man ______ invented the telephone.

b ~~Cross out~~ the extra word in each of the sentences.

1 Why don't you stay in the hotel where we stayed ~~there~~ last year?
2 He's the actor who he played the role of Sherlock Holmes.
3 Those are the students who they won first prize.
4 I'll go to the supermarket that it has the best offers.
5 She's the woman whose her daughter went to the same school as me.
6 What's the name of the store where we bought the USB cable there?
7 That's the computer that it isn't working.

c Complete the sentences with a relative pronoun and the phrases in the box. You will need to leave out one of the words in each of the phrases.

~~he has appeared in several James Bond movies~~
her voice will never be forgotten
his wife is the singer Beyoncé
Native Americans protected themselves from hot temperatures there
she is a human rights leader
it is in the Andes
the Mona Lisa can be seen there
it was opened in China in 2011

1 Daniel Craig, *who has appeared in several James Bond movies*, was born in Chester.

2 The Louvre, ______, is in the center of Paris.

3 Aconcagua, ______, is the highest mountain in South America.

4 Selena, ______, died in 1995.

5 Jiaozhou Bay Bridge, ______, is the longest bridge in the world.

6 Aung San Suu Kyi, ______, was under house arrest for 15 years.

7 Jay-Z, ______, is one of the most successful rappers of all time.

8 The Cliff Palace, ______, is in the US.

2 VOCABULARY compound nouns

a Write the compound noun for each picture.

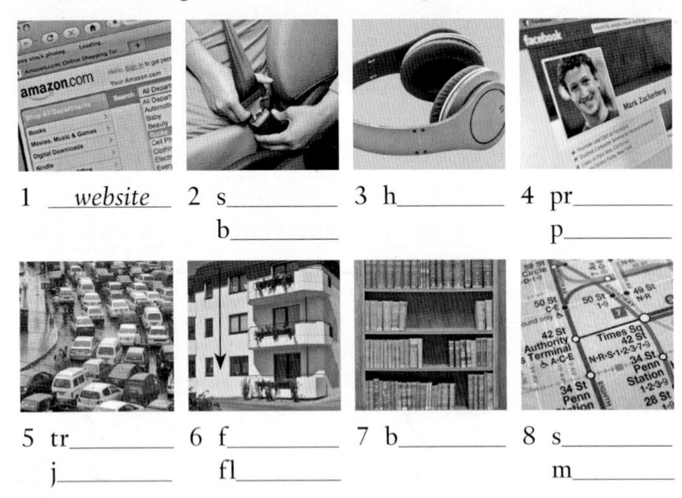

1 _website_ 2 s______ b______ 3 h______ 4 pr______ p______

5 tr______ j______ 6 f______ fl______ 7 b______ 8 s______ m______

b Match a word from A with a word from B to make compound nouns. Then complete the sentences.

A ~~bank~~ high bicycle room rush sound top training
B ~~account~~ course floor hour lane mate school track

1 My salary is deposited directly into my _bank_ _account_ every month.
2 They live on the ______ ______, so they have a great view of the city.
3 The ______ for the movie *The Hobbit* is awesome.
4 My brother is taking a ______ ______ to learn about health and safety.
5 Do you get along well with your ______ or do you argue about paying the bills?
6 The first year of ______ ______ in the US is usually ninth grade.
7 Bike riders should use the ______ ______ to keep away from traffic.
8 Commuters usually travel to work during ______ ______.

3 PRONUNCIATION word stress

a Match the words 1–8 with the words in the box to make compound nouns.

cam|era court drive map ~~pass~~
ti|cket tone walk

1 boar|ding _pass_	5 ring ______
2 cross ______	6 speed ______
3 flash ______	7 sub|way ______
4 par|king ______	8 te|nnis ______

b ONLINE Listen and check. Then listen again and repeat the words. Underline the stressed syllables.

4 READING

a Read some extracts from an interview with Usain Bolt once. What do you learn about his family?

1 He has ______.
2 He lives with ______.

Children, adults, old people... everybody wants to race me. I get challenged to races every day. I met Mickey Rourke in a dance club and we had a race in the street. I'll race the kids, but grown-up people need to get real.

I am an athlete and a doctor. I have received lots of honorary degrees, so my full official title is something like Dr. The Honorable Ambassador Usain Saint Leo Bolt. I have tried to make my friends call me it, but nobody does.

My father was my hero. He always worked so hard. People think I don't train hard, but I really do – and it's all because of him.

My earliest memory is playing in my yard. I'd play cricket, soccer, and basketball or just run around. As long as I was outside in the sun I was happy.

Your environment definitely changes your personality. I am similar to my sister. We are relaxed because we grew up in the country (in Jamaica), but my brother is different because he grew up in Kingston.

Sleep is beautiful. I live with my brother Sadiki and my best friend NJ in Kingston, and my only house rule is: never wake me up early.

I can't cook. I just know that vegetables are good for you.

What I enjoy most about my house isn't the big TV or the swimming pool, but the fruit trees in my yard. They remind me of my childhood. When I sit and stare at them I feel happy. I like to sit under trees.

Snakes and spiders terrify me. That's why I don't go to Africa very often. I also used to believe in ghosts when I was a kid and I would get scared, but not anymore.

Bob Marley is a legend. I have all his old albums, and he did a great job of bringing Jamaica to the world.

I can be emotional. I cried at a movie last year – but don't tell anyone.

I have always been young and fast...so the idea of being old feels weird. I do worry about it. My friend NJ is a couple of months older than me, so I will always be younger than him. That makes me feel better.

b Read the interview again and answer the questions.

1 Who doesn't Usain Bolt mind racing?
Children.

2 Which member of his family does he admire the most?
___

3 What did he enjoy doing when he was a child?
___

4 What doesn't he like doing?
___

5 What isn't he very good at?
___

6 What does he like most about his house?
___

7 What is he afraid of?
___

8 Which singer does he like?
___

9 What happened when he went to the movies last year?
___

10 What does he worry about?
___

c Look at the highlighted words and phrases. What do you think they mean? Use your dictionary to look up their meaning and pronunciation.

d Complete the sentences with the highlighted words.

1 We have a *house rule* that the person who cooks doesn't have to wash the dishes.
2 My car is making a ___ noise – I have no idea what it is, but it doesn't sound good.
3 I told my sister to ___ ___ – she'll never have a big house on the beach.
4 Miles Davis is a ___ of jazz music.
5 American colleges often give ___ ___ to celebrities who didn't study there, but who have done work for charities or have inspired students.

5 LISTENING

a ONLINE Listen to a radio program about a new exhibition at the Science Museum. Check (✓) the two inventions mentioned in the program and label the two pictures you check.

5 8 7 2 3 5 9 8 6

1 ___ 2 ___ 3 ___

4 ___ 5 ___ 6 ___

b Listen again and mark the sentences T (true) or F (false).

1 The exhibition shows very special things that we don't often use. *F*
2 Napoleon Bonaparte had a problem feeding all his soldiers. ___
3 A French soldier won the competition. ___
4 The first design was made of metal. ___
5 A later design killed a number of people. ___
6 In the past, people bought a big box of leaves to make tea with. ___
7 Thomas Sullivan sold the small bags of tea to his customers. ___
8 He told his customers not to open the tea bags. ___
9 Tea bags were really invented by some of his customers. ___
10 The exhibition closes on Sunday, July 25th. ___

c Listen again with the audioscript on p. 76.

USEFUL WORDS AND PHRASES

Learn these words and phrases.

icon /'aɪkɑn/
logo /'loʊgoʊ/
silhouette /sɪlu'ɛt/
incorporate /ɪn'kɔrpəreɪt/
manufacture /mænyə'fæktʃər/
be adopted /bi ə'dɑptəd/
drop out (from school) /drɑp 'aʊt/
found a company /faʊnd ə 'kʌmpəni/
a worldwide (Internet) sensation /ə wərld'waɪd sɛn'seɪʃn/

Poetry is not the most important thing in life. I'd much rather lie in a hot bath reading Agatha Christie and sucking sweets.

Dylan Thomas, Welsh poet

10B Two crime stories

1 VOCABULARY crime

Complete the text.

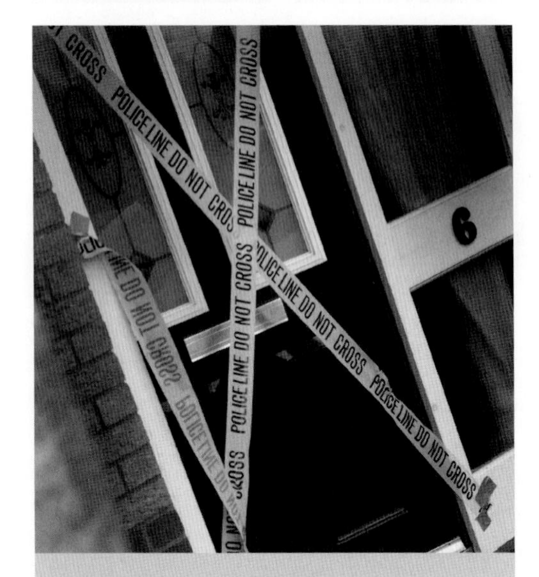

[1] D*etectives* are investigating a [2] m__________ in Millbrook. The [3] v__________ is a 26-year-old man whose body was found last night next to a quiet, back road. No [4] ev__________ was found at the scene and police are appealing to [5] w__________ who saw the man yesterday to help them with their investigation. They believe that the [6] m__________ was someone known to the man. The main [7] s__________ are the man's roommate, his girlfriend, and a neighbor. These people are currently being interviewed by the police in an attempt to [8] s__________ the crime. A police spokesperson said that they had a theory, but so far, they had been unable to [9] pr__________ who had committed the crime.

2 GRAMMAR tag questions

a Circle the correct answers.

1 You live in Seattle, *don't you* | *aren't you*?
2 But you weren't born in Seattle, *weren't you* | *were you*?
3 You moved to Seattle when you were ten, *weren't you* | *didn't you*?
4 That means you've been living here for twenty years, *haven't you* | *have you*?
5 But you're moving to Los Angeles next week, *won't you* | *aren't you*?
6 Your brother lives in Los Angeles, *doesn't he* | *isn't he*?
7 You've been in prison before, *aren't you* | *haven't you* ?
8 I guess you'd like to call your lawyer now, *don't you* | *wouldn't you*?

b Complete the tag questions.

1 Adam's living with his parents now, *isn't he*?
2 You don't like animals, __________?
3 It isn't difficult, __________?
4 He drives a van, __________?
5 They left yesterday, __________?
6 Kathy hasn't been home for over a week, __________?
7 I'm late, __________?
8 You'll see him tomorrow, __________?

3 PRONUNCIATION intonation in tag questions

a ONLINE Listen and repeat the sentences. Copy the rhythm.

1 You **called** her **last night, didn't you**?
2 He's **older** than **you, isn't he**?
3 They **aren't coming, are they**?
4 You'd **like** to **visit Paris, wouldn't you**?
5 She'll be **late, won't she**?
6 I **can't dance** very **well, can I**?

b Write the words in the box in the correct columns .

brutal suspect hurt ~~murder~~ prove truth discover suddenly weren't

1 ɜr bird	2 u boot	3 ʌ up
murder		

c ONLINE Listen and check. Then listen again and repeat the words.

4 READING

a Read part 1 of an extract from a novel once. Where does Hannay first think Scudder is from?

England ☐
Norway ☐
the US ☐
Greece ☐

The Thirty-Nine Steps

Introduction:
Richard Hannay, the narrator, has just returned to London from Africa. A mysterious man called Franklin Scudder appears outside his flat one night, and tells Hannay about a group of people he met who are trying to push Europe towards a war. He believes only the Greek Prime Minister, Constantine Karolides, can stop the war. Karolides will be in London soon, and Scudder believes there is a plan to kill him then. Scudder believes he can stop this plan, but only if people think he is dead...

Part 1
I was beginning to like this strange little man. I gave him another drink and asked him why he thought he was now in danger himself.

He took a large mouthful. "I came to London by a strange route – through Paris, Hamburg, Norway, and Scotland. I changed my name in every country, and when I got to London, I thought I was safe. There's a man watching this building and last night somebody put a card under my door. On it was the name of the man I fear most in the world.

"So I decided I had to 'die.' Then they would stop looking for me. I got a dead body – it's easy to get one in London, if you know how – and I had the body brought to my flat in a large suitcase. The body was the right age, but the face was different from mine. I dressed it in my clothes and shot it in the face with my own gun. My servant will find me when he arrives in the morning and he'll call the police. I've left a lot of empty bottles in my room. The police will think I drank too much and then killed myself." He paused. "I watched from the window until I saw you come home, and then came down the stairs to meet you."

It was the strangest of stories. However, in my experience, the most extraordinary stories are often the true ones. And if the man just wanted to get into my flat and murder me, why didn't he tell a simpler story? "Right," I said. "I'll trust you for tonight. I'll lock you in this room and keep the key. Just one word, Mr. Scudder. I believe you're honest, but if you're not, I should warn you that I certainly know how to use a gun."

"Certainly," he answered, jumping up. "I'm afraid I don't know your name, sir, but I would like to thank you. And could I use your bathroom?"

When I saw him next, half an hour later, I didn't recognize him at first. Only the bright eyes were the same. His beard was gone, and his hair was completely different. He walked like a soldier, and he was wearing glasses. And he no longer spoke like an American.

"Mr. Scudder – " I cried.

"Not Mr. Scudder," he answered. "Captain Theophilus Digby of the British Army. Please do remember that."

I made him a bed in my study, and went to bed myself, happier than I had been for the past month. Interesting things did happen sometimes, even in London.

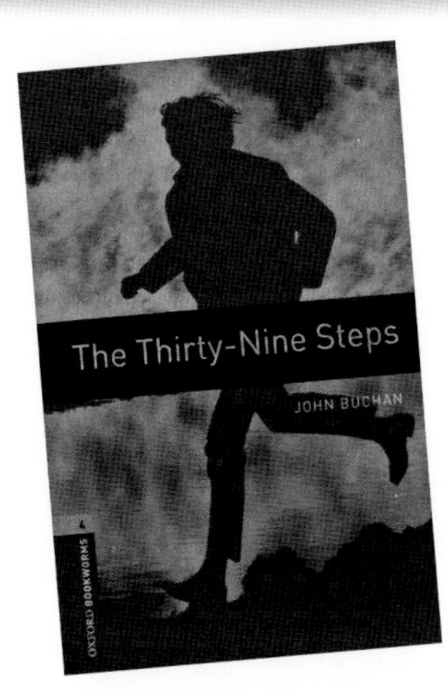

Extract from Oxford Bookworms Library:
The Thirty-Nine Steps by John Buchanan, retold by Nick Bullard

b Read the extract again and choose the best answers.

1 The man took a strange route to London because...
   a he wanted to see all the sights.
   b he got lost on the way.
   (c) he didn't want anybody to find him.
2 The person who sent him a card last night is...
   a a friend.
   b an enemy.
   c a colleague.
3 The man is pretending to be dead because...
   a he wants people to stop looking for him.
   b he owes someone a lot of money.
   c he doesn't want to talk to the police.
4 The narrator, Hannay, trusts the man because...
   a he knows him very well.
   b his story is so complicated.
   c he doesn't look like a murderer.
5 When the man went to the bathroom, he...
   a took a bath.
   b combed his hair.
   c put on a disguise.
6 The man spent the night...
   a in Hannay's apartment.
   b in a hotel.
   c in his own apartment.
7 The man changes his name to a...
   a French name.
   b British name.
   c German name.
8 Hannay now thinks that...
   a nothing exciting happens in London.
   b it's always interesting in London.
   c something exciting can happen in London.

c Underline six words or phrases you don't know. Use your dictionary to look up their meaning and pronunciation.

5 LISTENING

a ONLINE Listen to Part 2 of the extract. What happens to Mr. Scudder?

b Listen again and mark the answers T (true) or F (false).

1 The narrator told his servant who Scudder really was the next morning. _F_
2 Mr. Scudder's plan to pretend to commit suicide worked. __
3 Mr. Scudder was calm and relaxed all the time he was in Hannay's apartment. __
4 He gave Hannay more details about the plot to kill Karolides. __
5 Apart from Karolides, he mentioned one other person. __
6 The study light was on when the narrator got home. __

c Listen again with the audioscript on p. 76.

USEFUL WORDS AND PHRASES

Learn these words and phrases.

alibi /'æləbaɪ/
case /keɪs/
court /kɔrt/
the defense /ðə dɪ'fɛns/
the dock (of a court) /ðə dɑk/
the prosecution /ðə prɑsə'kyuʃn/
trial /'traɪəl/
plead (guilty / innocent) /plid/
swear (e.g., on the bible) /swɛr/
be acquitted /bi ə'kwɪtəd/

ONLINE **FILE 10**

Listening

6 A

Tour guide Hello, and welcome to the TV and Movie Walking Tour of Central Park in New York City. My name's Stacy Clinton, and I'm going to be your guide today. I hope you are all wearing comfortable shoes because the tour lasts for two hours. We'll end at Columbus Circle at around two o'clock.

We're going to start at Gapstow Bridge – a stone bridge originally built in 1874. From the bridge you have an amazing view of the Plaza Hotel. Does anyone know which movies the Plaza Hotel has been featured in? No? Well, you can see this famous hotel in *The Great Gatsby* and *Almost Famous* just to name two. So that's where we're going to go first. Then we're going to go to the Wollman Skating Rink—one of two rinks in the park. This skating rink was opened to the public in 1858, well over 150 years ago! You might recognize the rink from the movies *Home Alone 2* and *Love Story*.

After the rink, we'll walk to one of the most well-known attractions in Central Park—the Carousel. This carousel has 57 colorful wooden horses for children and adults to ride on, and it's only three dollars a ride! The original carousel was built in 1871. This one isn't the original, but it is beautiful. Maybe that's why director Mel Brooks chose to include it in his movie, *The Producers*.

As we walk toward the middle of the park, we'll pass by the Promenade and Bethesda Fountain where movies such as *The Avengers, Breakfast at Tiffany's,* and *Enchanted* shot scenes. Farther north, we'll take a look at the largest lake in Central Park and we'll visit the Boathouse Restaurant, which was featured in the movie *When Harry Met Sally*. Next, we'll visit the Bow Bridge—a graceful cast-iron bridge, which is considered one of the most romantic spots in New York City. Movie directors must agree because the bridge has been featured in *Spider-man 3,* on the TV show *Glee* and in one of the greatest love stories of all time—*The Way We Were.*

At this point, we'll visit Strawberry Fields, an area of the park dedicated to John Lennon and his music. We'll look at the beautiful memorial mosaic with the word "imagine" in the middle designed to honor Lennon's memory. Of course, this area of the park was also used for a scene in the movie *Little Manhattan*.

Finally, we'll walk to the Sheep Meadow. Don't worry—there haven't been any sheep in this meadow since 1934. However, we will see people sunbathing or relaxing in this 15-acre open area. This location was used in scenes for *Wall Street* and *The Fisher King*.

As we walk to our final destination, Columbus Circle, we'll pass by Tavern on the Green, once a famous restaurant in New York City and also used as a location for the popular movie *Ghostbusters*. And finally, we'll end up at Columbus Circle where scenes for *Taxi Driver* and *Borat* were shot. OK, so let's get going and head to our first stop, Gapstow Bridge…

6 B

Host Hello, and welcome to today's program. Have you ever wondered how women made themselves look beautiful in the past? Our beauty expert Olivia Johnson is with us today, and she's going to tell us all about beauty through the ages. Olivia, where are you going to start?

Olivia Well, I'm going to start with the Egyptians, but it wasn't only women who used cosmetics at this time. Both Egyptian men and women loved their cosmetics – we know that from the paintings and the powders they left behind. The women wore a powder on their faces to make their skin lighter, and they painted a big black line around their eyes to make them look bigger. Men put a cream made of fat and oil and other substances on their face to protect it from the sun – a very early version of sunscreen. Egyptian kings and queens also put colorful powders around their eyes. Their favorite color was green, which they got from a mineral called malachite.

Host How interesting! Who are you going to tell us about next?

Olivia OK! Let's move on to the ancient Greeks. Cosmetics were an important part of their life, too. The ancient Greek idea of beauty was very pale skin, blonde hair, and natural makeup. For them, pale skin was a sign of beauty and wealth. The women used a powder made out of a metal called lead to make their faces look lighter.

Host You mean lead? The lead that used to be in the pipes carrying the water in our houses?

Olivia That's right.

Host But lead is poisonous!

Olivia Yes, it is, and the ancient Greeks knew lead was poisonous, but it was so important for them to be beautiful that they used it on their face, and of course, it made them sick.

Host I can't believe they used lead on their faces! Anyway, who's next on the list?

Olivia The Romans. They were absolutely obsessed with beauty. A Roman philosopher once wrote, "A woman without paint is like food without salt," so it's clear that they really believed that women should wear a lot of makeup. The Romans believed that pink on the cheeks was a sign of good health, but they did not apply the makeup themselves. Instead, they used their servants to put on their creams and powders.

Host So, the servants were like modern makeup artists, then?

Olivia Yes, I guess you could say that.

Host I think I prefer putting on my own makeup. Olivia Johnson, thank you for joining us.

Olivia My pleasure.

7 A

Host And now for a review of last night's TV shows. The highlight for me was a new series called *The Unteachables*. It's a kind of reality show that tries to find out if it's really true that there are students who can't be taught. Last night, we were introduced to the students. There are 16 of them altogether, and they're all 14 years old. They've all been suspended from schools at least once, and their teachers think they're impossible to teach.

Watching the students on last night's show, it isn't hard to see why. We see the group during their introductory weekend at the study camp when they meet each other for the first time. At one point, one of the boys warns that he might set the building on fire. You couldn't imagine how their teacher was going to teach them.

And that's where 40-year old Philip Beadle comes in. Beadle used to be a rock musician, but he gave up music at the age of 32 to become a teacher. Since then, he has had a very successful career in education. His greatest achievement was when he worked at a high school where there were a lot of problems. He worked really hard, and his students got the best test scores in English that the school had ever seen – all of his students passed their exams, half of them with the highest score. But let me get back to the show.

In Beadle's first class, he manages to help the students learn to trust him by playing a game with the children. In the game, Beadle and the students point at each other and say an insult. This might not seem very educational, but Beadle had the attention of all the students, and everybody was joining in. And that was the point of the game.

You might think that Beadle's teaching methods are pretty unusual, and you'd be right. At one point on last night's show, he took the students out into the country. They found a field with cows in it, and he made them read poems and plays by Shakespeare to the cows! Remember that these are children who refuse to read in front of other people in a classroom. In another scene, they are in a different field, learning about punctuation. Beadle teaches this by going around to different students and shouting the names of the types of punctuation. So, for example he shouts "question mark," then "huh!" and at the same time moves his body into a shape like a question mark. The students learn by copying him, and it looks like a lot of fun. By the end of the first episode, the students are starting to accept their new teacher. Some of them even say he's "all right."

I really enjoyed *The Unteachables* and I really want to know what happens next. If you're fascinated by the experiment like I am, you'll watch the next episode at the same time next Wednesday. Personally, I can't wait!

7 B

Guide: Ladies and gentlemen, can I have your attention, please? Thank you and welcome to Graceland, the home of music star Elvis Presley. We start our tour here, at the front door of this impressive home. This is the perfect place to look closely at the outside of the house. It was built in the early part of the twentieth century, in a style that was popular at the time. The outside walls of the house are made of stone and wood, and the house has two floors as well as a basement. This house was Elvis's home from 1957 until 1977 when he died, which means he spent most of his adulthood here. He got married in 1967 and his wife, Priscilla, came to live with him here after they got married. Their only daughter Lisa Marie was born here. So you see, this house played an extremely important role in Elvis's life. Now, as you're walking through the house, I'd like you to pay special attention to how different rooms are decorated. One room is decorated to look like a jungle with green rugs, plants of all kinds, and animal-print decorations. Another room, the TV room, was one of the first "home theaters" in the US. Elvis placed three TVs side-by-side on a wall. On Sundays, he could watch three different football games at the same time! OK, if you'll come this way, we'll start on the first floor, and the first room we're going to visit is the dining room.

Are you all in? Well, this is the dining room where Elvis enjoyed meals with his guests. The large dining room table could seat about 12 people. The beautiful light hanging over the table is made of Italian glass. Elvis didn't usually wake up until four in the afternoon, so the dinner parties didn't start until ten at night! His full-time cooks made old-fashioned Southern food for the dinner parties – and when he wanted a snack, his cooks made him his favorite peanut butter, banana, and bacon sandwiches…which were probably the reason he gained weight as he got older! The dining room was also used by Elvis as a place to play card games with his friends.

Now, we're going to walk across the hall to the living room, and then we'll head to the music room right behind it. Please follow me.

The centerpiece of the living room is a 14-foot-long white leather couch and 10-foot-long coffee table. Quite impressive! The room has a wall covered in mirrors and is decorated in gold, blue, and white. If you look over here, you'll see a pair of stained-glass birds that lead into the music room. It was in this room that Elvis and his friends spent hours together creating and playing music. When you're ready, we'll continue with our tour of the first floor and visit the kitchen and Elvis's parents' room, where his father had a swimming pool installed in his bedroom along with a jukebox next to it!

8 A

Laura Hi, Sam! How was your trip to Chicago?

Sam It was great, thanks. But the flight back was awful! In fact, I made a complaint to the airline.

Laura What was the problem?

Sam Well, as you know, some airlines make you wait forever in line before you can board, which I can't stand. It also means that there's always a huge rush to get on the plane and there isn't any place to put your bags. I find all this so annoying that I usually pay for PreferredAccess – you know, when you pay extra to get on the plane first. You just get in line when they call the flight, and then they tell the passengers with PreferredAccess to come to the front and you get on the plane first.

Laura So what went wrong?

Sam Well, it was fine on the flight to Chicago. I stood in line, they called the people who had PreferredAccess, I boarded the plane, and I got to my seat with no problems. Perfect! But on the flight back from Chicago to New York, I was standing in line at the gate waiting to be called to board first, and nothing happened. I don't know if they forgot about PreferredAccess or what, but they didn't call us to the front of the line. That meant I had to board the plane with everyone else – in fact, I was one of the last to get on. As you can imagine, I wasn't very happy.

Laura So, what did you do?

Sam When I got home, I emailed the airline explaining what had happened. I told them that I had paid for PreferredAccess on both of my flights, but I had only received the service on one of them. I asked them, very politely, to give back the money I had paid for the PreferredAccess for the return trip. It was about $20 at the time.

Laura Did you get a response?

Sam Yes, I did. They were very quick. I sent my email at 5 p.m., and I received a reply the next morning.

Laura And did they give you your money back?

Sam Well, no, they didn't. I had a very nice message from a man in customer service saying he was concerned about the incident. But he didn't say he would give me my money back.

Laura Typical! They never do, do they?

Sam Wait a minute – I haven't finished the story yet.

Laura Oh. Sorry...go ahead.

Sam Well, I sent them a second email. But this time the tone was much stronger and less polite. And it worked! They refunded my PreferredAccess AND they gave me money for my return flight from Chicago. I was impressed!

Laura That's great!

8 B

Speaker 1 When I was about 15, I got a part-time job in a supermarket. The job was in the cash office, so I had a lot of responsibility. I had to collect the money from the registers, count it, and put it in the safe for the security people to collect the next morning. I was still in school at the time, so I worked for a couple of hours on a Friday evening and all day on Saturdays. During the holidays I worked more hours because I had more time and there were more customers. The girls in the office were a lot of fun, so the job wasn't at all boring. I worked there for about three years, until I left because I needed more time to study for my final exams at school.

Speaker 2 I studied Spanish in college and at the end of my first year, I went to Argentina to practice my Spanish. I found a job in a restaurant almost as soon as I arrived. The job was washing dishes, which I thought was going to be easy. Unfortunately, I was wrong. There was a machine in the kitchen that washed the plates and glasses and things like that. But my job was to clean the pots and pans that the chef had used. The saucepans were always completely black and it used to take me hours to get everything clean. I didn't enjoy working there very much, and I was really happy when I had learned enough Spanish so that I could stop working there.

Speaker 3 I don't know if you can call this a job, but I did get paid for it, even if it was only twenty dollars! When I was a teenager, I used to take care of my cousins when my aunt and uncle wanted to go out. The kids were a lot younger than me, so I had to babysit for them. I didn't do it every weekend, but it was probably about once a month. My uncle used to pick me up at about seven and take me back to their house. I had to bathe the kids, give them their dinner, and play with them for an hour or so before they went to bed. They were no trouble at all to babysit, and I absolutely loved being with them!

Speaker 4 My dad's a painter, and so the summer after I finished school, I went to help him for a few weeks. At the time, my dad's company had a contract to paint all the exterior doors and windows of some houses in a new development. The weather was great – not too hot and not too cold, so I didn't really mind it. The work was pretty tiring because I spent most of the day climbing up and down a ladder, but I earned a lot of money that summer. But the best thing was spending some time with my dad and his colleagues– we had a really good time!

Speaker 5 One of the first jobs I ever had was in a food processing company in San Diego. I was a student at the time, and I needed a temporary job during the holidays. Fortunately, the job was only for two weeks because it was really awful. The worst day was when we were packaging hamburgers. I had to stand on the production line and count the burgers into groups of five. Later, someone farther down the line put the burgers in a box. The problem was that the burgers were frozen and we weren't allowed to wear gloves. This meant that I had to pick up the ice-cold burgers with my hands. I've never had such cold fingers in all my life!

9 A

Speaker 1 I know a lot of people who are superstitious when they see somebody standing on top of a ladder on the sidewalk and they don't want to walk underneath it. Actually, I'm one of those people! Walking under a ladder is supposed to give you bad luck, so I never do it. Whenever I come across a ladder, I always walk around it – even if I have to walk out into the street. Come to think of it, that's probably worse than walking under the ladder because I could get hit by a car, but there's no way that I would ever walk under the ladder.

Speaker 2 I don't know if any other countries have this superstition, but where I live, you have to be very careful when you buy a new pair of shoes. Apparently, it's bad luck to put the shoes on your dining room table. This goes back to something that people did in the past when somebody died – in fact, it was the families of miners in the north of England who originally did this. The family always bought new clothes to dress the dead person in, and this included buying new shoes. So, if you leave your new shoes on the table, some people think that this could bring bad luck.

Speaker 3 In some countries, some people are very superstitious about going up or down stairs. If you're going down stairs, it's bad luck to pass someone who's coming up the stairs and the same thing happens the other way around. Someone once told me the reason for this. A long time ago, people carried swords so you had to be very careful of the people around you. If somebody passed you on the stairs you couldn't see them because they were behind you. That meant that they could turn around and kill you with their sword without you realizing.

Speaker 4 When I was planning my wedding a couple of years ago, I had my heart set on a beautiful outdoor spring ceremony in November. Unfortunately, my husband's brother was engaged at the same time, and in Chile it's considered bad luck for two brothers to get married during the same year. Since his brother is the eldest, he got to choose his wedding date first. Of course he chose November. We had to wait until January, in the middle of summer. Our wedding day was one of the hottest days of the year! It was so uncomfortable in my dress and my hair was out of control!

Speaker 5 In Brazil, if someone has an exam or is going for a job interview, we push our thumb between our first two fingers to wish them luck. I have some German friends who make a similar sign. They wrap the fingers of their right hand around their thumb and say, "I'm holding my thumb for you." And I know that in the US people cross their fingers and say "fingers crossed" when they wish people luck, which is also similar. Maybe they're all connected in some way.

9 B

Receptionist Good afternoon. Can I help you?

Guest Oh, hello. Yes – I need to ask you about Wi-Fi access in the hotel. I have some work to do while I'm here, so I'm going to need an Internet connection.

Receptionist Well, there's a Wi-Fi hotspot in the lobby of the hotel and all of the rooms have Wi-Fi.

Guest Great. And how much does it cost?

Receptionist It's free in the lobby, but we charge for the Wi-Fi access in the rooms. Are you interested in our standard connection or would you prefer our advanced service?

Guest Um, what's the difference?

Receptionist The standard service is available for a flat fee of ten dollars per day. However, it can be a little bit slow because everyone in the hotel uses it. We have a higher-level service for our guests who need a faster and more reliable connection.

Guest And how much is that?

Receptionist It's 25 cents per minute.

Guest That could get pretty expensive if I use it all evening.

Receptionist Not really, Sir. The maximum charge is 30 dollars for 24 hours.

Guest I see. So how would that work? Would I have to pay 30 dollars today and another 30 dollars tomorrow?

Receptionist No. The 24-hour period begins from when you checked in.

Guest Great! I'd like the advanced service, then. Oh, and one more question. What do I need to log on to your Wi-Fi?

Receptionist Just a moment. Could you give me your name and room number?

Guest It's Gray. Barry Gray. I'm in room 302.

Receptionist Thank you, Mr. Gray. Here's your Wi-Fi pack, which has the name of the connection…here, and… here's your password. Please try to keep it safe so that nobody else can use it. You checked in at ten after three today, so the connection will last until the same time tomorrow afternoon.

Guest Great. Is that all I need?

Receptionist Yes, it is.

Guest Thanks a lot for your help.

Receptionist You're welcome.

10 A

Host Welcome back to the show. Now, a new exhibition opens today at the Science Museum, and all of the exhibits are everyday objects that we couldn't live without. Charlotte Heath, who has been to the exhibition, is with us today to tell us more about it. Welcome to the show, Charlotte.

Charlotte Thank you.

Host So what kinds of objects can you see in the exhibition? Are we talking about modern gadgets like smartphones and tablets here?

Charlotte No, no, not at all. This exhibition is all about the little or important things we have in our house and use every day. We use them so much that we probably forgot, or don't even realize, that someone actually invented them.

Host Such as?

Charlotte Well, a good example is the container we use to keep food in: the tin can. But I bet you don't know how it was invented.

Host No, I don't.

Charlotte Well, there's a very interesting story behind it. It was the French leader Napoleon Bonaparte who was responsible for this one. In 1809, he was worried about how to feed all his soldiers when they were away from home, so he organized a competition to try to get ideas for how to solve the problem. The first prize was 12,000 Francs and the competition was won by a French chef who had the idea of using glass jars to store food. A year later, a British manufacturer, Peter Durand, improved the design by using thin sheets of metal to make the container that became what we now call a tin can. The only problem was that he used lead in the can, which as you know is poisonous. Several people died after eating food from his tin cans.

Host How unfortunate! Now, Charlotte, do we have time for one more story before the news headlines?

Charlotte Sure. I can tell you about the tea bag. In the past, if you wanted to buy tea, you had to buy the leaves in a big box. To make a drink of tea, you would put the leaves in water, and you would often find small pieces of tea leaves at the bottom of your cup. Anyway, in 1908, an American tea salesperson named Thomas Sullivan had the bright idea of putting the tea in very small bags to give to his customers to try. Sullivan thought that customers would take the tea out of the bags in order to try it, but some of the customers didn't. They found it more convenient to put the bag into hot water, without actually opening it. So, tea bags weren't really invented by a company, it was the tea drinkers who came up with the idea!

Host What an incredible story! And the Everyday Inventions Exhibition at the Science Museum will run until Sunday, July 25th . Right, Charlotte?

Charlotte Yes. The museum is open from ten to six every day, so there's no excuse not to go.

Host Thanks for joining us, Charlotte. And now it's time for the news headlines with…

10 B

The next morning when my servant Paddock arrived, I introduced him to Captain Digby. I explained that the Captain was an important man in the army, but he had been working too hard and needed rest and quiet. Then I went out, leaving them both in the flat. When I returned about lunchtime, the doorman told me that the gentleman in flat 15 had killed himself. I went up to the top floor, had a few words with the police, and was able to report to Scudder that his plan had been successful. The police believed that the dead man was Scudder, and that he had killed himself. Scudder was very pleased.

For the first two days in my flat, he was very calm, and spent all his time reading and smoking, and writing in a little black notebook. But after that he became more restless and nervous. It was not his own danger that he worried about, but the success of his plan to prevent the murder of Karolides. One night he was very serious.

"Listen, Hannay," he said. "I think I must tell you some more about this business. I would hate to get killed without leaving someone else to carry on with my plan."

I didn't listen very carefully. I was interested in Scudder's adventures, but I wasn't very interested in politics.

I remember that he said Karolides was only in danger in London. He also mentioned a woman called Julia Czechenyi.

The next evening I had to go out. I was meeting a man I had known in Africa for dinner. When I returned to the flat, I was surprised to see that the study light was out. I wondered if Scudder had gone to bed early. I turned on the light, but there was nobody there. Then I saw something in the corner that made my blood turn cold.

Scudder was lying on his back. There was a long knife through his heart, pinning him to the floor.

WORKBOOK ACKNOWLEDGEMENTS

The authors and publisher are grateful to those who have given permission to reproduce the following extracts and adaptations of copyright material:

p.19 Extract from http://www.roughguides.com/article/10-unusual-types-oftransport/. Copyright © *2013 ROUGH GUIDES LTD*. Reproduced by permission of Rough Guides Ltd.; p.47 Extract from 'Why houses with history will sell' by Christopher Middleton, The Telegraph, 20 June 2011. © Telegraph Media Group Limited 2011. Reproduced by permission; p.51 Extract from 'Ten tips for safe shopping online this Christmas' by Stephen Ellis, The Telegraph, 8 December 2008. © Telegraph Media Group Limited 2008. Reproduced by permission; p.57 Extract from 'Lucky it wasn't raining! Moment driver was catapulted through sunroof of flipping car…and walked away unharmed' by Emma Reynolds, The Daily Mail, 10 July 2012. Reproduced by permission of Solo Syndication; p.61 Extract from 'What to do when you spill a drink on your laptop' by Jack Schofield, The Guardian, 5 July 2012. Copyright Guardian News & Media Ltd 2012. Reproduced by permission; p.64 Extract from 'This much I know: Usain Bolt' by Mark Bailey, The Guardian, 17 June 2012. Copyright Guardian News & Media Ltd 2012. Reproduced by permission; p.67 Extract from 'Oxford Bookworms Library: The Thirty-Nine Steps' by John Buchan, retold by Nick Bullard, Series Editor Jennifer Bassett. © Oxford University Press 2007. Reprinted by permission; p.23 Extract from www.newyorktaxis.org. Reproduced by permission; p.62 Extract from Slate, © 12 November 2008 Issue, The Slate Group All rights reserved. Used by permission and protected by the Copyright Laws of the United States. The printing, copying, redistribution, or retransmission of the Material without express written permission is prohibited; p.36 Extract from 'USA Getting there & around', www.lonelyplanet.com. Reproduced with permission from the Lonely Planet website www.lonelyplanet.com © 2012 Lonely Planet.

Illustrations by: Satoshi Hashimoto/Dutch Uncle: pp.14, 57; Anna Hymas/New Division: p.20; Tim Marrs: p.13; Jerome Mireault/Colagene: pp.28, 40; Ellis Nadler: pronunciation symbols; Roger Penwill: p.59; Ron Tiner: pp.67, 68; Kath Walker: p.41.

We would also like to thank the following for permission to reproduce the following photographs: Cover: Gemenacom/shutterstock.com, Andrey_Popov/shutterstock.com, Wavebreakmedia/shutterstock.com, Image Source/Getty Images, Lane Oatey/Blue Jean Images/Getty Images, BJI/Blue Jean Images/Getty Images, Image Source/Corbis, Yuri Arcurs/Tetra Images/Corbis, Wavebreak Media Ltd./Corbis; pg.4 (2 across) studiomode/Alamy, (3 across) Gastromedia/Alamy, (5 across) Food and Drink Photos/Alamy, (1 down) Annabelle Breakey/Getty Images, (2 down) Dave King/Getty Images, (4 down) jon whitaker/Getty Images; pg.6 Mike Kemp/Tetra Images/Corbis; pg.7 (1) Sean Justice/Getty Images, (2) Image Source/Corbis, (3) JGI/Getty Images, (4) PhotoAlto/Eric Audras/Getty Images, (5) Jose Luis Pelaez Inc/Getty Images; pg.9 Stefano Ravera/Alamy; pg.10 Brian Hamill/Getty Images; pg.11 2020WEB/Alamy; pg.15 (bus) Thomas Cockrem/Alamy, (construction) Ryan Smith/Somos Images/Corbis, (orangutan) Andrew Watson/Getty Images; pg.16 (1) Lobke Peers/shutterstock, (2) LJSphotography/Alamy, (3) Rich Legg/Getty Images, (4) John Rowley/Getty Images, (5) Denis Scott/Corbis, (6) Everynight Images/Alamy; pg.18 (China) Ma Hailin/Xinhua Press/Corbis, (Mexico) Danny Lehman/Corbis, (Australia) John Gollings/Arcaid/Corbis; pg.19 (boat) Julia Rogers/Alamy, (sled) Accent Alaska.com/Alamy, (train) STRINGER/CAMBODIA/X80007/Reuters/Corbis, (jeep) Christian Kober/Robert Harding World Imagery/Corbis; pg.22 (man) Ann Summa/Corbis, (woman) Flashon Studio/shutterstock; pg.23 Bufflerump/shutterstock.com; pg.24 Erik Isakson/Blend Images/Corbis; pg.25 (Speilberg) Luc Roux/Sygma/Corbis, (Newton) The Gallery Collection/Corbis, (Gates) Peer Grimm/dpa/Corbis, (Edison) CORBIS; pg.27 (Liberty) Rubens Alarcon/shutterstock, (Times Square) Kobby Dagan/shutterstock.com; pg.32 Michael Regan/Getty Images; pg.34 (friends) Dreampictures/Image Source/Corbis, (couple) Monkey Business Images/shutterstock; pg.36 Car Culture/Getty Images; pg.38 (Knebworth House) Steven Vidler/Eurasia Press/Corbis, (Anna Karenina) 2012/Moviestore/Rex; pg.39 (carousel) Ambient Images Inc./Alamy, (table) Anna Clopet/CORBIS, (rink) Kiet Thai/Getty Images, (bridge) Andrew C Mace/Getty Images; pg.42 Dimitri Otis/Getty Images; pg.44 Ken Seet/Corbis; pg.45 epa european pressphoto agency b.v./Alamy; pg.47 (Graceland) Jon Arnold Images Ltd/Alamy, (cabin) jpbcpa/istock, (apartment) cdrin/shutterstock.com; pg.48 Jeff Morgan 12/Alamy; pg.51 auremar/shutterstock; pg.52 Mira Oberman/AFP/Getty Images; pg.53 Blend Images/shutterstock; pg.54 C. Devan/Corbis; pg.55 (dentist) Julian Abram Wainwright/epa/Corbis, (golf) Andrew Geiger/Getty Images; pg.57 Top-Pics TBK/Alamy; pg.58 Mathew Crowcoot/Newsteam/SWNS Group; pg.59 Tokyo Space Club/Corbis; pg.60 (keyboard) S.E.A. Photo/Alamy, (plug) Carsten Reisinger/Alamy, (outlet) Joe Belanger/shutterstock, (switch) Olivier Le Queinec/shutterstock, (headphones) Bryan Solomon/shutterstock, (USB) cristi180884/shutterstock, (speaker) arigato/shutterstock, (mouse) vasabii/shutterstock, (screen) yanugkelid/shutterstock, (remote) MNI/shutterstock, (flashdrive) bogdan ionescu/shutterstock, (adaptor) Freer/shutterstock; pg.61 R and R Images/Getty Images; pg.63 (Selena) AP Photo/Blanca Charolet, Premier Postage via Hispanic PR Wire, HO, (Jay Z) Ben Rowland/The Hell Gate/Corbis, (bridge) Imaginechina/Corbis, (Kyi) Anindito Mukherjee/epa/Corbis, (Craig) EON/DANJAQ/SONY/The Kobal Collection/Maidment, Jay, (Mesa Verde) MarclSchauer/shutterstock, (Louvre) Migel/shutterstock.com, (Everest) Pal Teravagimov/shutterstock; pg.64 (1) NetPhotos/Alamy, (2) leolintang/shutterstock, (3) Alexander Demyanenko/shutterstock, (4) Erkan Mehmet/Alamy, (5) Asianet-Pakistan/shutterstock.com, (6) Bernd Kohlhas/Corbis, (7) Ferenc Szelepcsenyi/shutterstock, (8) claudiodivizia/istock, (Bolt) Christopher Morris/Corbis; pg.65 (1) pockygallery/shutterstock, (2) Burdika/shutterstock, (3) Graphic design/shutterstock, (4) anaken2012/shutterstock, (5) Anton Prado PHOTO/shutterstock, (6) maniacpixel/shutterstock; pg.66 Arthur Turner/Alamy.